THE MONGOL CONQUESTS

TimeFrame AD 1200-1300

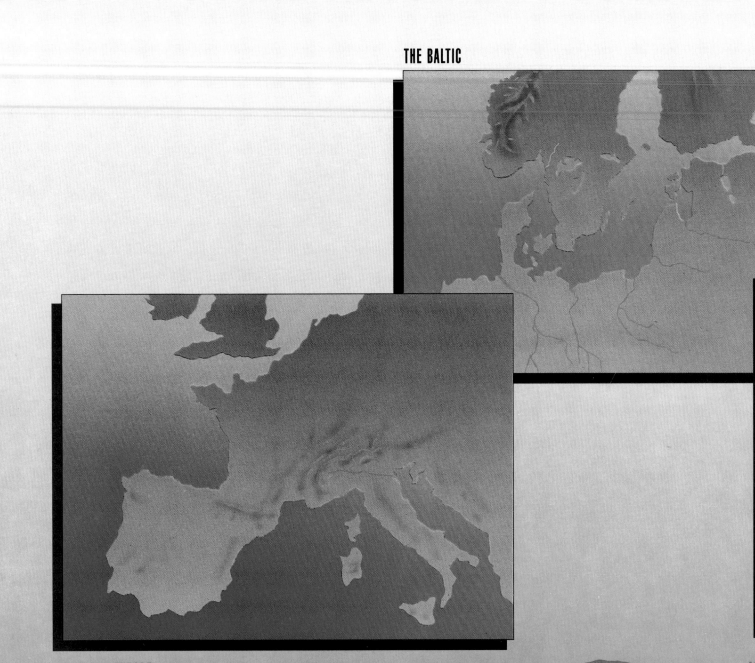

THE BALTIC

WESTERN EUROPE

TimeFrame AD 1200-1300

CENTRAL ASIA AND THE FAR EAST

ICA AND THE MIDDLE EAST

Other Publications:
WEIGHT WATCHERS® SMART CHOICE RECIPE COLLECTION
TRUE CRIME
THE AMERICAN INDIANS
THE ART OF WOODWORKING
LOST CIVILIZATIONS
ECHOES OF GLORY
THE NEW FACE OF WAR
HOW THINGS WORK
WINGS OF WAR
CREATIVE EVERYDAY COOKING
COLLECTOR'S LIBRARY OF THE UNKNOWN
CLASSICS OF WORLD WAR II
TIME-LIFE LIBRARY OF CURIOUS AND UNUSUAL FACTS
AMERICAN COUNTRY
VOYAGE THROUGH THE UNIVERSE
THE THIRD REICH
THE TIME-LIFE GARDENER'S GUIDE
MYSTERIES OF THE UNKNOWN
FIX IT YOURSELF
FITNESS, HEALTH & NUTRITION
SUCCESSFUL PARENTING
HEALTHY HOME COOKING
UNDERSTANDING COMPUTERS
LIBRARY OF NATIONS
THE ENCHANTED WORLD
THE KODAK LIBRARY OF CREATIVE PHOTOGRAPHY
GREAT MEALS IN MINUTES
THE CIVIL WAR
PLANET EARTH
COLLECTOR'S LIBRARY OF THE CIVIL WAR
THE EPIC OF FLIGHT
THE GOOD COOK
WORLD WAR II
HOME REPAIR AND IMPROVEMENT
THE OLD WEST

For information on and a full description of
any of the Time-Life Books series listed on this page,
please call 1-800-621-7026 or write:
Reader Information
Time-Life Customer Service
P.O. Box C-32068
Richmond, Virginia 23261-2068

THE MONGOL CONQUESTS

TimeFrame AD 1200-1300

BY THE EDITORS OF TIME-LIFE BOOKS

TIME-LIFE BOOKS, ALEXANDRIA, VIRGINIA

TIME-LIFE BOOKS

EDITOR-IN-CHIEF: John L. Papanek

Executive Editor: Roberta Conlan
Director of Editorial Resources:
Elise D. Ritter-Clough
Executive Art Director: Ellen Robling
Director of Photography and Research:
John Conrad Weiser
Editorial Board: Russell B. Adams, Jr.,
Dale M. Brown, Janet Cave, Robert
Doyle, Jim Hicks, Rita Thievon Mullin,
Robert Somerville, Henry Woodhead
Assistant Director of Editorial Resources:
Norma E. Shaw

PRESIDENT: John D. Hall

Vice President, Director of Marketing:
Nancy K. Jones
Vice President, New Product Development:
Neil Kagan
Director of Production Services:
Robert N. Carr
Production Manager: Marlene Zack
Director of Technology: Eileen Bradley
Supervisor of Quality Control: James King

Editorial Operations
Production: Celia Beattie
Library: Louise D. Forstall
Computer Composition: Deborah G. Tait
(Manager), Monika D. Thayer, Janet
Barnes Syring, Lillian Daniels
Interactive Media Specialist: Patti H. Cass

Time-Life Books is a division of Time Life
Inc.

PRESIDENT AND CEO: John M. Fahey, Jr.

EUROPEAN EXECUTIVE EDITOR:
Gillian Moore
Design Director: Ed Skyner
Assistant Design Director: Mary Staples
Chief of Research: Vanessa Kramer
Chief Sub-Editor: Ilse Gray

Correspondents: Elisabeth Kraemer-Singh
(Bonn); Maria Vincenza Aloisi (Paris);
Ann Natanson, Ann Wise (Rome); Dick
Berry (Tokyo).

TIME FRAME
(published in Britain as
TIME-LIFE HISTORY OF THE WORLD)

SERIES EDITOR: Tony Allan

Editorial Staff for *The Mongol Conquests:*
Editor: Fergus Fleming
Designer: Mary Staples
Writer: Chris Farman
Researchers: Caroline Lucas (principal),
Marie-Louise Collard
Sub-Editors: Diana Hill, Christine Noble
Design Assistant: Rachel Gibson
Editorial Assistant: Molly Sutherland
Picture Department: Patricia Murray
(administrator), Amanda Hindley (picture
coordinator)

Editorial Production
Chief: Maureen Kelly
Production Assistant: Samantha Hill
Editorial Department: Theresa John,
Debra Lelliott

U.S. EDITION

Assistant Editor: Barbara Fairchild
Quarmby
Copy Coordinator: Colette Stockum
Picture Coordinator: Robert H.
Wooldridge, Jr.

Special Contributors: Windsor Chorlton,
John Cottrell, Ellen Galford, Alan Lothian,
Deborah Thompson (text); Stephen Rogers
(research); Jane Clark (copy); Roy Nanovic
(index)

CONSULTANTS

General:
GEOFFREY PARKER, Professor of History,
University of Illinois, Urbana-Champaign,
Illinois

C. A. BAYLY, Reader in Modern Indian History, St. Catharine's College, Cambridge
University, Cambridge, England

Western Europe:
CHRISTOPHER GIVEN-WILSON, Lecturer
in Medieval History, University of St.
Andrews, Fife, Scotland

MICHAEL PRESTWICH, Professor of History, University of Durham, Durham,
England

The Baltic:
ERIC CHRISTIANSEN, Fellow of New College, Oxford University

Central Asia and the Far East:
I. J. McMULLEN, Lecturer in Japanese,
Oxford University

D. S. M. WILLIAMS, Lecturer in History of
Asiatic Russia, School of Slavonic and
East European Studies, London University

Africa and the Middle East:
ROBERT IRWIN, Author of *The Middle
East in the Middle Ages*

**Library of Congress Cataloging in
Publication Data**

The Mongol conquest.
 Bibliography: p.
 Includes index.
 1. Mongols—History. 2. China—History—
Yüan dynasty, 1260-1368.
I. Time-Life Books.
DS19.M58 1989   951'.025   88-29612
ISBN 0-8094-6437-3
ISBN 0-8094-6438-1 (lib. bdg.)

© 1989 Time-Life Books Inc. All rights reserved.
No part of this book may be reproduced in any
form or by any electronic or mechanical means,
including information storage and retrieval devices or systems, without prior written permission from the publisher, except that brief
passages may be quoted for reviews.
Third printing 1993. Printed in U.S.A.
Published simultaneously in Canada.
School and library distribution by Time-Life Education, P.O. Box 85026, Richmond, Virginia
23285-5026.

TIME-LIFE is a trademark of Time Warner Inc.
U.S.A.

CONTENTS

THE MONGOL HORDES

"I am the flail of God. If you had not committed great sins, God would not have sent a punishment like me upon you." The speaker was the Mongol leader Genghis Khan, and the year was 1219. He was addressing refugees huddled into the principal mosque of Bukhara, in central Asia. But there were few of them to hear him. Earlier his soldiers had burned the outer city and herded the inhabitants together to serve as a human shield for an assault on the citadel. All of the city's 30,000 defenders had been slaughtered. Civilians who survived were stripped of their possessions and driven before the invaders at the launch of their next campaign.

For some fifty years, from the first decade of the thirteenth century, the fate of Bukhara was shared by cities all across the Eurasian landmass—from China and Korea in the east through Persia, Iraq, and Turkestan to Bulgaria, Russia, Poland, and Hungary in the west. The sumptuous palaces of Zhongdu (now Beijing) were razed. Samarkand and Baghdad, resplendent capitals of Islam, were totally destroyed. Golden-domed Kiev, the most opulent city in Russia, was reduced to ashes. In those years, half the known world reeled under an onslaught of unprecedented ferocity.

Beyond the boundaries of their empire, the Mongols inspired dread. In the Christian West, the chronicler Matthew Paris described them as a detestable nation of Satan. "Piercing the solid rocks of the Caucasus, they poured forth like devils from the hell of Tartarus. They swarmed locust-like over the face of the earth and brought terrible devastation to the eastern part of Europe, laying it waste with fire and carnage." It was only chance that saved the lands west of Hungary from a similar fate.

Though spared Mongol invasion, the West was experiencing a metamorphosis almost as momentous. In Germany, Italy, and Sicily, the Holy Roman Empire was riven by quarrels between pope and emperor. Amid this discord there blossomed the glittering Sicilian court of Emperor Frederick II, one of the most enlightened and cosmopolitan rulers of his day. But after his death in 1250, his empire disintegrated into a collection of principalities, which would not reunite for another six centuries.

At the same time, the feudal territories that made up France and England were moving in the opposite direction. By the dawn of the fourteenth century, the two nations had almost taken on their modern-day shapes, and they were experiencing under strong monarchs the benefits of centralized governments and in England the birth of a democratic parliament.

In the frozen lands of northeast Europe, where the Mongols' yak-tail banner was seen as a demon "with a devil face and a long gray beard," a redoubtable Christian order, the Teutonic Knights, was clearing the southern Baltic coastlands of their pagan inhabitants. By the end of the century, these warrior-monks had created a rich and powerful military state in the lands of Prussia, Livonia, and Estonia.

To the Muslims, the Mongols were known as "the Accursed of God," and indeed

With his mount at full gallop, a Mongol hunter aims to the rear, demonstrating the mobility and firepower that made the steppe warriors unequaled on the battlefields of Asia and Europe. In combat, every Mongol carried on a wooden frame two bows made out of bone and sinew, one for short-range work, the other with a reach of almost 1,000 feet. His quiver could hold as many as sixty arrows, some armor piercing and some fitted with whistling heads for signaling. He could bend and string his bow in the saddle by putting one end between a foot and a stirrup, and he could shoot accurately even at speed, timing the release of the arrow to come between the paces of his horse.

9

the civilization of the old Islamic heartlands of Iran and Turkey was all but extinguished by their savagery. Only in Egypt were they successfully thwarted—by the Mamluks, a dynasty of Turkish-born warrior-slaves who would make Egypt the center of Islamic culture and their empire the most powerful in the Middle East. Half a world away in Japan, another emergent warrior class, the samurai, also successfully defied Mongol expansion, having earlier pushed imperial rule to one side and instituted a reign of military feudalism.

Despite these two setbacks, the Mongols carved out in less than half a century the largest empire the world had ever seen. At the root of their conquests lay the military genius and inspiration of one man: Temujin, the chieftain who rose from obscurity to be proclaimed Genghis Khan, "Lord of the Earth." Driven by a sense of divine mission, he forged the Mongol nation out of disparate nomadic peoples and created an army with the potential to conquer the world.

At the time of Temujin's birth, in the early 1160s, the Mongol world was confined to the central Asian plateau, varying from 3,000 to almost 5,000 feet above sea level, bounded by the snow-capped Altai and Tianshan mountains in the west and by the Great Khingan peaks bordering Manchuria in the east. The land was divided by nature into three terraces: the vast northern plain of Outer Mongolia merging into the forests at the edge of the Siberian tundra; a central region dominated by the Gobi Desert, some 1,200 miles wide; and the southern grasslands of Inner Mongolia.

East of the grasslands lay the Buddhist kingdom of Xixia, founded about 990 by Tangut nomads from Tibet. Farther east sprawled China, divided into two huge realms. In the north was the empire of the Jin dynasty, created in 1115 by the conquering Jurchen, a forest people from Manchuria, and in the south was the

In 1206, the mighty forces of Genghis Khan burst out of their Mongol homeland, and within half a century they had created the largest empire the world had ever seen. At its greatest, the Mongol Empire encompassed all of Russia and almost the entire landmass of Asia. The Mongol conquests were divided after Genghis's death into four separate khanates—the Ilkhanate of Persia, the Golden Horde in Russia, the Chagatai khanate in central Asia, and the lands of the great khan, which were made up of the Mongol heartland and China. Mongol armies also penetrated eastern Europe and India, as well as the jungles of Southeast Asia; only in Palestine and Japan was their advance halted.

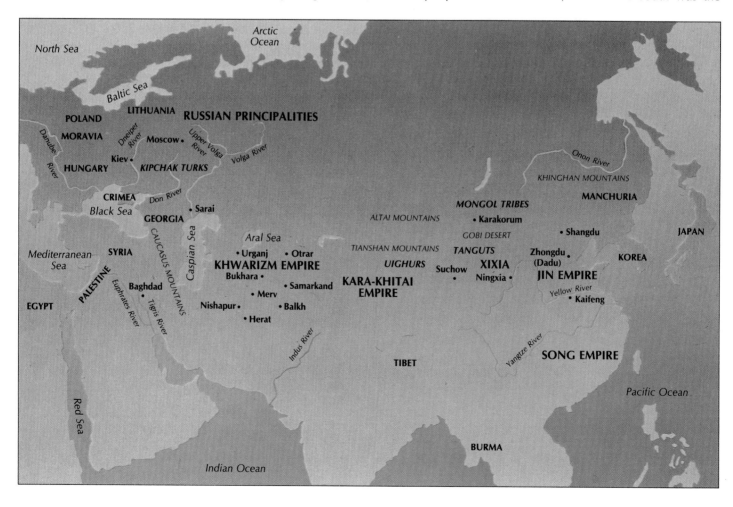

200-year-old Song empire, perhaps the world's most highly developed civilization.

Between the Mongols and China rose the Great Wall, a fortified serpent of stone stretching nearly 1,500 miles from the eastern coast at Shanhaiguan to Jiuquan near the Gobi Desert. Strategically, the wall was only as strong as the armies that manned it; at times, invaders had surmounted it without force, relying instead on political guile and the treachery of Chinese commanders. Symbolically, however, the wall never weakened. Dynasties rose and fell, but to the Chinese it always remained the last outpost of civilization. Beyond it were the lands of the barbarians, considered by the Chinese to be totally lacking in culture and artistic refinement.

Compared with the Chinese, the Mongols were certainly barbarous. Whereas the Song and the Jin built cities of palaces and prospered from an agriculture-based economy, the Mongols were tent-dwelling nomads whose primitive lifestyle was dictated by harsh climatic conditions. The greater part of their lives was spent on horseback. They eked out a living by driving cattle, sheep, and goats to the north for the brief growth of vegetation in the summer and then moving south at the onset of the long, hard winters. The desert and steppe lands could barely support them, and warfare between groups was a natural part of their struggle for survival.

Numbering perhaps two million, the Mongols were not so much a race as a confusion of tribes, each with a ruler known as khan and each comprising numerous clans whose members honored a common ancestor. They had been united once. At the dawn of the twelfth century, a great Mongol state had been formed by Kabul Khan of the Bojigin clan. But this unity had evaporated following defeat in wars against the Jin. By the 1160s, the Mongols were again hopelessly divided, with tribes and clans pursuing feuds passed down from generation to generation.

Temujin, as a descendant, possibly a great-grandson, of Kabul Khan, was born into a clan with a tradition of power. According to legend, his birth was auspicious because he entered the world gripping a clot of blood in his fist. In his early years, however, he seemed doomed to obscurity. He was nine years old when his chieftain father, Yesugei, was poisoned by members of the Mongol Tatar tribe in continuance of an age-old feud. Subsequently his clan abandoned Temujin, together with his mother and five younger brothers and half-brothers. For a time, they endured abject poverty in the harsh region of the upper Onon River, subsisting on berries and such small creatures as marmots and dormice.

The thirteenth-century *Secret History of the Mongols* is the only native source of information about Temujin. Compiled in 1240, possibly by a Mongol chief justice, it dealt with Temujin's ancestry and early life, emphasizing his exceptional courage by recounting various boyhood adventures. One such adventure was his escape after being captured by the rival Taichi'ut clan and fettered in a wooden collar. Still wearing his collar, Temujin used it as a club to crack the skull of his guard before fleeing with the aid of friends in the enemy camp who remembered his father.

The chronicler did not detail how the family's fortunes were revived; certainly the first step must have been the acquisition of horses and livestock from sympathetic clansmen. For all Mongols, herds provided the essentials of life: food, drink, and felt for clothing and makeshift housing. But the herding of these flocks would have been impossible without the help of one animal: the horse. Not only in peace but also in war the success of the Mongols depended on their wealth of horses and their consummate skill in breeding, training, and riding them. Accordingly, all young Mongols, boys and girls, were raised to be accomplished riders: It was not unusual

Mongol nomads, such as the two pictured here, eked out an existence from the steppe. Their food consisted primarily of mutton or beef, and game: gazelle, boar, and rabbit. They also consumed curds, butter, and cheese made from the milk of ewes, goats, cows, and mares. Mare's milk, when fermented, provided their favorite drink, kumiss. The women undertook most domestic chores, such as preparing skins and furs to make clothes and gear; converting animal sinew into thread; and producing felt by beating and oiling animal hair. Felt was needed for outerwear and for the construction of the Mongol home: a circular tent called a yurt.

for children to be tied onto the backs of ponies before they had learned to walk.

As a chieftain's son, Temujin would surely have been subject to this early initiation into horsemanship. In addition, from the age of three, he would have been taught by his father to handle a bow and arrow, eventually learning to shoot on horseback at a gallop while standing in the stirrups—a technique that was to make the Mongol cavalry the deadliest in all Asia.

Temujin badly needed proficiency in such fighting skills. On his majority, he inherited several feuds with other Mongol clans, notably the Merkits, from whom Temujin's father had forcefully acquired his future wife. The Merkits were to take revenge years later by snatching Temujin's bride, Bortei, and giving her to one of their own warriors. When Temujin finally tracked down the abductors, he killed every one of them and went on to defeat the entire clan. Nine months later, Bortei gave birth to a boy. His paternity was uncertain, but Temujin named him Jochi and claimed him as his son.

By now, as a renowned warrior and leader, Temujin had built up a large following. At the head of an army more than 20,000 strong, he set about systematically destroying his enemies with a combination of outstanding generalship and utter ruthlessness. He followed his victory over the Tatars by executing every Tatar male standing taller than the height of a cart axle. After defeating the Taichi'ut with massed cavalry charges, he had the enemy chiefs boiled alive. His overall aim was to destroy traditional divisions and unite the Mongol world under his supreme control, and he sought to achieve it by eliminating all rivals capable of challenging his authority.

By 1203, Temujin had achieved mastery of central and eastern Mongolia. Over the next three years, he completed his conquest of the steppes by marching west to defeat the great Naiman tribe. He also consolidated his position by capturing a chief named Jamuka, who had formed tribal coalitions to challenge Temujin. Jamuka was Temujin's blood brother, a friend since teenage days, when he had allied himself with Temujin against the Merkits. But there was no sentiment on his capture. Temujin ordered his men to crush Jamuka to death by piling rocks on his chest. Not one drop of blood was to be shed; otherwise, Temujin believed, his brother's spirit might escape and return to haunt him.

Like the majority of the Mongols, Temujin was deeply religious. The god that he and his people worshiped was known as Mongke Koko Tengri, "Eternal Blue Sky." This almighty spirit controlled the invisible forces of good and evil that emanated in infinite number from the North Siberian plain. According to the Mongols' animistic creed, powerful spirits lived in fire, in running water, and in the wind; they were to be treated always with the greatest respect. It was, for example, an offense—punishable by beating, sometimes by death—to thrust a knife into a fire, to urinate into a stream, or to launder clothes or even wash out food vessels with running water.

The Mongols offered prayers to idols of the various gods and spirits, most commonly to an image of the earth goddess, Nachigai, mistress of grass, crops, and herbs; and every clan had its own animal spirit, or totem (the Blue Wolf was the legendary ancestor of Temujin's family). They also believed in oracles, dreams, and visions, as interpreted by shamans, who served as prophets, spiritualist mediums, astrologers, wizards, and witch doctors.

The Mongols especially venerated their ancestors' spirits, and it was the sacred duty of every child to learn the names of his forebears, to strive to be worthy of them, and to ensure that their memory was honored. It was from such indoctrination that Temujin came to be driven by a sense of divine mission, by an unshakable belief that it was his destiny to emulate the greatness of Kabul Khan by uniting the Mongol tribes. In 1206, he fulfilled that mission. On the banks of the Onon River, at a *kuriltai*, or assembly of all the chieftains of the steppe lands, he was proclaimed Genghis Khan— Khan of Khans, or "Universal Ruler" of all the Mongol peoples.

At the age of forty-five, Genghis Khan had become more than the supreme ruler of the Mongol nation. Because of his achievements, he was, so the presiding shaman declared, the representative on earth of the Eternal Blue Sky, a veritable visitor from heaven, and it was popularly accepted that his destiny was to conquer and rule the world. The very definition of his divine status denied the existence of sovereign states equal to his. All were expected to recognize the supreme authority of Genghis Khan. They could pursue their own forms of religious worship, but any that offered resistance to his demands were automatically seen to be defying the will of God.

Genghis Khan has been recorded as saying: "The greatest joy a man can have is victory: to conquer one's enemy's armies, to pursue them, to deprive them of their possessions, to reduce their families to tears, to ride on their horses, and to make love to their wives and daughters." Yet he was by no means solely a destructive force. He was also a military organizer of genius, and by Mongol standards, an administrator and lawmaker of the first magnitude. He not only built the most efficient war machine of his time but within his own homeland created order and unity out of chaos. Under his rule, all internecine feuding abruptly ended. Old tribal loyalties were replaced by allegiance to a single people and a single ruler. A new pyramid of power, with Genghis Khan and his kin at its apex, was established by the appointment of some ninety-five senior governors, who with lesser commanders beneath them were responsible for law enforcement, taxation, and conscription within their domains.

At the same time, Genghis ordered the recording of all legal judgments to form a body of case law for the guidance of judges. These judgments dictated extremely high moral standards within the Mongol world, forbidding, among other things, blood feuds, adultery, sodomy, theft, the bearing of false witness, betrayal, sorcery, disobedience of a royal command, and bathing in running water—the last a reflection of the Mongols' animist beliefs. In most cases, the punishment for infringement was death. More lenient was the decree that no man was to be persecuted for his religion, provided that he acknowledged the ultimate authority of the great khan.

Genghis's new, disciplined Mongol nation was totally geared for war. It was not based on settled agricultural communities but on nomadic groups of hunters divided into military-style units of 100, 1,000, and 10,000. Warriors by nature, these people were unencumbered by material possessions and never needed to allow time for the planting and harvesting of crops. And a history of constant feuding made warfare an integral part of their lives.

When the Mongols were not actually engaged in warfare, they were practicing for it. Genghis Khan once stated, "When the Mongols are unoccupied by war, they shall devote themselves to hunting. The objective is not so much the chase itself as the training of warriors, who should acquire strength and become familiar with drawing the bow and other exercises." Thus, at the onset of every winter, all able-bodied Mongols were obliged by law to make themselves available for a great hunt, conducted over a specified area of several thousand square miles and involving many thousands of men. This annual event not only provided an enormous reserve of meat for the harsh months to follow but, more important, served as an elaborate military rehearsal; the hunters were deployed in regimental formations, and prominent individuals were assessed on their performance.

For an outstanding young hunter-warrior, the supreme accolade was promotion to the Imperial Guard, an elite, full-time corps of more than 10,000 men. In battle, the guard was always deployed in the center and used for the final, decisive thrust. Its members were so highly esteemed for their military skills that each one was considered qualified to take command of any fighting unit in an emergency.

Therein lay a key aspect of the Mongols' military might. Beyond the immediate royal family, promotion was by merit alone, and that merit was judged by martial ability. Important, too, was Genghis Khan's rare talent for delegating authority wisely. His own sons—Jochi, Ogedei, Chagatai, and Tolui—were well trained for command, and his chosen generals were men of outstanding ability and unswerving loyalty.

Within a year of his elevation to emperor, the great khan had an army of many tens of thousands, all strictly disciplined, expertly trained, and admirably equipped for open warfare. That year, driven to expansion by the inadequate pastures of their homelands and by their inbred love of war, the newly organized Mongol hordes burst out of the steppes. Fierce and merciless, they swept with hurricane force across the Tangut kingdom of Xixia. Next they struck directly across the Gobi Desert, lured east by the fabulous riches of the Jin empire and its imperial capital, Zhongdu.

Ahead of them lay the limitless rice plains of one of the richest agricultural regions in the world, whose great cities boasted artistic and scientific wonders. But the Mongols, steeped in nomadic tradition, gave no thought to the advantages of occupying such a bountiful land. Life in permanent settlements was alien to them. They conquered for conquest's sake, for a harvest of immediate booty.

On the other hand, the Mongols were far from savages limited to brute force. In open warfare they were tactically brilliant, dividing their armies for three-pronged advances and making frequent use of the feigned retreat before launching counterattacks. They were shrewd in negotiating alliances with non-Mongol tribes bordering the Jin empire, and they made artful use of spies, neutral merchants, and dissatisfied Chinese officials to gather intelligence. Moreover, they were quick to strengthen their war machine with materials and techniques acquired from their enemies. Most significant, with the aid of captured Chinese engineers, they gained the means of laying siege to cities: great rock-catapulting machines such as the mangonel and the trebuchet; a giant crossbow mounted on vertical stands; and gunpowder that could be fired in bamboo-tube rockets from a longbow.

Initially, however, lack of siege machines was the Mongols' one major weakness. In the kingdom of Xixia, they had been delayed by the resistance of the fortress capital Ningxia. They were also brought to a halt by the challenge of the Great Wall. For two years, Genghis chose to wait menacingly in the mountain region of Jehol to the north while the Jin emperor stalled the Mongol leader with gifts. The great khan demanded more, and he received more: 1,000 young men and women, 3,000 horses, vast quantities of gold, jewelry, and silk. Then, on learning that the imperial court had moved its headquarters to Kaifeng on the Yellow River, he ordered an all-out attack.

The Mongol hordes broke through the Great Wall by sheer force of numbers and at appalling cost to both sides. In May 1215, they finally stormed the walls of Zhongdu, leaving the imperial capital in ruins—its palaces stripped, every building razed, and almost the entire population exterminated. In the words of the Mongols' own *Secret History*, it was a "glorious slaughter"; its monument, as described by later travelers, was a mountain of human bones and horse skeletons.

Of the imperial officials remaining in Zhongdu, only a few survived the carnage.

The typical Mongol yurt, as depicted here, was almost fifteen feet in diameter, made from willow poles and latticework lashed together with rawhide and then covered with layers of greased felt. The layers varied in number according to the weather; the outermost was often whitened with lime or powdered bone. Inside, the floors were covered with felt, skins, or rugs, and horns were fixed to the latticework for hanging meat and weapons. Opposite the entrance, which always faced south, the head of the household sat on a couch behind a central hearth, with the women to the east and the men to the west. Most yurts could be taken apart quickly and carried by packhorses, but those belonging to great commanders were sometimes so large that they were kept permanently erected and were transported on huge wagons drawn by oxen.

Mongol cavalry moved in huge separate columns, often many miles apart, their advance coordinated by a sophisticated signaling system of flags, smoke, and burning torches. In battle, a huge camel-mounted kettledrum was used to sound the charge and a yak-tail banner was waved to indicate the commander's orders.

Every soldier was well equipped for battle, carrying bows, quivers, a wicker shield covered in thick leather, a lasso, and a dagger strapped to the inside of his left forearm. He also had a large hide saddlebag—a receptacle for food, spare clothes, and tools—that could be inflated to act as a life preserver, as shown in this illustration of a Mongol army fording a river. The light cavalryman, armed with a small sword and two or three javelins, wore a quilted tunic or a cuirass of lacquered leather strips. His heavier counterpart, clad in mail and a cuirass made either of ox hide or iron scales covered in leather, wielded a scimitar, a battle-ax, or a mace, as well as a lance that was equipped with a hook for dragging enemies from the saddle.

The whole column was followed by enormous, well-organized support units—ox-drawn carts carrying equipment, food, and fodder; Chinese technicians to operate siege machines; engineers to build or repair bridges; shamans to give spiritual and medical aid; officials to catalog the booty; and a host of female workers who not only prepared food and equipment but took part in mopping-up operations, such as slitting the throats of enemy wounded.

AN ARMY ON THE MOVE

Among them was one Yeh-lu Ch'u-ts'-ai, a twenty-five-year-old noble of Mongol descent, who greatly impressed Genghis with his dignity and loyalty to the Jin. The great khan, who valued such qualities above all else, promptly offered him a position in his service, which the young scholar-mandarin accepted. Soon he had become one of Genghis's principal advisers. As such, he exerted a moderating influence on the Mongol leadership. He discouraged needless destruction, counseled against plans to turn the cultivated fields of northern China into grazing land, and showed how the Mongols might greatly profit through taxation and trade if agriculture and the mining of salt and various metals continued to flourish.

Although Genghis Khan heeded much of this advice on the governing of China, he never again set foot in the country, withdrawing to his tented headquarters in Outer Mongolia. Over the next seventeen years it was his general, Mukali, who gradually brought all of northern China under Mongol domination. Genghis himself turned his attention westward, campaigning against the border empires of the Islamic world.

In 1217, Genghis's general Jebe subdued the neighboring kingdom of Kara-Khitai—sandwiched between Tibet and Lake Balkhash—which had earlier fallen under the rule of a fugitive Naiman chieftain. The Mongols later established trading relations with their new western neighbors in the state of Khwarizm, a Turkish-dominated empire that included Turkestan, Persia, much of Afghanistan, and part of northern India. The Mongols might have once more turned their attention eastward had it not been for outrageous provocation by Shah Muhammad, the ruler of Khwarizm. In 1218, Muslim traders traveling with a huge caravan under the protection of Genghis Khan were robbed and murdered by the Khwarizmian governor of the frontier town of Otrar. Perhaps the governor saw the caravan as a cover for espionage (a common Mongol ploy), or he may have been motivated by greed. In any event, the great khan demanded his extradition. Shah Muhammad not only refused but in defiance beheaded a Mongol ambassador sent to his court at Samarkand.

It was this action that impelled the Mongols into western Asia, stirring up a tidal wave of such irresistible fury that it swept on into eastern Europe. In pursuit of his vengeance, Genghis conscripted all Mongol men from the ages of seventeen to sixty, and he himself rode against Khwarizm at the head of some 200,000 men, including about 10,000 siege engineers from China. The great mechanized catapults constructed and operated by these men now proved indispensable. In Khwarizm, no army dared face the Mongol cavalry in open combat, and resistance was centered in the fortified cities, notably Bukhara, Samarkand, Nishapur, Merv, Herat, Balkh, and Gurgan. But none of them survived the wrath of Genghis Khan. In a war lasting only three years, literally millions of men, women, and children were put to the sword.

It was in this war against Shah Muhammad that the Mongols earned a reputation for infinite savagery. While the Mongols punished cowardice and rewarded courage among their own, the policy was reversed for foreigners. The prolonged and heroic resistance of cities ensured that the retaliation of the conquering armies was even greater. They stormed one great city after another, massacring the inhabitants or driving them ahead as human shields for subsequent sieges. When forces commanded by Chagatai and Ogedei finally captured the offending governor of Otrar, they killed him by pouring molten silver into his eyes and down his throat.

Indeed, the Mongols used slaughter and carnage as a means of demoralizing the opposition. The civilian inhabitants of defiant cities were sometimes rounded up like cattle to be massacred by troops who were required to bring back sacks containing

a designated number of ears as proof of having fulfilled their quota. After the fall of Nishapur, all the survivors were decapitated, the skulls of men, women, and children being piled into three separate pyramids. Even dogs and cats were killed; the city simply ceased to exist. Throughout the land, the stories of Mongol atrocities were legion; and historians of the time recorded astounding death tolls: 700,000 at Merv, 1,600,000 at Herat, 1,747,000 at Nishapur. If these figures were exaggerated, it was entirely to the satisfaction of the Mongols, who usually sent ahead agents to foster panic in their targeted cities.

Meanwhile, generals Jebe and Subedei led an army that pursued Shah Muhammad as far as the Caspian Sea; he died there of pleurisy, marooned on an offshore island On their way, the generals overran northwest Persia, routed a 10,000-strong army sent out by King George IV of Armenia, and then drove north, defeating in quick succession the Georgians, the Kipchak Turks of the Volga steppes, and the Bulgars of the upper Volga. By 1223, the Mongols had become entrenched in the Ukraine and the Crimea, where despite numerical inferiority they resisted all counterattacks.

At this point, the Mongols temporarily ended the extraordinary westward thrust that had brought them victory over the armies of twenty states. Recalling his generals, Genghis Khan concentrated on a new, urgent objective: the suppression of the Tanguts of Xixia, who had defied his call to arms against Khwarizm and were now in open revolt. It was his last military campaign. In 1227, after leading his army to a string of victories, he was waiting for the Tangut king to pay him homage when he developed a high fever and died.

It had been just twenty years since Genghis first led the Mongols out of their barren homeland. In that time, he had broken the power of Islam in central Asia and had destroyed the mighty Jin empire. He believed that it was his divine destiny to conquer the world. Now that mission was entrusted to his descendants.

Genghis had already divided his empire into subordinate khanates to be ruled over by his sons and grandsons under the supreme authority of Ogedei, his favorite child. It was two years, however, before a kuriltai was held in Mongolia to formally elect Ogedei as great khan. Then the Mongol war machine swung back into action with the same devastating effect as before.

In the first few years of Ogedei's reign, the Mongols completed the conquest of northern China, subjugated Korea, declared war on the Song rulers of southern China, and campaigned across northwest Persia, northern Iraq, Armenia, and Azerbaijan. Then, in 1236, eastern Europe was made the target of an army of 150,000 men. This great invasion force was under the nominal command of Genghis's grandson Batu, though largely reliant on the tactical genius of the veteran general Subedei. Its basic purpose was to secure the inheritance of Batu, who following the death of Genghis's eldest son, Jochi, shared the northwestern of the four khanates with his brother Orda. The latter received western Siberia, and Batu inherited a vaguely defined region beyond the Volga. Mongol authority in the region remained to be fully asserted.

To that end, Batu's horde drove north and west, defeating the Bulgars of the middle Volga region and the ferocious Cumans of the southern steppes before invading Christian Russia. In a lightning winter campaign, the invaders overwhelmed Rostov, Moscow, and Vladimir, pausing in 1238 to recoup. In 1240, they advanced again, destroying Kiev in December. Pressing on, they defeated a Polish army at Liegnitz in April 1241, devastated Moravia and Silesia, and turning south took Hungary.

The Mongols seemed poised to sweep across the Christian states of central and

A HARDY COMPANION

Prized throughout Asia for its courage and stamina, the Mongol horse was his master's most valued possession in both peace and war. Some fourteen to fifteen hands high, thickset, with broad forehead and short legs, the Mongol horse roamed wild in huge herds of 10,000 or more, from which Mongol tribesmen captured their chosen mounts using nooses attached to the ends of long, springy poles.

Treated with the utmost care, the steeds were broken young, not ridden until three years old, and whenever possible, kept rested on marathon journeys by the use of numerous remounts. Genghis Khan laid down strict rules for their welfare, one of which, for example, forbade leading a mount by a bit in its mouth.

It was the qualities of such steeds and the ingenuity with which they were used that gave the Mongols their military superiority. Although Mongol armies were often quite small, their maneuverability in battle could make their numbers seem doubled. And the rate at which they advanced could take even the most wary foe by surprise. When on the move, each soldier had at least three horses following him, and by regularly changing mounts he could ride at good speed for days, eating in the saddle or pausing when sustenance was scarce to slit a vein and drink the blood of his weakest animal. Batu Khan's vanguard was said to have advanced into Hungary at the rate of sixty miles a day.

Warfare aside, horses also played a prominent role in ceremonies and folklore. Although a weak horse might be eaten, one that had been ridden in battle could never be killed for food. Some Mongols worshiped mounts of rare speed and stamina, eventually preserving their skins and skulls as sacred relics. Indeed, according to the western missionary John of Plano Carpini, a great chieftain was customarily buried alongside a mare, a stallion, and a foal so that he might breed horses in the afterlife.

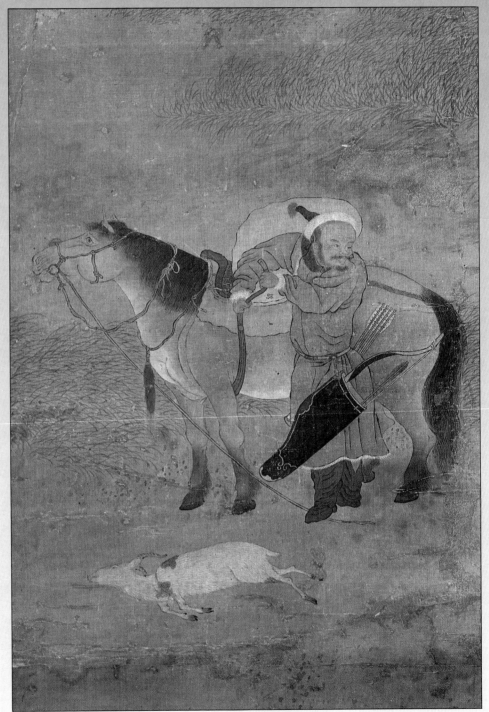

Seen through the eyes of a Chinese miniaturist, a Mongol hunter and his short, stocky horse stand, inseparable, alongside their felled quarry.

In a late-thirteenth-century Japanese scroll, Kublai Khan's soldiers are shown clad in luxurious Chinese tunics and bearing Chinese musical instruments. Despite the adoption of such foreign customs, the warriors are still mounted on Mongol horses.

A horse and groom feel the bite of north China's winter wind, as depicted by Zhao Mengfu, Kublai Khan's leading painter. Some Chinese artists refused to serve the Mongol conquerors; those who did found that their patrons seldom asked for anything but equestrian portraits.

In this Persian miniature, two clashing forces are represented wearing Mongol armor. Here, the artist has depicted slimmer, faster horses, which were the result of the crossbreeding of Mongol and Arab steeds.

A khan and his chief wife prepare to dine, their guards and courtiers arranged according to Mongol etiquette, with men on the khan's right and women on his left. The Mongols never lost their liking for the traditional boiled meats and kumiss, which they consumed in copious quantities. But they also developed tastes for the luxuries they encountered among their conquered subjects. During the invasion of Khwarizm, for example, Genghis Khan became particularly fond of wines from Shiraz.

western Europe. But in December 1241, the offensive was halted. The great khan Ogedei, his health impaired by debauchery, had died at Karakoram, the capital he had established in western Mongolia. The Mongol chiefs were called to a kuriltai to elect a new khan. The would-be invaders retreated to the steppes.

For a time, Ogedei's son Guyuk ruled as great khan, but in 1251 the title passed to Mongke, another grandson of Genghis's. In eight years, under Mongke's leadership, Mongol rule spread east and west. Under his brother Kublai, the Mongols advanced deep into Song China. And with another brother, Hulegu, at their head, they completed the conquest of western Asia, all but annihilating the Assassins, Muslim fanatics who had terrorized the Middle East for 160 years. Most notably, however, they destroyed Baghdad, the rich capital of Iraq. Among the two million deaths reported by the fourteenth-century historian Maqrizi was that of the caliph, world leader of Islam.

In 1259, Mongke died while campaigning in China. His death was as great a blessing for the Middle East as that of Ogedei had been for Christian Europe. At the time, Hulegu had advanced through Syria and was planning to attack Egypt, a powerful country ruled by the Mamluks, warrior-slaves who had recently seized power. At the news of the great khan's death, he hurried east to attend the kuriltai in Mongolia, leaving behind a depleted force, primarily of Mongol-led Turks, to continue the campaign. The result was disaster. On September 3, 1260, at Ayn Jalut near the Jordan in Palestine, the 10,000-man Mongol force was engaged by the army of Qutuz, Mamluk sultan of Egypt. It was outnumbered, outmaneuvered, and routed. The Mamluks then annexed Syria, driving the Mongols back across the Euphrates.

The Battle of Ayn Jalut destroyed the Mongols' reputation for invincibility. It also marked the end of their expansion toward the Mediterranean. Nevertheless, they continued to dominate central and western Asia, which yielded a rich booty of army recruits—in particular the nomadic Turks, who fitted well into the ruthless Mongol mold. And nineteen years later, under the leadership of Kublai, they achieved their ultimate victory over the Song, thereby bringing the entire Chinese nation of some 90 million people under their rule.

When Mongke died, the empire gradually began to disintegrate into virtually independent states that fiercely pursued their own interests. Hulegu and his successors, known as the Ilkhans, held sway over Persia. From their capital, Sarai, on a tributary of the Volga, the descendants of Orda and Batu controlled the Kipchak khanate—later known as the Golden Horde—from Batu's gilded and gold-embroidered tent, extracting tribute and military support from almost all of Russia. And in Samarkand, the descendants of Genghis's second son, Chagatai, ruled the central Asian steppes as the Chagatai khanate.

Meanwhile, control of the Mongolian heartland and of China was disputed between two of Mongke's brothers: Kublai and Arik-Boge. The former had been elected great khan by a kuriltai held, most unusually, at Shangdu, his summer palace in northern China, the latter by a kuriltai more traditionally convened in Mongolia. Four years of civil war ensued until, in 1264, Kublai finally won supremacy.

Though designated great khan, he was never to have the universal sovereignty over the Mongol people enjoyed by Genghis. Both the Chagatai khanate and the Golden Horde were openly opposed to him. This time, it was not merely tribal and family feuds that divided the Mongols. Fundamental religious and ideological differences were emerging between the traditionalists, who favored the old ways of the steppes, and progressive-minded rulers like Kublai in China and the Ilkhans in Persia, who had modified their lifestyle to suit their circumstances. It was a fatal dichotomy.

The new great khan of the Mongols was cast in an entirely different mold from his predecessors: They were rough, unlettered warriors; he was literate, cultured, politically astute, and adaptable. Genghis had been immutably bound to the nomadic way of life and regarded his beloved Asian steppes as the permanent base of the great khans. Kublai, however, aspired to create a new, more sophisticated Mongol civilization outside the inhospitable homeland of his ancestors.

Born in 1215, four months after his grandfather had destroyed the Jin capital of Zhongdu, Kublai grew up in an environment influenced by Chinese ideas. His education was largely the responsibility of a Confucian scholar, Yao Ji. Later, during years of campaigning against the Jin and the Song, he became increasingly Chinese in his tastes and manners, to the degree that he felt China to be his natural home.

In 1256, Kublai commanded the building of his north China summer palace at Kaiping, later renamed Shangdu. Four years later, following his election as great khan, he chose a site only marginally northeast of ruined Zhongdu for the building of his winter capital. By 1270, it had become a city of unrivaled splendor—a complex of palaces, courtyards, gardens, hills, and artificial lakes teeming with fish.

It was not until 1279, some seventy years after Genghis's first invasion, that Kublai completed the conquest of China. The final victory was delayed partly because Mongol cavalry methods were unsuitable to the paddies of the tropical south and also because the Mongols faced an enemy far more numerous, tenacious, and scientifi-

Leering Mongols devour their victims in an illustration from *Chronica Majora,* by the thirteenth-century English chronicler Matthew Paris; to the right, a horse feeds off a tree. During the invasion of Poland and Hungary, Europeans believed every fanciful tale of Mongol atrocities, which some priests proclaimed had been visited on man as God's punishment for the sins of the world. One terrified monk, Ivo of Narbonne, wrote from Austria, "Virgins were raped until they died of exhaustion; then their breasts were cut off to be kept as dainties for their chiefs."

Soon afterward, more realistic reports were written by friars John of Plano Carpini and William of Rubruck, the first Western emissaries to visit Mongolia. But even Friar John wrote of a land where, he had heard tell, "every male had the shape of a dog."

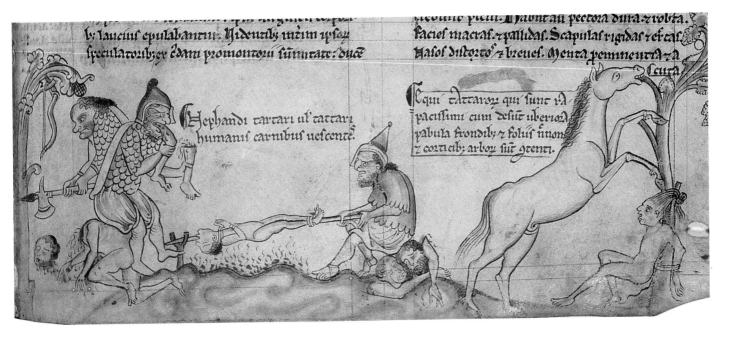

cally advanced than any in western Asia. Yet Kublai did not wait for victory before affirming his authority. In 1271, when the vestiges of Song power were confined to the southeast, he proclaimed himself first emperor of the Mongol Yuan dynasty.

Thereafter, Kublai lived in a style of dazzling opulence and refinement that belied his nomad origin. Bejeweled and robed in silk, he ruled from a palace whose walls were plated with gold and silver and decorated with the figures of dragons, beasts, and birds. He was surrounded by counselors and courtiers, both Chinese and Mongol; guarded by rotating shifts of 3,000 knights from his 12,000-strong personal guard; and attended by countless concubines, who in turn, were served by eunuchs. He gave audiences to ambassadors and merchants from all over Asia and beyond and held feasts in a hall that seated 6,000 guests.

This great khan of the Mongols saw himself in traditional Chinese terms: as the Son of Heaven, issuing edicts from the Middle Kingdom, to which all peoples of the earth owed tribute. By identifying himself so closely with the Chinese world, he fanned the fires of revolt in Mongolia and eventually had to send an army to regain the old capital Karakoram. His forces triumphed, but to no lasting effect. Kublai Khan would never reside in Karakoram, nor would he permanently station troops in the steppes. China had become more precious to him than all the domains of the Mongol Empire, more valuable even than Mongolia.

The West had made several overtures to the Mongols, with the aim of converting them to Christianity. Most notable among these ventures were the missions by the friars John of Plano Carpini and William of Rubruck. That of the former, in 1245, was the first recorded European exploration of Asia. It failed, however: The khan assumed that the pope was offering homage. That of William fared no better: He mourned his failure to convert Mongke in 1254 with the words, "Had I had the power of Moses to work miracles, perhaps I could have convinced him." But in 1266, another opportunity presented itself almost by chance. In that year, Kublai received at his court two Venetian merchants, who had been forced off their intended route by wars. Their names were Niccolo and Matteo Polo.

On a hunting expedition, Kublai Khan, clad in a magnificent ermine coat, is accompanied by a woman dressed in the Chinese fashion. Although he adopted the lifestyle of the Chinese court, Kublai never lost his Mongol passion for the hunt. The great khan did not stint his enjoyment, traveling in luxury and employing trained lions, leopards, and eagles, in addition to huge numbers of mastiffs and falcons. Nor were others to miss out on the fun: Marco Polo recorded that between the months of December and February, Kublai ordered all the people within fifty miles of where he was staying to devote their time to hunting and hawking.

Kublai was so impressed with these Europeans that he made them a startling proposition. Let the pope, he said, send 100 men learned in religion and the arts to his court. If the savants could prove the superiority of Christianity over other religions, then he and all his subjects would be baptized. The khan assured the Polos that there would be more Christians in his realm than existed in all their part of the world.

The Venetians duly traveled back to the West but were unsuccessful in the ambitious project; when they finally returned to Kublai's court in 1275, they could deliver only some papal letters and, as requested, holy oil from Jerusalem. With them, however, they brought Niccolo's twenty-year-old son, Marco Polo.

Kublai, it seems, took a liking to this bright young Venetian and employed him for seventeen years as a special envoy, sending him on missions throughout the empire. Those journeys, and his intimate knowledge of Kublai's court, gave Marco the material for *A Description of the World*, the story of his travels as dictated to a professional romancer, which gave an invaluable picture of Mongol China and its emperor.

Kublai Khan, as Polo described him, was of medium height, well proportioned in build, and had "a pink and white complexion like a rose, fine black eyes, and a handsome nose." He had perhaps more than 100 children, but only the boys were noted: twenty-five sons by numerous young concubines and twenty-two sons by four legitimate wives, each of whom had her own household with no fewer than 300 beautiful girls in attendance. Beyond the bedchamber, Kublai's chief pastimes were hunting and feasting. He rode to the hunt on the backs of four harnessed elephants in a richly timbered howdah, accompanied by trained leopards and hounds and the hawks of some 10,000 falconers. He observed numerous feast days, notably New Year's Day, when his 5,000 elephants were paraded, and his birthday, when he dressed in beaten gold and dined with 1,200 nobles cloaked in similar finery.

Marco Polo was overwhelmed by the opulence of Kublai's way of life. He marveled at the splendors of Dadu and Hangzhou, the greatest cities he had ever seen. He was amazed, too, by everyday things he had never encountered before—porcelain, asbestos, a "long-burning black stone" (coal), and the use of paper money, "made from bark collected from mulberry trees." But, in truth, his impressions emphasized how far in advance of Europe's civilization China's society was. Few of the wonders he observed could be attributed to Kublai Khan and the Mongols.

Among those few was a superefficient communications system. New roads, radiating from Dadu to the farthest corners of the Mongol Empire, greatly boosted international trade, making China more accessible to the outside world than ever before. Internal transport was much improved by extending the Great Canal—built in the fifth century BC to connect the Yangtze and Yellow rivers—until it stretched some 1,000 miles from Hangzhou to the capital in the north. There was also a remarkably swift courier service operated via some 10,000 well-appointed post houses, each about twenty-five miles apart and stabling hundreds of horses.

Marco Polo lavished praise on Kublai for these developments. He stressed, too, the emperor's generosity in distributing free grain to "people who are poverty-stricken because of illness or other misfortunes that prevent them from working." But his view of China was one-sided. To the Chinese themselves, already used to the benefits of their civilization, Kublai's reign was in many respects a disaster. Although the great khan was the first Mongol ruler to fully recognize the importance of agriculture and trade, his twenty-three-year rule brought progressive impoverishment to the Chinese peasantry. His efforts to expand the productivity of the land were a dismal failure, and in his energetic encouragement of commerce, he favored non-Chinese interests to such a degree that profits from foreign trade drained out of the country.

The fact was that the Mongols showed little talent for government. Ch'u-ts'-ai, the shrewd adviser of Genghis and Ogedei, had warned: "The empire was won on horseback, but it will not be governed on horseback." Although the great khans took heed, they could not set up efficient administrations of their own. In China, they found it convenient to retain the local ways of administering the country through a

The capering antics of this fifteen-inch-high pottery actor recall the many theatrical entertainments offered at Kublai Khan's court. Chinese drama flourished under the patronage of the nation's Mongol rulers, and districts with as many as a dozen theaters grew up in most of the principal cities. Simple entertainments with singers and dancers evolved into fully constructed plays that tackled serious subjects and used colloquial dialogue. Courtroom stories became particularly popular. Prestige was added to the profession by scholars who, no longer guaranteed a career in the khan's civil service, took to writing comedies and tragedies that became the foundation of Chinese classical drama.

Issued by Kublai Khan to one of his military commanders, this seal would also have been accompanied by a *paiza,* a metal tablet bearing a symbol of authority that could easily be recognized by illiterate soldiers. The seal's impress *(below)* reveals writing in the script known as 'Phags-pa, an early attempt to unite the Mongol lands linguistically. Since the Mongols had no alphabet and the Uigur script that they used on the steppe did not accurately represent Mongol sound, Kublai Khan commissioned a Tibetan lama to devise a script to represent not only Mongol but Chinese and the other major languages of the empire. The lama succeeded, yet his new alphabet never gained popular acceptance, and the Uigur script continued to be used.

bureaucratic elite. It was a sensible expedient. But now the centuries-old system operated inefficiently, largely because the number of Chinese officials was limited, and important offices were allocated to Mongols and privileged foreigners.

In addition, Kublai never abandoned the shamanistic beliefs of his Mongol ancestors. In Dadu, as Marco Polo noted, he maintained some 5,000 full-time astrologers and soothsayers, who fostered in him a deep mistrust of the native population. The result was that China acquired a racially and culturally divisive caste structure headed by the military: several hundred thousand Mongols who made no contribution to the economy and were exempt from taxation. A second class of privileged citizens comprised other non-Chinese, such as Persians and Turks, who operated as senior civil servants, entrepreneurs, and merchants. Like the Mongols, these foreigners enjoyed tax exemption and numerous privileges, including priority in the use of official trade routes and the post road services.

The majority of the population were third- or fourth-class citizens, with former subjects of the Jin taking marginal preference over the Song Chinese, who were treated as the lowest of the low. The Jin and the Song regarded their alien rulers as barbarians, yet they were the ones treated as inferiors both by custom and by law, forbidden, for example, to learn the Mongol language or to marry a Mongol. They could not walk the streets after dark or own weapons.

Kublai exacerbated the economic inefficiency of Mongol rule by waging costly wars that brought only modest gains. His political aim was to establish his Middle Kingdom as the center of the world. In its pursuit, he sent armies on inconclusive, often disastrous campaigns against Japan and kingdoms in the territories now known as Thailand, Burma, Vietnam, Malaysia, Java, and the Philippines.

Mongol military expertise, so dependent on cavalry strength, had little value in the jungles of Southeast Asia. Nor were the khan's men any more successful in the two great naval expeditions they launched against Japan. The last, in 1283, ended with tens of thousands of Mongols either enslaved or put to the sword. Kublai never managed to avenge this humiliation. He died at the age of seventy-nine, in 1294. Although he had failed to emulate his grandfather, Genghis, in uniting the Mongol peoples, his achievements as general and statesman had been considerable. His Chinese conquests brought about the reunification of a country that had been divided for 350 years. The Yuan dynasty survived another seventy-four years, but it was never powerful enough to seek new conquests. Its decline was hastened by rivalries among the descendants of Kublai, by the growing arrogance and oppressiveness of the Mongol nobles, by the greed and corruption of the landowning Chinese aristocracy, and by inflation, which rendered paper money worthless. Civil war was finally made inevitable by the combination of crippling taxes and a series of appalling floods and other natural disasters.

Many rebel groups rose up to defy their alien masters. The most powerful of them was led by the peasant-born Zhu Yuanzhang, a former Buddhist novice, who gradually gained control of the rural south. In 1368, a huge peasant army swept over the north, taking the great capital of Dadu in the face of only token resistance. The anti-Kublai conservatives in Mongolia had been proved right. After decades of exposure to the silk-cushioned court life of China, a new generation of Mongol warriors had emerged: soldiers not only poor in discipline but even lacking the traditional appetite

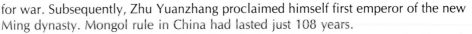

for war. Subsequently, Zhu Yuanzhang proclaimed himself first emperor of the new Ming dynasty. Mongol rule in China had lasted just 108 years.

The rot was not restricted to China. From the late thirteenth century on, the Mongol Empire went into rapid decline. Quarreling factions and weak hereditary leaders destroyed Genghis's dream of unity; the once-proud armies lost discipline when their purpose switched from conquest to occupation; and in China and Persia especially, power was eroded by the influence of more advanced cultures.

In the Ilkhanate of Persia, the Mongols devastated the land to such a degree that they were compelled to use a Persian bureaucracy to revive the economy. Here, even more rapidly than in China, the conquerors were absorbed into the culture. Confronted by the powerful Mamluks in Egypt and Syria, it became expedient for the Ilkhans to adopt Islam. The first to do so, ruling from 1282 to 1285, took the name Ahmad and the title of sultan. But in his successor's reign, Buddhist and Christian influences prevailed, bringing economic chaos: bureaucratic corruption, ruthless exploitation of the peasantry, and inflation fueled by the use of paper money. Order was restored in 1295, but on Islamic terms: The Ilkhan Ghazan declared his adherence to Islam, heralding an unbroken succession of Muslim Ilkhans until the male line of Hulegu's heirs ended in 1335. The Persian khanate had lasted eighty years.

The Mongols' rule in Russia and central Asia was more enduring: These lands had a less developed tradition of central government, making the Mongols' administrative inexperience less disabling. Compared with Persia and China, they were primitive societies, where the Mongols had no need of sophisticated bureaucracies. The sword was sufficient to harvest tribute and taxes.

The khanate of the Golden Horde prospered at the expense of Russia's disunited native principalities. Princes of local dynasties were allowed to keep their thrones if they journeyed to pay tribute and do homage at Sarai. The system operated without significant resistance for more than 130 years and existed, though on a diminishing scale, for two and a half centuries. It was only in the eighteenth century that the last independent Mongol state in the Crimea was overrun by the Russians.

In the meantime, the Chagatai khanate was fatally weakened by years of inter-Mongol conflict between the traditionalists in the eastern half and those in the west who had adopted the Islamic faith and, in many cases, the Persian language. Finally, in 1369, a new leader emerged: a soldier who seized power in Samarkand and ultimately asserted his authority over nearly all the Mongol lands in both the Chagatai and Golden Horde realms. Commonly called Timur Lang, "Timur the Lame," he was destined to become infamous throughout Europe as Tamerlane, the scourge of all central and western Asia.

Made in China for a high-ranking officer, this silver-inlaid Mongol helmet was of the same standard design as the iron or leather headgear worn by Mongol cavalrymen. Like the hats and helmets of all the khan's soldiers, it would have originally been adorned with two red ribbons hanging down the back from the top.

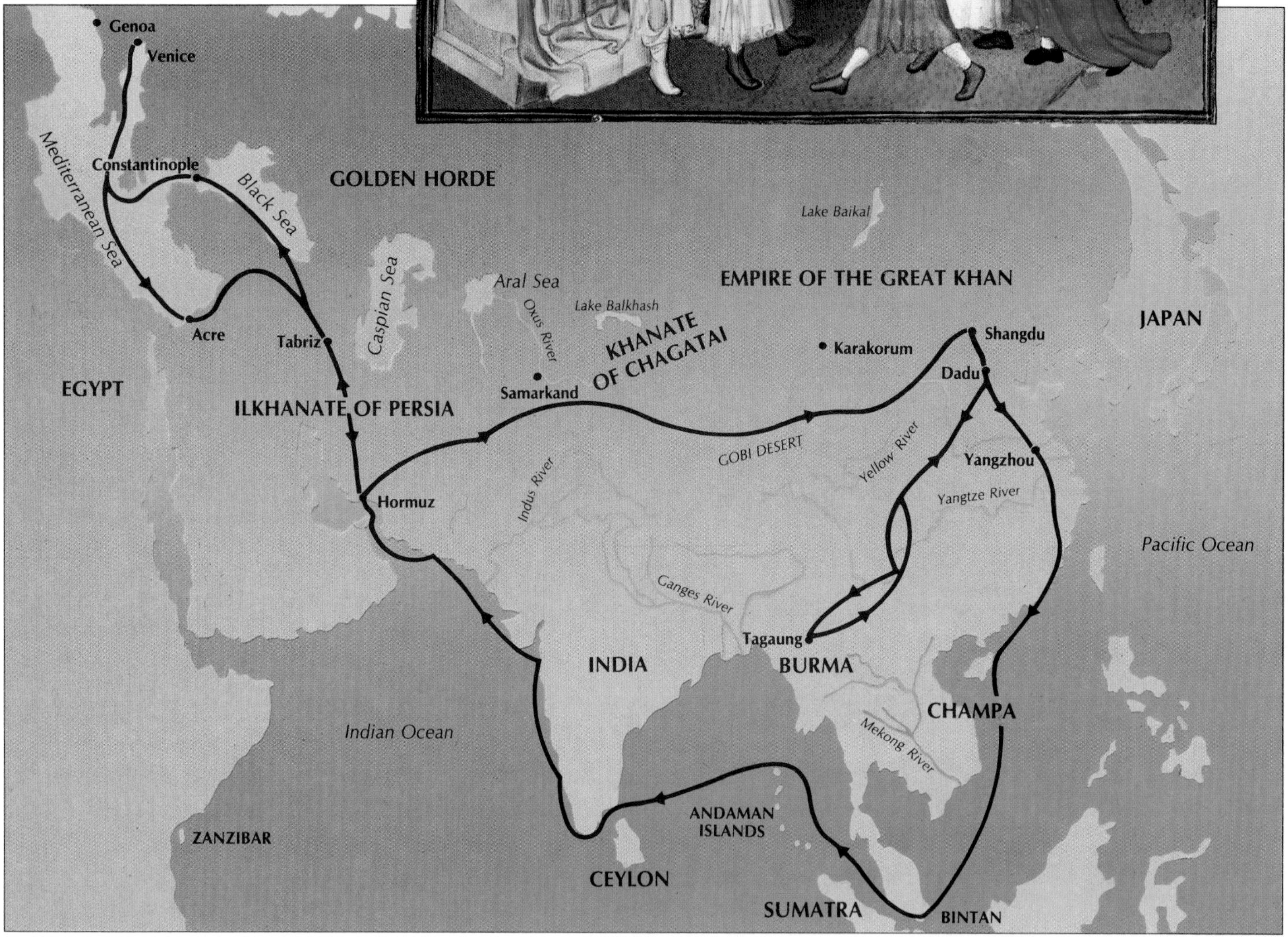

Genoa

Venice

Mediterranean Sea

Constantinople

Black Sea

GOLDEN HORDE

Lake Baikal

Aral Sea

Oxus River

Lake Balkhash

EMPIRE OF THE GREAT KHAN

JAPAN

Shangdu

Karakorum

Acre

Tabriz

Caspian Sea

KHANATE OF CHAGATAI

Dadu

EGYPT

ILKHANATE OF PERSIA

Samarkand

GOBI DESERT

Yellow River

Yangzhou

Yangtze River

Pacific Ocean

Hormuz

Indus River

Ganges River

Tagaung

INDIA

BURMA

CHAMPA

Indian Ocean

Mekong River

ZANZIBAR

ANDAMAN ISLANDS

CEYLON

SUMATRA

BINTAN

The rise of Timur signaled the end of the Mongol Empire proper. By the dawn of the fifteenth century, the conquerors from the steppes had become so integrated with the conquered that they ceased to exist as a separate race. In Russia, they had merged with Turks, Slavs, and Finns to create a new Turkish-speaking race loosely known as Tartars. In central Asia, they had become indistinguishable from the masses, predominantly Turkic or Persian in origin. The destructive force unleashed by Genghis Khan in 1207 had swept across Eurasia and finally worn itself out.

At its height in 1260, the Mongol Empire stretched from the Pacific Ocean in the east to Russia's Dnieper River in the west, from the Arctic Ocean in the north to the Strait of Malacca in the south. In their conquests of Persia and China, the Mongols had gained control of the two most advanced civilizations in the world. Yet in carving out this colossal realm, they themselves contributed nothing to methods of organized government or the advancement of arts and sciences. Indeed, they had nothing to give their conquered peoples apart from a keener appreciation of the methods of war.

As military conquerors, however, the Mongols were catalysts for many changes, among which was the alteration in strength and distribution of the world's leading religions—Islam, Christianity, and Buddhism. Under the Mongols, Buddhism took a far stronger hold in eastern Asia, especially in China, where it was viewed sympathetically by Kublai and his descendants. Islam suffered a shattering blow with the sack of Baghdad, only to flourish anew with the Cairo of the Mamluks as its new capital. Meanwhile, under the aegis of a flourishing Persian culture, the Muslim religion was adopted by a majority of the Mongols, and it spread far and wide in their western territories. And although this expansion represented a lost opportunity for Christianity, the western half of Christendom had escaped Mongol conquest. With its natural development undisturbed, the West was eventually able to flourish, whereas the Mongol-influenced East was held back by a heritage of tyranny.

In addition, the vastness of the Mongol Empire allowed, for the first time, an intercontinental traffic in goods, knowledge, and ideas. For a while in the mid-thirteenth century, the main arteries of Asia and Europe were thrown open by the so-called Pax Mongolica, a terror-enforced peace so effective that merchants and missionaries under the nominal protection of the great khan could journey east and west in relative safety. Thus, at its zenith, the empire oversaw international intercourse on an unprecedented scale. Representatives of all nations and faiths were received at the great khan's court in Karakoram. And in Kublai Khan's Dadu, there was a comingling of papal envoys from Rome and Buddhist priests from India, of artisans from France, Italy, and China, of merchants from Persia, Java, and Ceylon.

Asia was crisscrossed by caravan routes, and China was thrown open to the world by both land and sea. Each year, so Marco Polo recorded, 20,000 cargo ships sailed up the Yangtze River, bringing diamonds and pearls from India; ginger, cotton, and muslin from Ceylon; black pepper, white walnuts, and cloves from Java. More significant, the gradual westward flow of eastern artifacts, knowledge, and expertise worked in favor of a Europe that was far behind China in the arts and sciences.

Ultimately, the barbarian rule of China led to a backlash of xenophobia. Under the fiercely nationalistic Ming, China became more isolated than ever. By then, also, the great trans-Asian trade routes had been closed by political upheavals during the decline of the Mongol Empire. But no matter. The wonders and wealth of the Far East were no longer secret, and the West would not be denied them forever.

Voyaging overland through Persia and the Gobi Desert with his father, Marco Polo arrived at the court of Kublai Khan in 1275. For the next seventeen years he acted as Kublai's envoy, traveling on fact-finding expeditions as far afield as Burma and southern China and possibly even acting as governor of the northern city of Yangzhou.

Polo returned to Venice in 1295, voyaging via Champa (present-day Vietnam), Sumatra, Ceylon, and India. With him he brought not only a fortune in precious stones but a series of notebooks in which he had recorded detailed observations of all he had seen and reports of lands as distant as Zanzibar and Japan. Later, during a brief imprisonment by the Genoese, he dictated the story of his travels to a fellow prisoner. After his release, it was published as *Divisament dou Monde,* "A Description of the World." The prologue claimed that Polo had traveled more extensively than any man since Creation; indeed, he revealed a world that was almost wholly unknown to Western Christendom, and some parts of his route would not be traveled by Europeans for another 600 years.

The wonders that he described captured the imagination of the masses, and the book was reprinted many times. From one fourteenth-century version came the picture shown at left, above, depicting the khan's men exchanging paper money—then an unknown commodity in the West—for bullion. The idea of paper being valued as much as silver seemed fantastic to many Westerners, as did such other reports as that of rocks—coal—being burned for fuel. Indeed, it is related that Polo was asked on his deathbed, in 1324, to retract his invented fables. His reply was that he had barely told half of what he had seen.

RISE OF THE SHOGUNS

On a spring morning in the year 1185, so chroniclers claimed, the sea in the narrow Strait of Dannoura, between the Japanese islands of Honshu and Kyaeu, turned red with blood. Pounding war drums echoed off the cliffs; shouted commands and the screams of the wounded all but drowned out the relentless clattering of arrows hitting armor as the warships of two rival clans met in battle. The prize they sought, apart from each other's destruction, was domination over the rocky, volcanic archipelago, off the eastern flank of Asia, that formed the isolated realm of Japan.

The contending armies were led by the Taira and Minamoto, the mightiest of Japan's warrior clans. Numerically, the Minamoto forces were superior, with a fleet two or three times as large as the Taira's. But the Taira troops were far better at naval warfare, or so their commanders reassured them: The Minamoto might be good cavalrymen, but they had little experience at sea. In addition, the Taira possessed what they saw as the moral advantage. For behind the fighting fleet stood ships carrying the cream of the Japanese nobility, connected by birth or marriage to the Taira clan. In their midst was the emperor himself, the seven-year-old Antoku, with his mother and grandmother. Both Taira, they carried the imperial regalia—the Sacred Seal, the Sacred Mirror, and the Sacred Sword—which since time immemorial had been the triple emblems of imperial power. But even with such impressive patronage, a Taira victory was uncertain. Soothsayers on both sides claimed to have seen omens—a mysterious white banner drifting out of the sky, the sudden appearance of a school of dolphins—suggesting that heaven might favor the Minamoto.

The omens did not lie. The Minamoto bided their time, taking only defensive action, until the tide turned in their favor. Then they bombarded the enemy with hurricanes of arrows; their warriors boarded one Taira ship after another, slew the sailors, and seized the helms. Escape was well-nigh impossible: Heavy seas and the high cliffs lining the strait made landing quite difficult, leaving would-be fugitives at the mercy of Minamoto grappling hooks.

Even to the imperial party, defeat now seemed inevitable. But Antoku's Taira grandmother would not allow herself, the royal child, or his imperial regalia to fall into the enemy's hands. She dressed herself in a gown of dark gray mourning and instructed Antoku to press his palms together and recite his prayers. Then, enfolding Antoku in her arms, she seized the Sacred Sword and plunged into the sea. Following this example, the boy-emperor's mother weighted down the sleeves of her kimono with stones and flung herself overboard, with a host of other courtiers—male and female—who preferred death to humiliation.

The boy-emperor sank below the waves and quickly drowned, but not all his elders succeeded in their wish to join him. Minamoto boatmen plied their grappling hooks to catch the women by their long, black hair and hauled them, painfully and un-

Glaring ferociously at potential evildoers, this wood-carved *kongo rikishi,* or "thunderbolt-wielding strong-man," originally stood guard at the portals of a Buddhist temple. As an official state religion, Buddhism was already widespread in Japan when the military came to power in 1185. In the following century, the ranks of its adherents swelled dramatically as an increasing number of sects offered simple paths to enlightenment for prince and peasant alike.

ceremoniously, to safety. The Sacred Seal and the Sacred Mirror were also recovered: The Taira woman who had tried to jump overboard with the mirror in her arms was stopped by a Minamoto arrow that pinned her gown to the deck. But the Sacred Sword was lost forever, and no number of prayers at the country's greatest shrines or forays by the most skilled and courageous divers could bring it to light.

The sword's disappearance marked an irrevocable change in the fortunes of its owners and indeed of all Japan. The victory of the Minamoto at Dannoura heralded radical transformations in nearly every aspect of national life. The way the country was governed, the identity and nature of those in power, the system of values these rulers espoused, the distribution of wealth, even the ways of worship were all about to be changed beyond recognition. The days of unchallenged imperial rule were over: The provinces' warriors, who prized martial discipline over courtly etiquette and bravery in battle over patrician pedigrees, now controlled the kingdom's destiny.

Separated from the Asian mainland by the dangerous currents of the Sea of Japan, the islands of Japan lay 125 miles from their nearest neighbors, with the easternmost parts some 500 miles from the continental landmass. Although the country comprised countless islands, the bulk of the population resided on the major southernmost cluster of Honshu, Kyushu, and Shikoku. The terrain of Japan was spectacularly

Japan entered the thirteenth century as a powerful nation under the hegemony of a military government, or shogunate, ruling from the town of Kamakura. The shoguns nominally took their authority from the emperor, residing with his court in the ancient city of Kyoto, 300 miles to the west, although the monarch's duties were mainly ceremonial. Centered on the three major islands of Honshu, Kyushu, and Shikoku, the Japanese population enjoyed a period of stability under the shoguns in which the country prospered and merchants plied a lucrative trade with mainland Asia. But the cost of meeting two unsuccessful Mongol invasions, launched from Korea in the latter half of the century, proved too much: By 1333 the Kamakura shogunate had fallen, and the country was once more at war with itself.

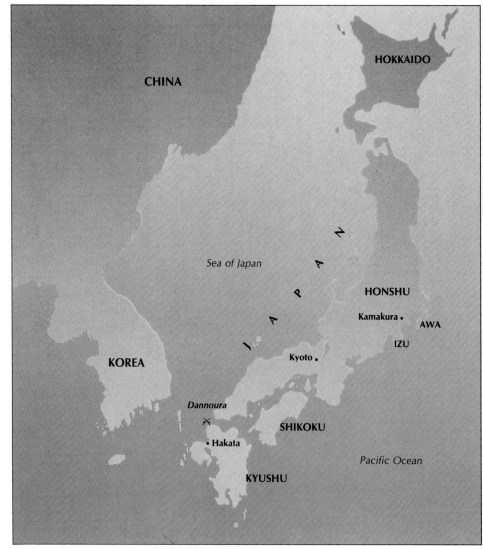

beautiful, with steep mountains—the highest being some 12,000 feet above sea level—deep gorges, and fast-flowing rivers that poured into innumerable rocky bays. Yet for all its beauty, it was an inhospitable landscape: The very earth underfoot was unsteady, lying precariously on fault lines, prey to earthquakes, volcanic eruptions, and tidal waves. Most of the land surface was unreceptive to agriculture, and despite concerted efforts to clear new territory and painstaking terracing of the lower mountain slopes, less than one-sixth of the total area could be placed under cultivation.

Compensation for these difficulties was a climate ideally suited for rice cultivation. Seasonal winds came with almost clockwork regularity, bringing heavy rains in the summer and drier but cooler weather in the winter. These conditions, along with plentiful sunshine and subtropical temperatures for much of the growing season, were perfect for rice. No other grain gave so high a yield within so restricted an area— an important advantage where farmland was in short supply. Other crops, such as millet, barley, wheat, soybeans, and various vegetables, were grown, but the Japanese—whether prince or peasant—essentially lived on rice.

In turn, rice was the basis of the entire economy. The coasts supported small fishing communities, whose catch might be traded for a share of the precious grain from the hinterland, but the vast majority of the population were peasants, living on the food they grew for themselves. Agricultural land was carved up into large manorial estates, generally held by the aristocracy, by the imperial house itself, or by the great temples and monasteries. These landowners were remote figures, based mainly in the capital, Kyoto, whose sole link with the land was the receipt of the quota of rice it yielded or the income from the sale of the crop. The people who actually ran the estates were the powerful local landlords—members of warrior clans such as the Taira and Minamoto. Serving as stewards and overseers, they organized the work of the manors and collected the crops for the proprietors. But they were more than mere hired managers: In troubled times, they took up arms and marshaled troops to defend their territories; in more peaceful periods, they ruled the countryside, dispensing justice and enforcing law. At all times they were a formidable power, whose influence and authority far outstripped that of the absentee landowners in Kyoto.

Antoku's predecessors had reigned over this land for possibly a thousand years. For the last four hundred of them, known as the Heian period, the fountainhead of power had been Kyoto—home to the imperial court and the inbred network of aristocratic families who dominated it. By the twelfth century, the aristocrats had become increasingly dependent on the two great clans of the Taira and the Minamoto. In the capital, these warriors shielded the emperor and kept the peace; in the countryside, they quashed rebellions, pacified the outlying provinces, and defended the rural manors whose income sustained the urban nobility in their opulent, leisured lives at court. Although the patricians relied on the warriors for protection, they treated them with contempt. But before the century ended, the control of Japan would slip from the soft and perfumed hands of the nobility into the rougher palms of the military.

By the mid-twelfth century, the imperial court at Kyoto was no longer the hub of the political universe. The emperor had become a figure of largely ceremonial significance, whose ritual functions were so time-consuming that it was the practice for any monarch seeking effective political involvement to abdicate. The ex-emperor would then set up his own separate, fully staffed court and hold sway from behind the scenes. Meanwhile, his successor, who might be only a child, would preside as the official monarch. Coexistence was not always peaceful; rivalries between court factions often boiled up into power struggles between the old emperor and the new.

A cumbersome bureaucracy developed about these twin poles of government. Senior posts remained in the hands of often incompetent hereditary officeholders, and promotion was less a matter of merit than of patronage. The lives of all members of this rank-obsessed hierarchy were ruled by rigid etiquette, governing everything from the size and shape of their carriages to the fabrics and colors of their gowns.

In contrast, Japanese spirituality reflected tolerance: Buddhism, which declared that man could attain enlightenment by destroying fear, hatred, and delusion, had come from India by way of China and had been adopted as a state religion in the eighth century, but its adherents never presented it as the one true faith. In Japan, it

In a picturesque incident from the civil war waged in Japan during the latter half of the twelfth century, Minamoto cavalrymen attack the fleet of their Taira foes in the shallow strait of Fujito, off the southern coast of Honshu. The conflict between the two rival factions climaxed at the battle of Dannoura in 1185, which ended in victory for the Minamoto. During the following century, tales of the clan struggles were added to national legend. Part of an oral tradition later committed to paper using a recognizably modern Japanese script, the accounts formed the basis for the thirty-six individual scrolls that make up the 2,300-foot-long *Heike Monogatari* scroll, from which this detail is taken.

coexisted comfortably with other traditions, such as Shinto, in which a random collection of ancient native deities, representing mountains, valleys, localities, and forces of nature, were worshiped in modest shrines with simple ceremonies. People saw no contradiction in honoring these native gods, making pilgrimages to Buddhist shrines, and paying deference to the codes of Chinese Confucianism—a formalization of ethical and behavioral rules that espoused harmony and respect for superiors.

But it was the great Buddhist temples and monasteries that dominated the religious establishment. Their abbots were actively engaged in politics, their monks and nuns were often members of the nobility—even emperors—who had opted for a religious life, and their considerable landholdings made them prodigiously wealthy. To protect their interests, the religious houses had private armies consisting of warrior-monks whose spiritual service was based partly on their skill with a sword. These troops were volatile: If they felt that the prestige of their monastery was compromised or their revenue endangered, they would not scruple to march on the capital or to fight secular soldiers or the monks of other houses with considerable ferocity. Buddhist strictures against shedding blood did not appear to enter into their theology.

The willful warrior-monks were just one sign of a country that was gradually drifting out of the court's control. The roads were dangerous—the haunts of impoverished soldiers who lived by robbery and theft. On the seacoasts, piracy was rife. And the countryside was dominated by strong local lords and their bands of well-armed horsemen. Provincial officials, originally appointed by the court, did little to restrain the chieftains and their clansmen: They were more interested in garnering local wealth and prestige than in carrying out their public duties.

The leaders of these provincial warrior clans boasted princely origins. By ancient custom, all descendants of the imperial house except eldest sons or direct heirs to the throne lost their noble status after six generations. For the ex-nobles, military life offered a means of making their way in the world. Of such stock were many of the Taira and Minamoto. Generations of soldiering had removed their courtly polish but given them a different kind of pride: They were *samurai* (literally, "those who serve"), fighting men who lived by a code of discipline, self-sacrifice, and courage. And while their followers were not necessarily their kin, they were attached by ties of loyalty as powerful as bonds of blood.

For a time, the Taira and Minamoto had lived side by side in wary rivalry, gathering patronage at court and furthering their material and political interests in the countryside. But a succession of brief yet savage internal conflicts had turned the two clans into enemies. In the 1150s, the court had split into two warring parties, enlisting Taira and Minamoto to fight each other on their behalf. The Taira triumphed, crushing the Minamoto so completely that few believed their clan could ever rise again.

The victors quickly established themselves in Kyoto as virtual dictators, packing key offices with their own kin and dispatching their followers to govern the provinces. Forsaking their spartan military existence, they insinuated themselves into the innermost circles of court society and married into the aristocracy. Any doubts about their newfound prestige were silenced when the daughter of their chief became the consort to the emperor and, in due course, mother to his successor. Their arrogance became a byword; indeed, one of their clan was heard to say that anyone who was not a Taira was simply nobody at all.

But while the Taira leaders reveled in the soft life of the capital, the Minamoto forces began to regroup in the provinces of eastern Japan, under the formidable Minamoto Yoritomo. A contemporary portrait of Yoritomo reveals a man of grave demeanor, determined jaw, and intelligent, unsmiling eyes. Born in 1147, he had ample reason to hate the Taira. At the age of twelve, he had accompanied his father, a Minamoto leader, into combat against the Taira. The Minamoto were defeated, his father was killed by a traitor in his own ranks, and the boy was captured and subsequently exiled to the eastern province of Izu. There he found a benefactor and eventually a father-in-law in Hojo Tokimasa, a local warlord who, though connected to the Taira, was friendly to the Minamoto. With Tokimasa's support, he was able to gather an army of some 300 men, and in 1180 he once more marched against the Taira to aid an imperial prince who had tried to break their stranglehold. But the rebel forces were defeated by an overwhelmingly superior Taira army at the battle of Ishibashi Mountain, and Yoritomo fled east, by sea, to the remote peninsula of Awa.

Distant and difficult of access, Awa offered a secure base from which Yoritomo began to regroup his forces, reestablishing contact with old Minamoto followers and gaining support among other warrior families opposed to the Taira.

As his strength grew, Yoritomo needed a more accessible base of operations, and on the advice of his new allies, he chose the small coastal town of Kamakura. Strategically, the site made sense: Some 300 miles east of Kyoto, it was far from the reach of the Taira and the imperial court, easy to defend, and surrounded by the lands of Minamoto loyalists. Historically, too, there were Minamoto connections: Yoritomo's ancestors had built a shrine there 100 years before.

Yoritomo set out from Awa with a few hundred followers on horseback. But as he traveled west toward Kamakura, more and more allies joined him. Even disaffected Taira supporters fell in behind him. One warlord, so the chroniclers say, brought an army sixty times as large as Yoritomo's own. By the time Yoritomo entered Kamakura in the autumn of 1180, he had 27,000 men at his command. Those lords who cast their lots with Yoritomo did not necessarily do so because of any particular belief in the greater virtue of his cause. They were more likely to be motivated by sheer self-interest and the realization that Yoritomo's star was now in the ascendant.

Before the end of 1180, Minamoto troops had defeated a Taira force and wiped out a formerly powerful provincial family that in spite of its Minamoto connections had stood against the clan. But Yoritomo was in no hurry to plunge into all-out war. His first priority was to bring strength and unity to his cause. To this end, he forgot old enmities and welcomed former opponents, even Taira, into his following. He used his influence to effect reconciliations between ex-rivals who now found themselves side by side in the Minamoto camp. Those of his supporters with no existing blood ties to Yoritomo's house were turned into honorary Minamoto; where possible, these bonds were cemented by marriage or by adoption into families within the clan.

The new vassals had a clear understanding of their obligations to their lord. In times of war, they rendered military service, but that service was not the end of their responsibilities. During peacetime, they were required to stand guard at Yoritomo's headquarters; act as his escorts and attendants when he traveled or took part in religious ceremonies; accompany him on hunting trips; and participate in all manner of martial contests, ranging from archery competitions to trials of horsemanship. At Kamakura, military skills were not allowed to rust.

In addition to these services, Yoritomo's followers made more material contributions to the cause. They were expected to present gifts to the lord and his family on special occasions and offer hospitality in their country houses. They also contributed timber to Yoritomo's construction projects, horses for his cavalry, and funds toward various good works, such as a roof repair to their leader's favorite shrine.

Yoritomo recompensed his warriors for their efforts. The most significant rewards were land rights—a share of the rice crop from one of the ever-growing number of rural estates under Minamoto control—or a lucrative stewardship on a Minamoto manor, with an automatic entitlement to a healthy portion of all profits from the land.

Yoritomo's efforts, or so he maintained, were dedicated to protecting imperial interests. Those who served him also served the emperor. But at the same time, he demanded his adherents' unswerving loyalty. A man whose father had been murdered by a traitor would brook no infidelities: Soldiers caught deserting were beheaded on the spot, and anyone whose devotion seemed lukewarm was the target for his imprecations and accusations. "He has the eyes of a rat," murmured Yoritomo of

Ceremonial robes and an elaborate coiffure lend gravity to the stern-eyed figure of Japan's first warrior-ruler, Minamoto Yoritomo, as captured on silk by a twelfth-century courtier-artist. A charismatic leader who defeated the rival Taira with the aid of his brother Yoshitsune, Yoritomo was ruthless in his search for power: He declared his brother a rebel in 1185 and eventually pursued him to his death. After his victory at Dannoura, Yoritomo ruled the country from his headquarters at Kamakura and in 1192 was awarded the supreme title of Seitaishogun, or Barbarian-Subduing Generalissimo. He died seven years later at the age of fifty-two.

one suspected waverer. "Rarely might one find a more villainous lieutenant." And to enforce this loyalty and keep order among his many followers, Yoritomo established an office for military management, known as the Samurai-dokoro, or Warriors' Bureau. It handled the assignment of ranks and duties, maintained military discipline, and supervised the activities of the Minamoto vassals.

Between 1181 and 1183, Yoritomo gradually built up his administration at Kamakura and consolidated Minamoto control over the eastern provinces. The Taira, lacking influence in that part of the country, could do little to stop him. At the same time, he was winning increasing support in Kyoto from members of the nobility who looked to the Minamoto to rid them of Taira hegemony. Confident that he now had friends at court, Yoritomo proposed that the policing of the country be divided, with the Taira named Protectors of the West, where their own influence was strongest, and his own clan made Protectors of the East. The imperial court seemed amenable to the idea, but the Taira spurned it.

By the end of that year, however, the Taira were on the run. Aware that Minamoto support was growing and that their enemies at court were gathering strength, they departed en masse from the capital to seek greater safety within their own western strongholds. They took with them their most important kinsman, the child-emperor Antoku, and the imperial regalia. The ex-emperor, Go-Shirakawa, nursing bitter grievances of his own against the Taira, declared them outlaws and sent Yoritomo to put them down. As a rueful Taira clansman observed, "Every single warrior in the east must have answered Yoritomo's call to arms."

The pursuit of the Taira was carried out under Yoritomo's brother Yoshitsune, whose military exploits made him a hero of folklore and literature for centuries to come. It was Yoshitsune who led the forces that crushed the Taira at Dannoura. While his brother did battle, Yoritomo continued the development of his administration at Kamakura. In 1184, the Samurai-dokoro was joined by two establishments: a bureau for running civil affairs in clan territories and a legal department for settling land disputes and seeing that justice was done on all Minamoto manors.

By the time the Minamoto won their decisive victory at Dannoura, Yoritomo had become the acknowledged defender of the imperial house, the man who would cleanse the land of Taira corruption. He was given supreme authority over all armed forces and used the exigencies of winning and keeping the peace as justification for extending his control. The country was soon being managed by a military elite consisting of Minamoto vassals, whom Yoritomo appointed as land stewards in charge of former Taira manors and as constables to police the provinces.

The court felt comfortable with Yoritomo, and he, in turn, felt comfortable with the court. Although his own upbringing was in the stern martial tradition of his clan, he had spent his earliest years among courtiers. Unlike his bluff and often illiterate fellow warriors, he valued scholarship and recruited many of the ablest court officials for his own staff at Kamakura. He appreciated the niceties of court etiquette, understood its

A WARRIOR'S ESTATE

As military retainers of the feudal lords who governed large domains within Japan, the samurai were pledged to defend their master's territory. In return for this service, they were often granted their own lands, occupying substantial houses set on self-supporting estates.

High-ranking samurai dwelt in secure stockades that were well equipped for both peace and war. As in the typical example shown here, stables, storehouses, and the living quarters of servants and lesser warriors stood grouped around the samurai's residence, which was thatched in reeds and equipped with extensive verandas. The walls of the buildings, made of expensive white cedar, were paneled with translucent paper screens. A plot within the compound provided space for a grove of maple trees and for cultivating vegetables. Food was cooked and eaten outdoors or in open-sided sheds. Water would have come from a nearby spring, beside which a small shrine might be erected.

In times of peace, the samurai's warriors practiced the martial arts of archery and swordplay within the fenced enclosure in front of the houses while laborers tilled the surrounding land. This tranquil compound, however, was also a fortress, constantly guarded, and protected by a moat, stout fences, and steep banks of earth planted with trees. When the compound was under attack, mud was spread on the roofs to protect them from incendiary arrows, and archers were hurried to the raised platform above the single gateway.

Skilled in the use of bow and sword, the samurai was a fearsome fighting machine whose loyalty lay first and foremost with his lord. To protect himself he wore an elaborate but efficient suit of armor. Over a light silk robe with baggy pantaloons and sleeves, the warrior donned a single garment composed of metal scales and plates, laced together with cords and suspended from the body by leather straps. For ease of movement, the right arm was left unprotected, and the armor below the waist was divided into a loose, four-part skirt. On his head the samurai sported a flared helmet, designed to intimidate the enemy as much as to deflect the blows of an opponent's sword. Compact, easily mended, and weighing less than twenty-five pounds, such armor was unparalleled for lightness and flexibility.

traditions, and was punctilious in following its procedures. He also had a reputation for fairness and justice: The smooth functioning of his own legal bureau had not gone unnoticed. With such effective administrative and judicial structures already in place, it seemed only sensible for Yoritomo to extend their reach beyond his own vassals, to embrace the country as a whole.

Both Kyoto and Kamakura stood to gain from this sharing of power. Freed of the humiliating yoke of Taira control, the imperial house was no longer compelled to restrict appointments and promotions to that clan's puppets. With peace restored in the countryside, nobles grew rich from the increased rice production of their estates. The monks of the great shrines and temples also approved of Yoritomo's respect for their rights; they, too, had been victims of the Taira, with their rice lands expropriated and their sanctuaries burned. The provincial warrior clans were equally enthusiastic. They felt secure under a strong government run by men of their own kind, and greater centralization was a small price to pay: With order restored, they had less need to render military service and could get on with the far more attractive business of clearing new land and increasing their estate revenues.

Yoritomo's prestige grew in proportion to his power. A contemporary historian, the abbot Jien, described his entry into the capital on a ceremonial visit from Kamakura:

> Everyone had waited expectantly for his arrival. But because it was raining on the day Yoritomo planned to enter the capital, he stopped over at a place outside the city. Then, when he entered the capital on the seventh day of the month—the rain having stopped, just as he wanted—his soldiers came riding into the city three abreast. Over 700 horsemen preceded him, and more than 300 were grouped behind him. Riding a black horse, and wearing an apron of deer's summer fur over a glossy tricolored robe of dark blue, light blue, and red, he was an impressive figure. After entering Kyoto, he paid his respects to Retired Emperor Go-Shirakaw and called at the imperial palace. In the eyes of Go-Shirakawa, no one was the equal of Yoritomo.

Other witnesses remarked that Yoritomo drew greater crowds, and engendered more excitement, than any public appearance by a retired or incumbent emperor. And it was felt to be no more than his due when in 1192 he was honored with the title Shogun, or in full, Seitaishogun, meaning Barbarian-Subduing Generalissimo.

His moment of glory was relatively brief: He died only seven years after the title was conferred. But the *bakufu* (literally, "tent headquarters"), the system he had created to govern his vassals at Kamakura, and the legitimate status and power he had won for the warrior caste would survive long after him, shaping the politics and culture of Japan for centuries to come.

On Yoritomo's death, real power in Kamakura passed into the hands of his widow, Masako. Like many highborn women of the age, she had taken religious vows upon widowhood. But her official renunciation of the world and its illusions did not stop her from taking an active part in government, and she equaled, if not surpassed, her late husband in ruthless efficiency. Her son Yoriie, nominal successor to the shogunate, was a weak reed: She provided the power behind the throne and set up a council of thirteen ministers—including her father, Hojo Tokimasa, Yoritomo's old benefac-

tor—to help her govern. She and her father soon conspired to remove Yoriie from the shogunate, but their alliance disintegrated when Tokimasa, without informing his fellow plotter, had Yoriie assassinated. When Tokimasa was revealed to be plotting against her second son, Sanetomo, as well, Masako and her brother, Hojo Yoshitoki, joined forces to drive out their father and made Sanetomo the new shogun. He did not win universal approval. The monk-historian Jien disparaged him as "foolishly careless, indulging himself in learning, and disgracing the offices he held."

But public favor was immaterial. Real power remained in the hands of Masako. On Sanetomo's death in 1219, she set up another underage member of her family as puppet shogun and made her brother the official regent, to run the Kamakura government on the child's behalf. After her brother's death, the regency would become a hereditary post, passing to his heirs and remaining in the hands of the Hojo family for more than a century. Some chroniclers found the irony amusing, recalling that although the Hojos were in the Minamoto camp, they were actually of Taira blood.

The intricate political structure of Kamakura Japan was now in place. The titular head of state was the emperor, whose court functions were largely ceremonial. Behind him stood the retired emperor, whose freedom from ritual responsibilities allowed him to devote more attention to furthering the interests of the imperial house. Meanwhile, many administrative responsibilities were officially in the hands of the shogun, presiding over the military establishment at Kamakura. Yet he, too, was in fact a figurehead: The regent was the real power in the land.

Not all parties were satisfied with the arrangement. Relations between Kyoto and Kamakura soured. In 1221, the retired emperor Go-Toba began to raise and train an army of his own with a view to restoring the dominance of the imperial house. The provincial monasteries, with their large troops of warrior-monks, sympathized with his cause. With this force behind him, he denounced the Hojo regent as a rebel and called upon the whole country to rise up in support. The bakufu responded swiftly. A large army made the long march west to Kyoto and suppressed the uprising in a matter of weeks. The regent banished the emperor, the retired emperor, and various members of the imperial family to remote islands, where in true aristocratic tradition they passed the time composing poetry. Former Emperor Go-Toba wrote:

> Sorry not to see
> Some people and sorrier
> To see some others,
> In my inmost self I feel
> The world has lost its savor.

Back in Kamakura, the regent did not pause for any such lyrical reflection. He was busy stamping out the last traces of dissent, exiling or executing the nobles who had taken part in the disturbances and seizing their manors.

These parcels of land fell into the regency's hands at an opportune moment. The military government was responsible for maintaining a growing population of warriors, many with little or no title to their own lands; to keep their loyalty, the regent was now able to reward them with stewardships of the confiscated manors. Although the vassals were not given the properties outright, they enjoyed a generous portion of the profits: Of every twelve acres of land under their stewardship, they were awarded two acres they could call their own, with no need to share its income. On the other ten acres—whose yields had to be apportioned among the actual cultivators of the land, the overseers, and their feudal masters in Kamakura or Kyoto—the stewards were allowed to impose a tax.

The regent scrupulously followed the policy, laid down by Yoritomo, of gaining the exiled emperor's permission for these arrangements. A certain amount of diplomatic arm-twisting may have been needed, but resistance by the court had been thoroughly broken. And to prevent any future misunderstandings, a branch office of the bakufu, backed up by a large armed force, was installed in the former Taira headquarters.

Culturally, Kyoto and Kamakura were worlds apart. The Kamakura society was based on traditional martial values: self-discipline, loyalty, honor, and austerity. By courage and devotion to duty, the samurai brought credit to his clan. Whenever he went to war, the ghosts of his ancestors stood at his shoulder. The fighting man proudly inscribed his name and origins on the shafts of his arrows and loudly recited his pedigree as he stepped onto the battlefield. "I who say this," declared one combatant, as he flung a challenge to the foe, "am a descendant of the Emperor Kammu in the tenth generation, grandson of the Minister of Justice Tadamori, second son of the governor of Aki, Kiyomori. My name is Motomori, my age is seventeen."

In the middle of the thirteenth century, a member of the regent's family, the Hojo, wrote a manual of good conduct entitled "Family Instructions" for the guidance of his son, who was about to take up a post in Kyoto as a deputy of the military government. It enjoined him to avoid bad companions, to fear all gods, to obey his lord and his parents without question, to be generous to the needy and cautious in his dealings with strangers, to avoid showing fear, and to practice his horsemanship and other martial skills on a regular basis. "The warrior," wrote the father, "must always bear in mind his moral duty. A good heart and the faith of a warrior are like the two wheels of a carriage."

The love of luxuries and an undue interest in matters of dress were to be avoided. Everyone in Kamakura remembered the reaction of their first shogun to an extravagantly dressed vassal: Yoritomo had borrowed the man's own sword, used it to lop off the rainbow-colored skirts of his robe, and excoriated him for squandering his wealth on silken garments instead of spending it for the good of his underlings.

The aristocrats in Kyoto had no such scruples. Aesthetics obsessed them. They poured the wealth of their manors into exquisite costumes; they expressed their emotions and arranged their assignations in allusive verse inscribed in beautiful calligraphy. Expeditions to view the full moon, admire the autumn leaves, or observe the first blossoms of spring occupied their abundant leisure hours. Court life consisted largely of a round of ceremonies, religious rituals, official banquets, and poetry competitions. Much behind-the-scenes activity went into the allocation of court privileges and promotions and the acquisition of the visible symbols of rank that went with them. Lady Nijo, a thirteenth-century courtier, proudly quoted the emperor's declaration of her status: "Nijo has publicly been granted permission to wear thin silk gowns and white pleated trousers anytime. She has even been given permission to board her carriage at the palace door."

The aristocrats privately called the Kamakura warriors "the Eastern Barbarians." But even the most supercilious courtier could not deny the effectiveness of the Kamakura administration. Pragmatism was the order of the day: Untrammeled by centuries of precedents and protocols, the bakufu ruled by trial and error. Decisions

SOUL OF THE SAMURAI

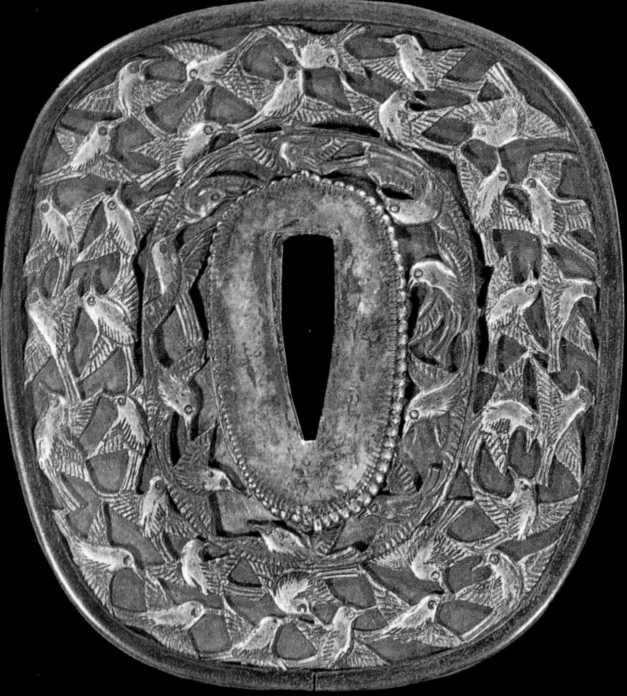

All that was important to a warrior in thirteenth-century Japan was symbolized by his sword. Awesome weapons requiring strict training and a meticulous etiquette for their use, they were also revered emblems of the samurai code of honor, bravery, and respect.

The creation of a blade was imbued with all the ritual of a religious ceremony. Swordsmiths did not eat any food derived from animals and abstained from sexual intercourse and intoxicating drink for several months while working on the weapon; they then donned ceremonial costumes for the final forging that created the razor-sharp edge of the perfect blade.

All disputes and problems were resolved by the sword, and the warrior lived and died by its laws. Strict decorum was involved: It was an offense to touch or step over another man's weapon, and to lay one's own on the floor and kick its guard in anyone's direction was tantamount to a challenge to the death.

Fashioned in traditional rice-cake shape, this guard of silver overlaid with gold adorned the blade of the ceremonial sword shown below. The guard's swirling bird design, possibly indicating spiritual longing, underlines the sword's use as a religious offering.

Worn suspended from two woven chains, this richly decorated sword was specially commissioned by a Kamakura warlord family for dedication to the Mishima shrine in the Izu Peninsula. Many such blades never saw combat but were placed in temples for worship or offered up as thanks for winning an important battle or fulfilling wishes.

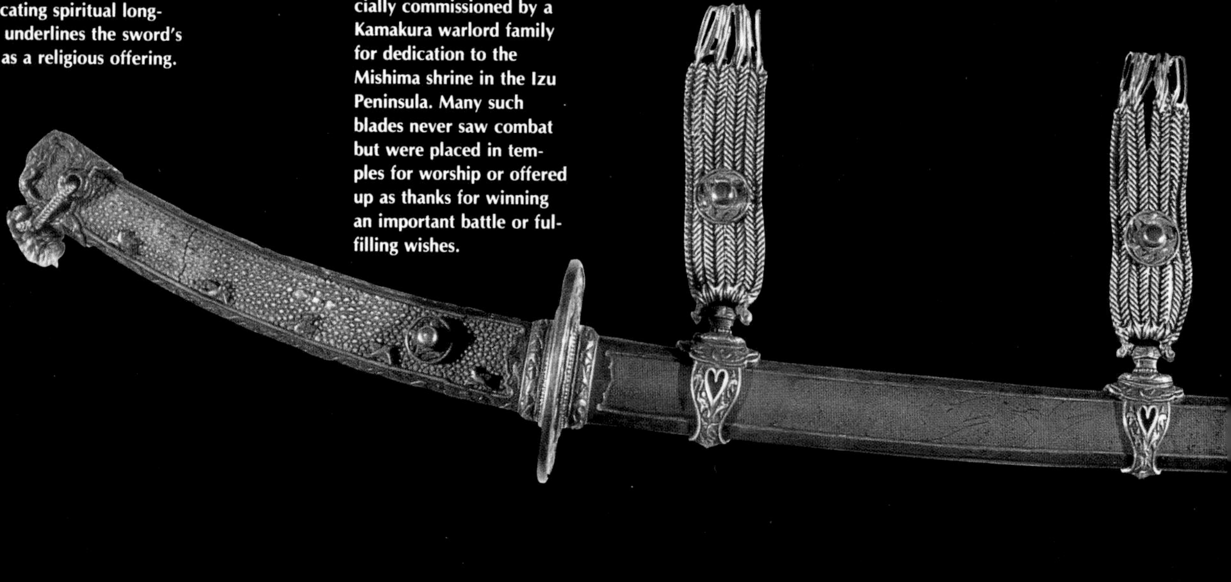

In a fragment of a screen depicting the battle of Rokuhara during the civil war of the late twelfth century, a warrior pulls back the head of an enemy to slit his throat with a short sword. Worn, cutting edge up, through the sash or belt of a samurai, the short sword was indispensable for the rapid maneuvering of close-quarter combat. Such weapons were produced in great numbers during the late thirteenth century, after the Mongol invasions of Japan had proved the unwieldy nature of the traditional long blade.

were made collectively by the Council of State, presided over by the regent. Members' discussions were held in secret and the results of their deliberations presented as unanimous decrees.

The policies devised in Kamakura were translated into action by the agents of the bakufu. Its inspectors traversed the country to supervise the military constables who policed the provinces and to oversee the land stewards who controlled the manors. The conduct of these local officials was examined, their accounts were thoroughly scrutinized, and any corruption was severely punished. The central administration took charge of revenue gathering and varied the tax rates according to the success or failure of the rice harvest. When disputes over land or water rights could not be settled locally, Kamakura stepped in to adjudicate.

The military administration, though never lenient, strove to be fair. In 1232, the Council of State issued a document known as the Joei Formulary, a collection of rules, recommendations, and legal wisdom. The formulary was based on the principles that Yoritomo and his clan had used for dispensing justice to their own vassals. Several decades of experience had proved their worth, and the bakufu now chose to extend these benefits to the country as a whole, to the feudal estates of the Kyoto aristocracy as well as those of provincial lords. Even the lowliest peasant, wading through his rice paddy, had a hope of being treated justly. He had rights that he had never enjoyed before: He was no longer tied to a particular parcel of land; he could sell his holdings and migrate to new districts that were being cleared for cultivation.

With the constant flow of traffic between Kyoto and Kamakura, a certain amount of cross-fertilization was inevitable. Career-minded scholars and administrators, stultified at court, came to Kamakura to make better use of their talents in the bakufu. There they learned that not all men of action were necessarily philistines. A prominent figure in the shogunate during the mid-thirteenth century, for instance, was Hojo Sanetoki, a military leader who was also a passionate bibliophile. His vast store of Japanese and imported Chinese texts contained many literary treasures, including thousands of rare works he had ordered copied at his own expense. He placed the entire collection in a favorite temple in Musashi Province and organized a system for enabling readers to consult or even borrow volumes for their own use, creating the most famous library in Kamakura.

A cautious respect began to replace the ancient mutual contempt between soldiers and cultured courtiers. As the Kamakura warriors established themselves as the ruling class, a new literary genre developed that glorified the deeds of their ancestors and extolled the samurai values of loyalty, courage, honor, and obedience. These martial epics originated in tales of the old Taira-Minamoto conflicts, which were recited aloud by storytellers with musical accompaniment. Eventually written down and embellished by scholarly compilers, such prose romances provided a new mythology, a cultural encyclopedia for an era dominated by military men.

Indeed, the formerly unlettered samurai were rapidly acquiring the ability to read and write. China had always been the source of religious and secular learning, and for centuries literacy had been the exclusive province of a leisured elite who had the time and the tutors necessary to master the complexities of Chinese script, with its thousands of characters. But a greater use of the considerably simplified syllabic script, which evolved in the early Heian period, now made it easier to read and write Japanese. Nevertheless, the historian Jien felt the need to apologize to his readers for using their native language instead of Chinese in his chronicle: "Since this book has been written in Japanese it will sound common. But meaning may be deeply embedded in Japanese words."

The younger generations of the warrior caste began to lose their contempt for the sybaritic patricians of Kyoto and to develop a taste for luxury. Artisans prospered as never before with the widening market for fine textiles, ceramics, and lacquer ware. Sculptors, carving the wooden statuary that wealthy patrons liked to bestow upon their favorite temples, displayed fresh exuberance and energy: Their gods and demons were no longer untouchable abstractions but actual personalities, with faces expressing the gamut of human emotions and naturalistically modeled bodies revealing superhuman power. Painters created vibrant, realistic picture scrolls depicting the lives of heroes and sages, the histories of important shrines, or episodes from the newly popular military romances. Dignitaries of the imperial court and the bakufu commissioned portraits of themselves, their carriages, and their favorite horses.

An emerging mercantile class made itself available to meet the increased demands. In the countryside, smiths and other artisans no longer worked simply to meet the needs of a private manor: They sold their wares, in company with itinerant traders, at local markets held three times a month in settlements that soon became small commercial centers with resident artisans and permanent shops. Merchants also gathered in provincial capitals and in Kamakura itself; in 1251 the Hojo regent established a specific commercial district and gave the merchants residing in that quarter the exclusive rights to hold markets.

In town and country alike, traders and artisans began to band themselves into trading associations or guilds, called za. In Kamakura alone, for instance, there were za for the merchants of silk, rice, charcoal, fuel, fish, salt, and horses, as well as for those who worked in woodcarving and joinery. These bodies flourished under the patronage of powerful protectors—members of the Kamakura government, local landlords, Kyoto aristocrats, or the abbots of important temples—who helped their protégés to acquire monopolies, exemptions from taxes or custom fees, and other commercial privileges.

Foreign trade also flourished. Links established between Japanese Buddhist monks and mainland religious centers helped forge a more comfortable relationship with South China under the Song dynasty. The Chinese themselves were quick to take advantage of advances in shipbuilding and navigation techniques to brave the China Sea with large cargoes of brocade, incense, and medicines, which they exchanged for gold from the newly opened mines of northern Japan. Copper coins from the Song dynasty became common, and by mid-century the markets were beginning to operate on a cash economy instead of barter.

Alarmed by the growing tendency toward materialism among their vassals, the military leaders passed various sumptuary laws. Undeterred by fines or other penalties, the warrior class's appetites grew ever closer to those of the old metropolitan aristocracy. But as this new group of potential consumers swelled in numbers, so too did the pressure on Japan's precarious agrarian economy:

Created in 1306 to hold the ashes of a Zen Buddhist monk, this pot was one of many such items made at Seto in eastern Japan. The town's artisans rose to prominence in the 1230s, using Chinese technology to fashion the region's fine white clay into glazed stoneware that was prized for both its durability and its distinctive green "autumn-leaf" glaze. With demand fueled by the newly wealthy warrior class, Seto rapidly became Japan's foremost pottery-producing area. Indeed, the goods produced there were traded so widely throughout Japan that the word *Setomono*, or "Seto things," became the accepted term for pottery.

More people were demanding more luxury goods, but the rice lands that would ultimately pay for these purchases could yield only a finite amount of income. New lands might be cleared in times when there was sufficient labor; the demand for rice and other basic commodities nonetheless far outstripped the limited quantities these islands could provide.

Economic stresses were not the only difficulties facing the Hojo regents. A massive earthquake shattered the Kamakura region in 1257, followed two years later by widespread plague and famine. It was said that the streets of Kyoto were filled with the bodies of the dead and that the peasants in the countryside were subsisting on roots and fistfuls of grass. To ameliorate rural suffering, the bakufu ordered its land stewards to give back the taxes they had gathered and to refrain temporarily from collecting any more. With so many dead, there was a shortage of able-bodied people to work the land and perform other necessary labors. Criminals were released from custody and even murderers given amnesty to supply the manpower. Kyoto seemed on the verge of anarchy. Graffiti appeared on the walls of the imperial palace:

At the New Year, ill omens.
In the land, disasters.
In the capital, soldiers.
In the palace, favoritism.
In the provinces, famine.
In the shrines, conflagrations.
In the riverbed, skeletons.

Temples and monasteries throughout the land were enlisted to conduct marathon prayer sessions beseeching a return of Heaven's favor. But these institutions also added to the bakufu's burdens. The great landowning monasteries quarreled frequently—with each other, with the nobility, and with the imperial house over territorial rights and privileges and over the payments due for religious services rendered. To reinforce their arguments, they sent out their fierce battalions of warrior-monks: The army of one monastery marched on Kyoto more than twenty times in the course of the thirteenth century. Whenever possible, the bakufu stood back and let these conflicts take their course until the monks' grievances had been answered or their honor satisfied. During the famine period, however, when the imperial court appeared to be in serious danger from a brigade of angry monks, Kamakura was compelled to intervene. It took several hundred soldiers, dispatched by the bakufu, to force the holy warriors back to their cloisters.

If the monks were restive, it was only a symptom of the dramatic changes taking place in the religious life of Japan. Years of clan warfare and disruption had given the common people a hunger for hope and consolation. The corrupt and arrogant clergy, more interested in enriching their temples and furthering their interests at court, offered little comfort to a man whose rice crop had been expropriated by soldiers or to a woman raped by bandits. And as political power shifted from the patricians to the samurai class, new popular forms of Buddhism emerged. No longer were the Buddha's teachings obscured by theological disputation and arcane scholarship. The spread of a simplified Japanese script made the basic tenets of Buddhism more widely accessible: Life was painful and transient, the world a kaleidoscope of shifting illusions. Through self-discipline and compassion for all fellow creatures, the seeker would eventually achieve enlightenment, escaping forever the weary round of deceptions and unfulfilled desires. New sects arose, and older ones revived, offering their own paths to nirvana for anyone, prince or peasant, who cared to follow them.

Salvation, said adherents of the Pure Land sect, formed in 1175 and named after the paradise to which its followers hoped to go, did not require a lifetime of rigid asceticism, constant meditation, or retreat from the world. It was attainable by anyone who faithfully repeated the name of Amida Buddha, the Lord of Boundless Light, as he or she went about the tasks of daily life. Even women, previously denied all hope of salvation until they underwent successive rebirths as a man, could achieve enlightenment in their present existence if they assiduously repeated the *Nembutsu* prayer: "Homage to Amida Buddha." All classes of society embraced the practice: It was reported that the former emperor Go-Shirakawa uttered the prayer several million times and died with it on his lips.

The orthodox Buddhist clergy were scandalized. So simple a faith would completely obviate the need for temples, priests, and ceremonies, and they launched into a violent persecution of the upstart creed. In 1201, they persuaded the emperor to take their part. The leader of the sect was exiled and some of his most prominent disciples beheaded. The utterance of the *Nembutsu* was banned. Nevertheless, so potent was the hope the Pure Land sect offered that these measures ultimately proved fruitless. The sect went through various schisms and modifications but survived—with its basic premises intact—to become a permanent part of Japan's religious life.

More rigorous in its demands but equally influential was the form of Buddhism known as Zen. Like the Pure Land sect, it rejected ritual and scholarship as roads to salvation. Enlightenment—the virtual transformation of a human being into a Buddha—was achieved by a simple monastic life of meditation and hard physical labor. Such enlightenment could come at any time in a sudden, ecstatic flash of light; intellectual effort, reason, philosophizing had nothing whatever to do with it. The Zen master devoted much energy to kicking, beating, and shouting at his disciples to purge them of self-deception and shake them into a state of higher consciousness.

The warrior class, with its own tradition of self-discipline, found this approach particularly sympathetic. The samurai appreciated a religion that emphasized and rewarded individual effort, especially one that did not make literacy a prerequisite for spiritual success. Monks from more conventional religious establishments put several Zen monasteries to the torch, but despite official hostility, the young sect flourished under the protection of the samurai.

Although their advocates believed themselves in sole possession of religious truth, neither Zen nor Pure Land Buddhists espoused the eradication of other branches of the faith. Such aggressive proselytizing was the preserve of a third force, the Lotus sect, founded by the monk Nichiren. Combative in spirit and colorful in his invective, Nichiren had begun religious life as a traditional scholar, steeped in classic Buddhist literature and theology. Like proponents of the Pure Land sect, he, too, preached that salvation was accessible to all and that the key to enlightenment lay within a particular sacred text, in this case the Lotus Sutra, an ancient Buddhist scripture written in India. It was not, however, necessary for the faithful to read or understand the text as long as they followed the path of righteousness and, more important, repeated a certain prayer: *namu Myohorengekyo,* or "salutation to the Lotus Sutra."

Nichiren was convinced that a new, reformed, and truly national Buddhism was

Carved in wood, an arch-browed attendant to one of Buddhism's ten Kings of Hell prepares to record a sinner's fate. According to the tenets of the Pure Land sect, hell was one of six realms into which man could be reborn.

The military shogunate governing Japan in the thirteenth century imposed a peace in which the nation's culture as a whole could flourish. Nowhere was this condition more evident than in the field of religion. The Buddhist faith, brought to Japan in the sixth century, spawned a number of sects whose teachings appealed to the masses. One such was Zen, whose rigorously monastic doctrines reached Japan from China at this time; others were the Pure Land movement, which promised its adherents rebirth in a paradise after death, and the Lotus sect, fiercely nationalistic in tone.

The effects of spiritual ferment were also felt in the arts and above all in sculpture, which attained a peak of craftsmanship and expressivity. Working under the influence of the new beliefs and often depicting Buddhist holy men, Kamakura sculptors toiled to produce masterpieces that reflected a relaxed and tender realism; dark-centered crystals were even used to give life to the eyes. The idealized forms of earlier carvings were replaced by those displaying a sincerity emphasizing the individual.

Bearing a mysterious wrapped object, possibly an offering, the saint Mu-chaku, attendant to the Buddha, mirrors the suffering of humanity in his eyes. Carved in 1208, the statue was the work of Unkei, one of the greatest artists of the time.

the only way forward for the Japanese people, and he censured all other versions of the faith as pernicious influences that drained the lifeblood of his compatriots and allowed the state to wallow in its own corruption. He denounced all his religious opponents as "the greatest liars in Japan," condemning Zen as "a doctrine of fiends and devils" and the Pure Land *Nembutsu* prayer as "a hellish practice." Only when the Japanese abandoned all these heresies would the country thrive. He himself would spearhead national regeneration: "I will be the pillar of Japan. I will be the eyes of Japan. I will be the great vessel of Japan."

Preaching in the streets of Kamakura three years after the great earthquake of 1257, during a period of plague, near anarchy, and famine, Nichiren found a receptive audience. The troubles in the land, he asserted, were punishment for years of religious corruption. If Japan did not embrace the one true faith he offered, worse horrors would follow. His warning was specific: A foreign army would invade Japan.

Displeased by the presence of this troublemaking priest, the Hojo regency banished Nichiren from the city. Undeterred, he carried his gospel through the eastern provinces, winning many samurai adherents. He had his supporters even within the bakufu, and in 1263 he was allowed to return to Kamakura. He did not refrain from constant criticism of the government, was tried for high treason, escaped execution—possibly through the intercession of influential friends—and was banished again. But only a few years would pass before the Hojo regents would be faced with an alarming fulfillment of Nichiren's prophecy: A formidable enemy was massing to the west.

For more than 300 years Japan, inward-looking and isolationist, had exchanged no official missions with its massive neighbor, China. But even without state envoys, communications of a less formal nature had persisted. Chinese merchant ships plied the sea, carrying exports to Japan and ferrying back the monks and students for whom the mainland was still the chief source of religious and secular learning. Korea, adjoining China and separated from Japan by a much narrower stretch of water, was similarly neglected by the Japanese rulers, although Kamakura's westernmost vassals occasionally plundered its vulnerable coasts.

But in the middle of the thirteenth century, Japanese isolation came to a sudden and unwelcome end. In 1264, Kublai Khan, grandson of the Mongol conqueror Genghis Khan, became great khan of the Mongols and established his capital at Beijing. Bowing before superior might, Korea rapidly became a vassal state to the khan. Kublai then cast his eyes eastward.

In 1268, he sent an emissary who carried a letter addressed to the "King of Japan." The Japanese officials who received the communication sent it, without hesitation, to the shogun at Kamakura rather than to the emperor. In his missive, Kublai Khan proposed that Japan buy his friendship with tribute—and suggested that the only alternative was war. Over the next few years, the khan peppered Kamakura with similarly veiled threats: The bakufu did not deign to reply.

Kublai bided his time until November 1274. In that month, a Mongol army carried in Korean ships traversed the straits separating the southern tip of Korea and Japan's southwestern island of Kyu. Chroniclers estimated that 15,000 Mongol troops supported by as many Koreans and carried in 450 warships landed in Hakata Bay.

The local chieftains, with the bakufu's own land stewards and law officers, sent off urgent messages to Kamakura and banded together to hold off the invaders until reinforcements arrived. For two days they battled successfully against unequal odds.

They were vastly outnumbered and terrified by the Mongols' use of strange new weapons—burning projectiles that exploded with an earsplitting bang. The rules of warfare were about to change forever: Gunpowder, previously the preserve of Chinese firework manufacturers, had come to the attention of the military.

The defenders suffered many losses but fought valiantly until sundown of the second day. With every expectation of resuming the engagement in the morning, the Mongols returned to their ships to wait out the hours of darkness. But during the night, a typhoon blew up and devastated the invasion force within a matter of hours. Those Korean vessels not shattered by giant winds and waves were driven out to sea, and 13,000 men were lost.

To guard against further invasion, the Kamakura leaders hurriedly raised vast numbers of troops, built new ramparts, and strengthened existing defenses. Responding to the call to mobilize, local lords and chieftains, especially on the vulnerable western island of Kyushu, required all their vassals to submit lists of the men, arms, and other resources at their disposal. An aged warrior named Saiko, for example, sent an inventory of his rice lands and described the members of his household:

> *Saiko, aged eighty-five. Cannot walk.*
> *Nagahide, his son, aged sixty-five. Has bows and arrows and weapons.*
> *Tsurehide, aged thirty-eight. Has bow and arrows, weapons, corselet, horse.*
> *Matsujiro, aged nineteen. Has bows and arrows, arms and two followers.*
> *Takahide, aged forty. Has bows and arrows, weapons, corselet,*
> *horse and one follower.*
> *These are at His Lordship's orders, and will serve faithfully.*

And despite initial hesitancy, the imperial court, too, by the end of 1280 began to appreciate the implications of the Mongol threat. The emperor placed all revenues from royal estates at the bakufu's disposal and ordered prayer sessions, offerings, and other placatory rites at the country's shrines. Religious services were conducted day and night, nobles and priests joined together in vigils, and crowds gathered at the shrine of the ancient Japanese war god. The emperor and former emperor deposited letters in the tombs of their ancestors, begging the intercession of the dead on behalf of their realm. Not to be outdone in zeal, the Hojo regent, Tokimune, was said to have copied out certain sacred texts in his own blood.

Kublai Khan, occupied with conquering the still-resistant southern China, waited for several years before resuming hostilities. Twice he sent letters to Kamakura, demanding that Japan become a vassal state. The bakufu's response was the same in both cases: The letters were destroyed and the Mongol envoys beheaded.

Finally, in June 1281, the long wait ended. A combined force of 150,000 Mongol, Chinese, and Korean troops landed on Kyushu. This time the Japanese were ready. Their newly formed navy consisted of small vessels that were swift and light enough to attack and harry the cumbersome Chinese troop transports. Their warriors, defending an imperiled homeland, fought with an intensity that could not be matched by a Mongol force largely made up of southern Chinese and Korean conscripts. Yet the defenders' will was not matched by their experience: Apart from those in the west, the Japanese warriors had seen little active service since the revolt of the former emperor Go-Toba nearly sixty years before.

The battle continued for fifty days. Then, once again, a great wind came roaring out of heaven. For two days, massive storms pounded the jagged Kyushu coastline. On land, trees were uprooted; at sea, enormous waves engulfed the Mongol ships. The ships that were not swallowed up were rammed together, and Japanese archers easily picked off the frantic soldiers as they clung to their splintered vessels. The Mongols beat a desperate retreat, and only a fragment of the khan's forces survived to carry the news of their failure back to China. According to the Japanese chroniclers, four-fifths of the invaders perished.

Japan exulted. Its people gave thanks for the typhoon that had saved them, calling it *kamikaze* (divine wind) and claiming it as proof that they were favored by the gods. Celebrations notwithstanding, the bakufu did not relax its vigilance: For twenty years Kamakura kept its warriors on full military alert. Only in 1300, six years after the death of Kublai Khan, was the danger acknowledged to have passed.

But the aftermath of victory was chaos. Kamakura's treasury was almost empty, with little money to pay the vassals who had defended the land during the war and through the years of wary peace that followed. In this instance, triumph was not accompanied by conquest: There were no rebels' rich estates to be confiscated, no spoils of war to be awarded. The priests, no longer engaged in round-the-clock prayers for peace, grew petulant. They claimed that they were far more deserving of reward than the warriors, for had not their chants brought forth the heavenly wind?

The bakufu could do little to meet these demands. The entire country was impov-

His horse spurting blood, the Japanese general Takezaki Suenaga collapses under a hail of arrows in this detail from a scroll depicting the attempted invasion in 1274 by the forces of Kublai Khan, Mongol emperor of China. Confronted with superior numbers, the Japanese forces also had to contend with advanced weaponry: The shell exploding over Suenaga's head is the first known depiction of the use of gunpowder in artillery. Such advantages availed the invaders little in the face of stout resistance and a devastating typhoon dubbed *kamikaze*, or "divine wind," by the grateful Japanese. Suenaga survived to commission the scroll, most of which focuses on his own heroic deeds; it is believed that the proud general himself added the red arrow piercing his helmet after the scroll was completed.

erished. The expenses of maintaining troops had been ruinous. Kyushu had suffered great loss of life during the invasion, and its warlords had used their own resources to build up the coastal defenses. Throughout the country, agricultural production had come to a virtual standstill: Such rice as there was had been requisitioned to provision the army, and many able-bodied men had been taken off the land to join the troops. A historian of the period reported that "during the last few years, owing to the Mongol attacks, in both east and west warlike arts have not been neglected, but agriculture has practically been abandoned by the peasants and the landholders."

Discontent spread. The only way the bakufu could compensate its vassals for their expenditures would be to take the money from one deserving group to pay another. Those who did not receive sufficient recompense were forced to mortgage their estates to pay their debts. For a while, the bakufu tried to ban any sale or mortgage of its vassals' estates, but those who had money to lend—and those who needed it— found ways around the law, and the ruling was soon rescinded. In Kyoto, there were nobles who were no friends of the Kamakura regime. They made common cause with the unhappy military vassals and gradually began to subvert the bakufu's influence.

The Hojo regents were losing their grip. The simplicity that characterized the early days of Kamakura rule had truly vanished. The law courts, once admired for their fairness and efficiency, had become as cumbersome and corrupt as any organ of the pre-Kamakura imperial bureaucracy. The regime did not come to an abrupt standstill, but even the most dedicated members of the bakufu knew they presided over a government in decline.

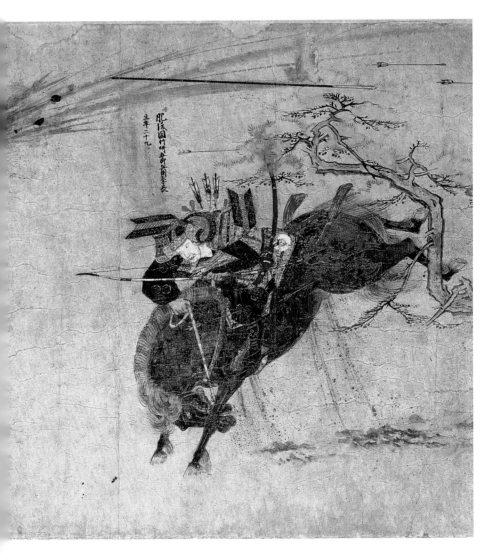

For the first three decades of the fourteenth century, the military government still ruled in Kamakura. But by 1333, its enemies had forged a coalition: Disaffected provincial warlords conspired with members of the nobility and the faction-ridden imperial and ex-imperial households to raise an army. This force marched on Kamakura, captured the city, and put it to the torch. The last Hojo regent, along with 200 of his loyal followers, committed ritual suicide rather than surrender, in the tradition of that warrior class their predecessors had elevated to new heights of dignity and power.

The death of the last Hojo regent did not mark the end of the shogunate. For fifty years Japan was rocked by a power struggle between the aristocracy and the provincial warriors, until in the 1390s the Ashikaga clan gained control. Once more the country was ruled by a bakufu, this time from Kyoto, and once more the imperial court was relegated to the shadows. Military rule in Japan had come to stay.

SLAVE SULTANS OF EGYPT

3 Shortly after sunrise on the morning of September 3, 1260, an insistent thunder of drums filled the air in the three-mile-wide Palestinian valley between Mount Gilboa and the hills of Galilee. An Egyptian army was advancing down the Plain of Esdraelon toward Ayn Jalut, the "Spring of Goliath," where waited the world-conquering Mongols, triumphant from a series of bloody victories that had brought them all of Iraq and Syria. The Mongols' next goal was the conquest of Egypt, which would ensure that the entire Islamic civilization of the Middle East was theirs.

When the two armies clashed, the Mongol confidence seemed well founded; their first furious charge swept the Egyptian advance guard aside, overrunning its left flank. But the Egyptians rallied. Their sultan, Qutuz, rode out before his troops, removed his helmet so that all could recognize him, and crying, "O Muslims! O Muslims! O Muslims!" led his army headlong into the Mongol ranks. The impetus was overwhelming: Mongol leader Kitbugha was killed, and his troops were driven into flight, to be pitilessly slaughtered by the pursuing Egyptians. After the battle, Qutuz dismounted, offered two prostrations to Allah, then sent Kitbugha's severed head back to Cairo as proof of victory.

Ayn Jalut was the battle that marked the limit of Mongol expansion in the Middle East. Although the steppe warriors returned five times to Syria during the next fifty years, they never again threatened Egypt itself. In addition, the victory was a turning point that marked the emergence of a new power in the region: the Mamluks, Turkish slave-warriors who for the next two and a half centuries—a bloody era of coup and countercoup—would rule over all Syria and Egypt. They would stem the Mongol tide, destroy the remaining Christian enclaves set up by the Crusaders of the twelfth century, and raise Cairo to a position preeminent in the Muslim world.

The empire that the Mamluks controlled had previously been run by the Kurdish Ayyubids, who in 1171 had deposed the Fatimid rulers of Egypt and founded their own dynasty under their leader, Saladin. By the first half of the thirteenth century, Ayyubid rule extended beyond the borders of Egypt to Syria, Yemen, and parts of Iraq. The Ayyubids' realm was a prosperous one. On the banks of the Nile River and in its fertile delta, the rich silt produced by annual floods yielded a bountiful harvest of wheat, cotton, and rice. The drier lands of Upper Egypt provided good grazing pastures for Bedouin herds. And in Syria, the cities of Aleppo and Damascus grew wealthy from an abundance of fruit and olives. Whatever commodities the empire lacked—such as iron and copper—could be bought from the Western merchants who flocked to the bustling port of Alexandria at the mouth of the Nile.

Despite its riches, the Ayyubid empire was far from stable. In Iraq its rule was contested by the hostile Islamic dynasty of the Abbasids; in Syria rival Ayyubid factions disputed the sovereignty of Saladin's successors; and along the coast of

Carousing subjects of the Mamluks, Egypt's Turkish ruling elite, are depicted in this miniature from a Mamluk version of *Maqamat*, a popular collection of picaresque tales by the twelfth-century writer al-Hariri. Following their rise to power in 1260, the Mamluks imposed an austere military regime on Egypt and Syria. Despite the Islamic ban on alcohol, many towns offered relief for imbibers. Native Arabs could find wine and beer in taverns, which were usually run by Christians and often attached to monasteries. The Turkish sultans and soldiers preferred kumiss, a highly alcoholic brew made from fermented mare's milk.

Palestine the Christian Crusader states were a constant threat. Since the First Crusade had arrived from the West in 1098, Muslim and Christian forces had been engaged in a struggle for possession of what each regarded as their holiest places. At the dawn of the thirteenth century, the Christians—or Franks, as they were known to the Muslims—were still established in the states of Tripoli, Antioch, and Jerusalem, excluding the Holy City itself, which had been taken by Saladin in 1187. Both Christians and Muslims profited from the trade brought by these coastal enclaves, and in the lower strata of society, members of both religions went about everyday life in comparative peace. Despite an uneasy coexistence, the situation was volatile, and when a particularly warlike batch of Crusaders arrived, or when a Muslim ruler saw a chance to exploit some Christian weakness, blood was inevitably spilled.

Nor were the Christians the only religious threat. The Ayyubids were Sunni Muslims, who saw the caliph in Baghdad as their spiritual leader. Yet there remained in Egypt and Syria a few communities who clung to the Shiite faith of the Ayyubids' predecessors, the Fatimids, denying the authority of the caliph and believing in a line of hidden redeemers who would one day return to claim the caliphate. In the towns, where they could be easily controlled, the Shiites were tolerated, but in the remote countryside they were seen as a threat to civil order and were frequently repressed by the military. The greatest menace, however, was that presented by the Assassins, a group of Shiite extremists who had terrorized both Christian and Muslim inhabitants of Syria since the early twelfth century. To the Ayyubids, the heretical Assassins were a graver danger than the Frankish Crusaders.

To keep order in their volatile empire, the Ayyubids, like other Muslim rulers since the ninth century, made extensive use of imported slave-warriors acquired as tribute, as booty, or by purchase. Saladin replaced the African infantry of the Fatimids with a 500-strong Turkish corps, which he dressed in distinctive yellow uniforms. His successors continued the practice, and by the reign of the last great Ayyubid sultan, al-Salih Ayyub, Mamluk warriors had become the mainstay of the Egyptian army. Foremost among them were the sultan's personal elite corps, the Bahris—so called because they were garrisoned on an island in the Nile River, Bahr al-Nil, just outside Cairo.

With few exceptions, the Mamluks were members of the Turkish Kipchak tribe recruited from the Crimea and the southern Russian steppes. Islamic law sanctioned the enslavement of all heathen, non-Arab peoples, but for military service it was the Turks who were prized above the others;

trained to ride a horse and draw a bow almost as soon as they could walk, they were natural warriors. According to the ninth-century Arab author of the *Epistle Concerning the Qualities of the Turk*, "They care only about raiding, hunting, horsemanship, skirmishing with rival chieftains, taking booty, and invading other countries. Their efforts are all directed toward these activities, and they devote all their energies to these occupations. In this way they have acquired a mastery of these skills, which for them take the place of craftsmanship and commerce and constitute their only pleasure, their glory, and the subject of all their conversation. Thus they have become in warfare what the Greeks are in philosophy."

A newly acquired Mamluk learned all aspects of the military arts, concentrating especially on improving his native skills with the short Turkish bow and mastering such cavalry tactics as the feigned retreat—a stratagem that had drawn many enemies into fatal traps. Conversion to Sunni Islam was an important part of his education, and he would probably be taught to speak Arabic and possibly to read and write it. Far from home and family, he inevitably developed strong bonds of kinship with both his fellow recruits and his master, whom he might address as father. Although the word *mamluk* signifies "something that is possessed," he was treated not as a menial but as a valuable part of his master's extended family. While his master lived, the Mamluk's duty first and foremost was to him alone. An important Mamluk might act as his equerry, cupbearer, or falconer. If he was ambitious and well favored and belonged to an important household, he could aspire to even higher office, for once he had embraced Islam, he was effectively emancipated, and no formal obstacles barred his advancement. It was not inconceivable that he would be named heir if his master was childless. If the warrior belonged to the Bahri elite, he might entertain hopes of elevation to the rank of emir, commanding an army in the field.

In the mid-thirteenth century, however, a short, broad-chested Bahri named Baybars al-Bunduqdari was to raise Mamluk status to an even higher level. His destiny was to be far more than an emir: He was to become sultan of all Egypt and Syria. Born in about 1220, Baybars was a member of a Kipchak tribe that had fled from the Mongols into the Crimea, where he had been taken into captivity, then sold at the age of about fourteen in the slave market of Aleppo. Although Turks were generally prized for their beauty, Baybars was disfigured by a cast in one eye, and he had been bought for the relatively low price of 800 dirhams—an estimated 2,000 grams, or about four pounds, of silver—by an Egyptian emir. His master was later disgraced and forced to hand over his Mamluks to the sultan al-Salih Ayyub, who recognized the youth's intelligence and fighting skills and placed him in the guard section of his Bahri troops. Within a few years, Baybars had become the deputy of the Bahri commander Aqtay.

Having used his Bahri Mamluks effectively against the Crusaders and hostile Ayyubid kinsmen in Syria, al-Salih Ayyub encouraged his son Turanshah to maintain the relationship. In a letter written shortly before his death in November 1249, he bemoaned the poor quality of his regular troops and urged Turanshah to treat the Bahris with generosity. "I strongly recommend them to you," he wrote. "I owe them everything." And, indeed, Turanshah himself owed a debt of thanks to the Bahris, who had successfully defeated a Crusader army at Mansura in February 1250, leading to the capture and ransom of the French king Louis IX. But Turanshah had his own slave household, which included black Sudanese soldiers as well as Turks. After his father's death, he set about appointing his men to key posts, ignoring the resentment of the

A MANUAL OF MARTIAL INSTRUCTION

Taught to read and write as part of their training, Mamluks studied the theory and practice of combat in military manuals such as the one from which the illustrations on these pages are taken, *The End of the Quest Concerning the Techniques of Horsemanship*. Its title notwithstanding, the book covered more than just horsemanship, containing sections on archery, lanceplay and swordplay, strategy, tactics, ambushes, inspection parades, the employment of poisonous smokes and chemicals, the use of fireproof clothing, the treatment of wounds, the law regarding the division of booty, and even the use of magic to gain forewarning of unseen military dangers.

Such works placed particular stress on thorough training, which was essential if the Mamluk cavalry was to function successfully in battle formation, particularly if it was to perform its favorite tactic, the feigned retreat and the rally. Exercises were regularly carried out on the open concourses of hippodromes at Cairo and Damascus, where warriors would give public demonstrations of their prowess; the great sultan Baybars would daily visit the Cairo site at noon to inspect his troops' progress. Mamluk warriors would also hone their skills on hunting expeditions through the Syrian countryside, chasing quarry that included lions, panthers, wolves, hyenas, wild boars, deer, and gazelles.

Four novices, their lances shouldered, gallop in simulated combat around a hippodrome pool.

A warrior demonstrates the effectiveness of an iron shield against "Greek fire." A Byzantine invention widely used in medieval warfare, the incendiary's composition is no longer known.

A lancer stabs a bear on a hunting trip. Mamluks placed great value on the chase as a method of training; sometimes such expeditions also served as cover for reconnoitering the borders of the neighboring Crusader states.

الخيل وازكنت ممن تحرز العمل بها فافعل واعمل الرفايد

Wheeling swordsmen practice their art. Strengthened by repetitive exercise, a Mamluk warrior could slice through lead bars or heaps of clay hundreds of times a day, using a sword weighing more than four pounds.

Bahris. They were particularly incensed by the promotion of Sudanese to the influential posts of master of the royal household and master of the royal guard. Turanshah confidently disregarded their pique: A contemporary Arab historian recorded that when warned of a possible rebellion, he drew his saber and began chopping the tops off candles, shouting, "So shall I deal with the Bahris!"

They struck first. On May 2, 1250, a group led by Baybars burst into his tent and tried to cut him down. He escaped, but on hearing of the coup attempt, the rest of the Bahris hunted him to a wooden tower by the Nile. Forced out by fire, he managed to reach the river before his assailants killed him. Then the Bahri commander, Aqtay, cut him open, plucked out his heart, and took it, dripping, to the captured French king, who was still negotiating the terms of his release. "What will you give me now that I have killed your enemy?" he demanded. "Had he lived, you can be sure he would have killed you." The Crusader lord who reported the gory incident noted that King Louis (who was released five days later) maintained a dignified silence.

Following the death of Turanshah, Egypt saw a decade of conspiratorial maneuvering, during which the Ayyubid empire began to collapse. In Egypt, Mamluk and Ayyubid factions jostled for control of puppet sultans. In Syria, rival Ayyubid princes united to form their own separate state. The Bedouin tribes of Upper Egypt were in rebellion. And the streets of Cairo were terrorized by the Bahris. Under Aqtay and Baybars, they acted as a law unto themselves, creating disorder, robbing citizens, and—as one chronicler noted with alarm, raiding the women's public baths. Cairo, it was said, would be better off under the Franks than these rowdies.

But relief for the townsfolk did not come until 1254. In that year, a non-Bahri Mamluk emir named Aybak—who had briefly held supreme power four years earlier, only to be pushed to one side—killed Aqtay and forced most of the Bahris, including Baybars, to flee to Syria. Those who remained were arrested, and their wealth was confiscated. With the Bahris out of the way Aybak now felt confident enough in his own strength to reclaim his former position, and in September 1254 he declared himself sultan of Egypt.

Aybak did not enjoy his throne long. Four years previously he had married Shajar al-Durr—al-Salih's widow and former harem slave, who had herself ruled for a short while. In 1257, having come to suspect that he intended to replace her as chief wife, she had him strangled in the bath by her servants.

Shajar al-Durr, however, profited little, for Aybak's supporters soon came seeking vengeance. Chroniclers relate that she held out for several days in the Red Tower of the Cairo citadel, grinding her jewels to dust so that no other woman might wear them. At last, forced by hunger to quit her sanctuary, she was beaten to death by the clog-wielding concubines of her late husband and left for the dogs to eat. And in November 1259, the throne was seized by Aybak's Mamluk officer, Qutuz.

Qutuz had barely secured his position against internal rivals when the country was threatened by a looming menace from outside: the Mongols. By mid-century the vast Mongol Empire built up by Genghis Khan had been divided into four parts, the southwestern share being allotted to the Ilkhan dynasty, based in Persia. In 1258, the Ilkhan Hulegu, grandson of Genghis, had struck westward, taking amid terrible bloodshed and devastation the city of Baghdad, seat of the caliph, who was among the dead. Two years later the Mongols stormed into Syria; Aleppo fell in January 1260, Damascus in March. The Mongol army, which according to some accounts numbered more than 100,000 men, seemed unstoppable.

Confronted by so formidable a foe, even the turbulent Mamluks put aside their quarrels and prepared for a showdown. They were saved by a twist of fate. After taking Damascus, Hulegu heard news of the death of the great khan in distant China. At once he set off eastward to defend his position in the forthcoming succession dispute, taking the bulk of his army with him. He gave command of the remaining 10,000 to 20,000 troops to Kitbugha, a Mongol who had adopted the Christian faith. Believing in the intrinsic superiority of his warriors, the new commander proceeded to overplay his hand. That summer a Mongol embassy arrived at Cairo with a demand that Qutuz submit to the Ilkhan. But the Mamluks, having heard of Hulegu's departure, were not accommodating. The Mongol ambassadors were halved at the waist and decapitated. Their heads were nailed to the Zuwaila Gate of Cairo.

On July 25, 1260, Qutuz rode out of Cairo to take overall command of a combined army that may have been 100,000 strong. His forces were swelled by refugees from Syria, among them Ayyubid princes outraged at their losses and, more important, Baybars, to whom Qutuz had guaranteed safe conduct in return for Bahri support against the Mongols. Even though the Egyptians outnumbered the Mongols ten to one, they could not be certain of victory; for all their martial valor the Mamluks were still only a small elite, and most of the army consisted of poorly equipped troopers and undisciplined Bedouin cavalry. Nevertheless, Baybars, as commander of the advance guard, easily defeated his opposite number at Gaza, then waited for the main Egyptian force and with it advanced up the coast of Palestine.

The Mamluks' route took them through the Crusader principalities. Although the Mongols had shown themselves to be sympathetic to Christianity, the Frankish leaders were distrustful of this new Oriental power and chose to grant Qutuz free passage and to furnish his army with supplies. It was while resting with their somewhat nervous Frankish hosts outside Acre that the Mamluks heard of Kitbugha's arrival in Galilee. Qutuz wheeled his army southeast, sending Baybars ahead with the advance force. And at Ayn Jalut the fate of the Middle East was decided.

The battle of Ayn Jalut confirmed the Mamluks not only as the dominant force in the Middle East, masters of both Egypt and Syria, but as champions of the faith, the last and most powerful bastion of Islam. As Qutuz followed Kitbugha's head back to Cairo, he had every reason to bask in the glory of his success. Beside him, however, rode a smoldering Baybars. After the battle, in which he had played an important part, Baybars had asked to be given the governorship of Aleppo or Palestine and had been brusquely refused. And on October 23, his anger became bloodily manifest. While camped near Gaza, Qutuz was slain by a group of Mamluk emirs in league with Baybars; by the account of one court chronicler, it was Baybars himself who struck the lethal blow. The ensuing debate over Qutuz's successor was ended, according to another chronicler, when one of the senior emirs declared, "He who kills the ruler should himself be ruler."

Few rulers were as ruthless as Baybars, a man of ferocious energy uninhibited by any notion of honor or scruple. During his stay at Acre, for example, he had noticed the weakness of the Frankish stronghold and suggested to Qutuz that they capture it before tackling the Mongols—a suggestion that Qutuz, thankful for the help of the Franks, had dismissed. But at the same time Baybars was a realist, and he took care to promote the interests of the Mamluks who had acclaimed him sultan. "When it pleased God to grant the advent of the sultan's reign," wrote his court biographer, "he gathered the fugitives and brought in those who were afar; he promoted those who lacked advancement and gave office to those who had been set aside. He returned to them the possessions, wealth, and favors of which they had been deprived. He appointed the deserving to emirates and promoted the competent."

Not all his appointees were Bahri Mamluks. In many cases he was obliged to leave Qutuz's powerful supporters in office, which may have contributed to the nightmares that allegedly disturbed his sleep and the stomach upsets that troubled his digestion. In order to forestall a possible coup, he set up an elaborate espionage system under the control of a Mamluk official whose other functions included the supervision of the postal service as well as of foreign affairs. Not content with that, Baybars made it his habit to spring surprise visits on his officers and walk the streets of Cairo in disguise to discover what was being said about him. What he heard could not have been flattering. The ordinary citizens disliked the Mamluks in general because of their bullying, swaggering behavior; and they well remembered Baybars for his leading role in the disturbances of the early 1250s. Baybars wooed them by reducing taxes, with only limited success; brave as he was, it was a couple of months before he dared ride through Cairo in public procession.

In Mamluk eyes, Baybars had earned the throne by virtue of his ability and the acclamation of the leading men of the realm. Nevertheless, perhaps remembering his slave origins, he sought a more formal way to legitimatize his position. One method was to revive the caliphate, the supreme expression of Sunni Muslim unity and legality. Theoretically, the caliph was the figurehead to whom all sultans owed their allegiance and from whom they derived their right to rule. Because the last Abbasid caliph had been killed by the Mongols, Baybars was obliged to find a new spiritual leader. He discovered a man who claimed to be an uncle of the last reigning caliph

The Metalsmith's Intricate Art

As Mongol armies swept through Persia in the 1250s, Egypt and Syria played host to a throng of Muslim refugees. Among the newcomers were Iranian goldbeaters and Iraqi smiths, under whose influence the art of metalworking reached new heights throughout the empire.

Commissioned by the wealthy Turkish elite to produce high-quality luxury items, these craftsmen vied with one another to make ever larger and more impressive pieces, most commonly of brass inlaid with precious metals. Using mineral ore imported chiefly from Europe, artisans cast the decorative objects, then carved grooves and hollows into which were hammered inlays of gold, silver, or niello—a compound of sulfur mixed with silver, lead, or copper. Abstract arabesque patterns and calligraphy featured prominently in their decoration, and although some Muslims disapproved of artists portraying living things, the shapes of humans, animals, and monsters also adorned the masterpieces.

Inlaid with gold, silver, and niello, this costly brass pen box was possibly commissioned by a high-ranking official in the Mamluk chancery. Carried under the waistband, it would have contained all the tools of a scribe's trade—reed pens, threads for cleaning the reeds, ink, and sand for blotting.

and brought him to Cairo, where his name was mentioned in public prayers and stamped on the state coinage. To Baybars's anger, however, the caliph proved less pliant than he had imagined, so he dispatched him on a deliberately underequipped expedition to retake Baghdad from the Mongols. The caliph and his followers were slaughtered almost to a man. The sultan immediately installed a new caliph who also claimed Abbasid kinship and placed him under dignified house arrest, bringing him out only on ceremonial occasions.

But while the caliph remained innocuously in the background, Baybars's chief religious counselor, Shaykh Khadir al-Mihrani, reveled iniquitously in his position. A professed mystic, he had fled his native Iraq to evade a noble who wished to castrate him for sleeping with his daughter. In Aleppo he again aroused the wrath of his conquests' male relatives and hastily moved to Damascus, where Baybars, then still an emir, fell under his influence. As sultan, Baybars came to rely heavily on the advice and predictions of Khadir, who used his privileged position to divert money intended for the sultan into his own coffers. In 1263, a group of some of Egypt's most powerful men pressed for his trial on the grounds of embezzlement, unlawful fornication, and sodomy. Found guilty, he escaped the death penalty by prophesying that the sultan's death would follow closely on his own, a prediction that made his judges limit his sentence to life imprisonment.

Among Khadir's unsavory acts was the instigation of pogroms and riots against Jewish and Christian subjects—ostensibly as part of the jihad, or holy war, that Baybars declared on all unbelievers but in reality for loot. Under the Fatimids and the Ayyubids, Jews and Christians had lived in relative peace with their Muslim masters, and many had become important and wealthy members of the administration. Now, under the Mamluks, their position took a distinct turn for the worse. The Christians

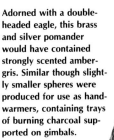

Adorned with a double-headed eagle, this brass and silver pomander would have contained strongly scented amber-gris. Similar though slightly smaller spheres were produced for use as hand-warmers, containing trays of burning charcoal supported on gimbals.

in particular were associated with the Mongols, who not only used Christian auxiliaries in their army but when sacking cities often spared Christians in preference to Muslims. And both Jews and Christians aroused popular jealousy for their prominent civil posts. This ire frequently manifested itself in protests and lynch mobs. At such times, the Mamluks chose to appease the majority rather than to protect the threatened minorities. The Christians were forced to wear blue turbans and belts, the Jews yellow; both were forbidden to ride horses or mules in the towns; and churches and synagogues were sacked or shut down. Many Christians were dismissed from their offices for refusing to convert to Islam. Both religious communities managed to survive despite this persecution because the Mamluks relied heavily on their bureaucratic skills and wealth.

Aside from the persecution of Jews and Christians, Baybars extended his jihad to Muslims, expressing his religious zeal in campaigns to purge immoral behavior—which he defined as including prostitution, hashish eating, beer drinking, and the wearing of immodest dress. The main targets of his holy war, however, were military rather than spiritual foes: the Mongols, the Crusader magnates of the Levant, and the Assassins, who still terrorized Syria. Besides these enemies of Sunni Islam, Baybars was also determined to smash the power of the surviving Ayyubid princes in Syria.

During his seventeen-year reign he went a long way toward achieving his goals. By a combination of force and treachery he brought the Ayyubids to heel and subdued the Assassins. He did not entirely dissolve the order; from then on they were to work for him. In addition, during a series of bloody campaigns he succeeded in reducing the Crusader presence to a few footholds on the coast. His most telling victory, and his most brutal, was the sack of Antioch in 1268, which fell after more than 150 years of rule by the Norman house of Hauteville. When his army breached

One of the finest examples of Islamic art, this basin's gold and silver inlay depicts Mamluk emirs and royal servants hunting. The sultan himself is not shown—perhaps because the political instability of the time prompted the artist to omit a potentially short-lived ruler.

the walls and poured in, he ordered the gates to be shut so that none of the inhabitants could escape. Most were massacred in the streets; the rest were taken for slaves—so many that the bottom virtually dropped out of the market. Four years later, when the English prince Edward landed at Acre to campaign in Palestine in league with the Mongols, Baybars employed an Assassin disguised as a native Christian to stab him with a poisoned dagger. The prince was seriously ill for some months and left Palestine as soon as he had recovered, never to return.

For all his ferocity, Baybars was an astute diplomat. In 1261, he concluded an alliance with Berke Khan, leader of the Mongol Golden Horde. Based in Russia, the Golden Horde had inherited the northwestern quarter of Genghis's empire, but after a dispute over the succession of the great khan in Mongolia, the Horde had become increasingly hostile to the Ilkhan Mongols; more important, from Baybars's point of view, these Mongols held sway over the Kipchak steppe, where most Mamluks were recruited. To ensure the safe passage of slaves through the Bosporus, Baybars also struck an agreement with the ruler of Byzantium, Michael VIII, who controlled the route. And he came to mutually profitable arrangements with the Genoese, who were the main slave-shipping agents, and with the Venetians, who were the sultan's chief suppliers of war matériel.

While strengthening his position abroad, Baybars also found time for internal consolidation, reorganizing the army, rebuilding the navy, strengthening forts, digging canals, and improving the major harbors. Superb communications were the key to his empire. His two capitals, Damascus and Cairo, were linked by a mounted postal service that took only four days to carry mail the 400 miles that separated them. Mail reached Cairo twice a week from all the cities and towns of his empire, and urgent news was dispatched by carrier pigeons. Flying in relays between homing lofts, the birds delivered most messages within a day. Whenever a carrier pigeon—perfumed if it brought good news—arrived at its loft in the citadel, Baybars was notified immediately, even if he was at dinner or on the polo field. The speediest pigeons with the best pedigrees might sell for 700 dinars—about 3,000 grams, or six and a half pounds, of gold—more than Baybars had cost his first master.

With his empire running so efficiently, Baybars felt confident enough to launch his most ambitious campaign. It was to be his last. Early in his reign, he had been asked by the exiled sultan of Rum to help him win back his realm, which had been a Mongol protectorate since 1243. In the spring of 1277, Baybars took up the invitation and invaded Asia Minor. He handily defeated a Mongol army in the frontier region of Elbistan, then swung west and occupied Caesarea, where he had himself crowned sultan. His reign was short, though, for he was unable to enlist sufficient local support to take on a second Mongol army, sent by the Ilkhan to expel him, and he was obliged to retreat to Damascus, abandoning his new subjects to the wrath of the Mongols. That June he was taken sick after drinking kumiss, fermented mare's milk—by one account a poisoned draft he had intended for someone else. He lingered for thirteen days and died on June 20.

By its very nature, the Mamluk system discouraged hereditary succession. Mamluk status, after all, could not be inherited. Sons of emancipated Mamluks grew up as Arabic-speaking Muslims, with Arabic rather than Turkish names..Although the military rulers regarded them more highly than native Egyptians, these sons were effectively assimilated into the local culture. They could pursue a military career if they wished but only in the broad body of troops of free birth, whose senior officers were almost entirely Mamluk emirs. Moreover, it was virtually impossible for the son of a Mamluk to establish the military and economic base from which he could mount a bid for the throne. The sultan rarely consented to let him inherit his father's slave corps or his father's *iqta,* a royal grant conferring the right to the income derived from a certain piece of land but not ownership of the land itself. Many rulers attempted to ensure the succession of their sons; however, unless the sons were strong and capable of mustering popular Mamluk support, their reigns were short-lived. In general, the Mamluk sultans were drawn from the ranks of first-generation foreign slaves.

Trained and educated in an environment where martial ability was all, the Mamluks brought their barracks-room principles to politics. If a Mamluk aspired to supreme power, he had simply to make himself stronger than the incumbent sultan. As a result, factions formed like bubbles in a heating teapot, and the pot frequently boiled over. The Mamluk political arena became strewn with the corpses of deposed sultans, whose average rule lasted a mere five years.

Despite this quick turnover of rulers, the system in some ways promoted administrative stability. Politics and ideology hardly entered into Mamluk succession struggles; rival candidates were not competing to change the system, only to control it. And while the Men of the Pen—native administrators who ran the day-to-day affairs of the country—might be discomfited by the violent methods of these Men of the Sword, they acknowledged with gratitude their firm government. Some even saw the benign providence of God in the coming of these aliens who had saved Egypt and Syria from the Mongols. In an age when most countries suffered the disruption of hereditary rule, which produced incompetent monarchs as often as it produced the great and the good, Mamluk society enjoyed the benefit of being a meritocracy—albeit a meritocracy dominated by the most ruthless.

Accordingly, it took just two years after Baybars's death for disaffected Bahri factions to overthrow the son he had appointed as his successor. In November 1279, following three months of political horse trading, they chose as his replacement a senior and respected emir, Qalawun. Like Baybars, Qalawun was a Kipchak Turk; the two had been born around the same year, making Qalawun nearly sixty when he became sultan. He had not been enslaved until his late twenties and as a result had never fully mastered Arabic. Tall, thick-necked, and broad-shouldered, he was nicknamed al-Alfi, "the Thousander"—a reference to the exceptionally high price of 1,000 gold dinars that his first master had paid for him. He had come into al-Salih Ayyub's possession during the last years of the sultan's life and fled to Syria with Baybars after the murder of his commander. More cautious than Baybars, he was just as ruthless and equally unpopular with the Egyptian citizenry. When he finally dared to ride in ceremonial procession through his capital, the crowds pelted him with offal.

Soon after ascending the throne, he purged Baybars's private entourage, then launched an attack on Sunqur al-Ashqar, an emir who had taken advantage of the factional infighting following Baybars's death to declare himself ruler of Damascus. Sunqur's army, however, was no match for Qalawun's, and after a heavy defeat on June 21, 1280, he fled to northern Syria. From there he apparently appealed for assistance to the Mongol Ilkhan of Persia, one of whose tribeswomen he had married. The Mongols were only too pleased to exploit the Muslim rift, and in 1281, the Ilkhan's brother rode into Syria at the head of 50,000 Mongols, in addition to 30,000 Armenian, Georgian, and Turkish auxiliaries, with the full expectation of supple-

INSIGNIA OF IDENTITY

Though bitter foes, the Mamluks and Western Crusaders enjoyed an exchange of trade and culture. One product of this mutual influence was the spread of distinguishing insignia to denote title or ownership. Originated by the Crusaders as a means of identifying different groups of heavily armored knights, such insignia developed into Western heraldry—the hereditary use of distinctive devices on shields, surcoats, and banners.

In Europe, a complex system of rules evolved on such matters as which colors could be placed upon others and how the shields could be divided. Colleges of heralds were established to adjudicate on these issues and also to judge between individuals who claimed the same device.

In the Middle East, Muslim warriors soon adopted the designs and colors of Western heraldry. The fleur-de-lis, for example, emblem of both the French royalty and the Virgin Mary, was sported in the Middle East as the *faransiya,* or Frankish symbol; lions and eagles, representative of power and dominion, adorned the property of Muslims and Christians alike.

Lance-bearing Christian forces struggle against a Muslim army in a manuscript illustration of the Second Crusade from 1147 to 1148. The fleur-de-lis, displayed here by the French king Louis, was adopted almost simultaneously by his opponent, the ruler of Aleppo.

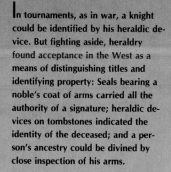

In tournaments, as in war, a knight could be identified by his heraldic device. But fighting aside, heraldry found acceptance in the West as a means of distinguishing titles and identifying property: Seals bearing a noble's coat of arms carried all the authority of a signature; heraldic devices on tombstones indicated the identity of the deceased; and a person's ancestry could be divined by close inspection of his arms.

Used to authenticate documents, this seal portrays a knight on whose shield are displayed the arms of Robert Fitzwalter, a prominent English Crusader.

In this thirteenth-century miniature of a chivalric joust, some of the knights and their steeds bear distinctive rosettes—a device popular with both Muslims and Christians.

Made around the end of the thirteenth century, this casket bears the enameled devices of its owner, the English earl of Pembroke.

As in Europe, Mamluk emirs and sultans used distinguishing insignia to indicate rank or title. Sometimes a Mamluk emir chose his own emblem; sometimes it was conferred on him by the sultan. Baybars, for example, granted a Mamluk who had distinguished himself at the siege of Antioch in 1268 the right to bear the arms of the city's defeated constable. Quite often a Mamluk's blazon reflected his offical post at the sultan's court. Because of the nonhereditary nature of Mamluk succession, however, and a devastating invasion by the Ottoman Turks, the use of such Islamic insignia died out in the sixteenth century.

Donated for use in a mosque, this glass lamp displays the crossbow emblem of its donor, Ala al-Din Aydakin, crossbow-bearer to the sultan al-Salih Ayyub.

Made for the Nuri hospital in Damascus, this ceramic pot sports the fleur-de-lis, an emblem adopted by several members of Sultan Qalawun's family.

menting this force with Sunqur's Syrian rebels. While the population of Damascus prayed for deliverance from the Mongols, Qalawun camped outside the Syrian town of Homs and waited for the invaders. Among his troops were those of Sunqur, who had been persuaded to change his allegiance with the promise of land in North Syria.

In size and quality, the armies that confronted each other outside Homs on October 29, 1281, were roughly equal. They also adopted a similar battle order; both sides placed their best troops in the center and their auxiliaries on the wings. In the fray, the Mamluk right triumphed over the Mongol left while the Mongol right inflicted a similar defeat on the Mamluk left. Amid the confusion both sides imagined they had lost the day. But at this critical moment, a senior Mamluk emir galloped to the Mongol center, calling out that he was a deserter. Brought before the Mongol leader, he drew his sword and managed to wound him before being hacked down. Encouraged by his bravery, the Mamluks launched an all-out attack that broke the Mongols' nerve and scattered them in a hectic retreat across the Euphrates. By sunset, Qalawun was master of the field. But the cost had been severe. Although one chronicler was probably exaggerating when he reported that only 500 of Qalawun's horsemen had survived, the histories of the time were littered with obituaries of dead officers and notable civilian volunteers who had died in the fray.

Qalawun's intention had been to drive the Crusaders out of the Holy Land after he had dealt with the Mongols, but first he had to rebuild his army. He did this so diligently that by the end of his ten-year reign his personal Mamluk corps numbered as many as 12,000—more than any other Mamluk sultan possessed before or after and possibly as many as one-third of the total number of military slaves then in service throughout Egypt and Syria. It may have been Qalawun's pressing need for slaves,

Arab traders haggle over the price of black slaves in a picture illustrating al-Hariri's *Maqamat*. Imported by North African slavers or captured in campaigns against Nubia to the south, such unfortunates were a common sight in Mamluk slave markets, where sultans and emirs purchased them for use as domestic servants or, less frequently, as military instructors or harem guards. Gang warfare between such slaves and young Mamluks was a major civic problem in medieval Cairo.

as well as a desire to keep the dominant Turkish element in check, that made him recruit Mamluks from beyond the Kipchak steppes—mainly Circassians from the eastern coastlands of the Black Sea. Most of these Mamluks were organized in an elite corps consisting of 300 emirs and 3,000 members of other ranks stationed in the citadel and therefore known as the Burjis, or Mamluks of the Tower.

Though recruited from a different region, these new Mamluks fitted easily into the established military organization of the Turks. Indeed, so numerous were Qalawun's new recruits that they soon occupied every important post in the strict Mamluk hierarchy. At the top were the members of the sultan's personal corps, dominated by the two *naibs*, or vice-regents, who governed Egypt and Syria in his absence. Other senior officers of this household guard included the head chamberlain, in charge of screening and presenting visitors; the emir of weapons, who had responsibility for the armory; and the emir of the stables. Outside the narrow elite of the household unit, there was a large body of emirs who were ranked according to the number of Mamluks under their command—from emirs of 100 down to emirs of 5.

According to his rank, each Mamluk received certain perquisites from his master. Senior emirs who maintained their own Mamluk establishments were given grants of land tax at the sultan's discretion, donations of money and horses before a campaign, and gifts on the accession of a sultan who wanted their support. In turn, some of this money was passed on to the junior Mamluks in the form of pay and rations.

In addition, more ostentatious signs of favor were bestowed; government regulations laid down in detail the type of ceremonial uniform each rank was entitled to wear. Emirs of 100 were invested with sumptuous robes of red and yellow satin, embroidered with gold thread and trimmed with fur. They wore turbans of muslin ornamented with strips of silk and gold belts inset with precious stones, and they carried swords in gold-inlaid scabbards. An emir who had won royal approbation might also be given a horse with an ornate harness and saddlery prepared by a special court official. Officers of lower ranks wore robes stitched from multicolored bands and bordered with a gold fringe. The striking uniforms distinguished all Mamluks from the civilian notables, who usually wore white or black.

Emirs with at least forty men under their command had the right to maintain a small orchestra, consisting mainly of percussionists, to encourage their men on the battlefield—many Crusader chroniclers wrote of the terrible and intimidating cacophony made by a Mamluk army as it attacked. Nor was the racket restricted to wartime; as audible proof of his exaltation, the emir was entitled to have the band play outside his house at sunset.

Although Qalawun's own men filled all the important military posts, the threat of a coup was nevertheless ever present. Accordingly, Qalawun took pains to train his Mamluks thoroughly and promote them slowly, and he was careful to move his Syrian vice-regents from post to post to prevent them from establishing an independent power base. During Qalawun's visits to Syria, Egypt was governed by his son, acting with Qalawun's vice-regent and according to stringent guidelines that were to form the basis for most subsequent Mamluk administrations. Cairo was patrolled by armed police, with special attention given to the area around the citadel, and local governors ensured that the populace traveled only by day. Troops sent to join the sultan in Syria were sped on their way by the issue of special laissez-passer documents. The Bedouin of the Nile delta were detailed to provide horses for the postal service, and regular contact with Damascus was maintained by pigeon post. In addition, the Christian merchants in Alexandria were locked in their caravansaries at night and at midday on Fridays to prevent a coup while Muslims were at prayer.

The cost of maintaining this administrative machinery and at the same time financing the army was exorbitant, and to meet the expense the sultan looked to his three main sources of income: taxation, tribute, and trade. The chief source of tax revenue was the iqta. In Ayyubid times, the revenue from one-sixth of the cultivable land had formed the royal treasury, with that of another five-twelfths allotted for the maintenance of the Mamluk emirs' establishments, and the rest going to the army of freeborn soldiers. By the early fourteenth century, the Mamluk sultans had more than doubled their share to over five-twelfths, effectively concentrating the wealth of the state in their hands.

War booty and tribute from weaker neighbors also swelled the sultans' coffers.

After the battle of Homs, for example, King Leo II of Armenia, an ally of the defeated Mongols, bought a peace treaty from Qalawun at the cost of an annual tribute of 500,000 Armenian silver dirhams, payable in advance, in addition to 25 horses, 25 mules, and 10,000 horseshoes with nails—this last a desirable commodity in mineral-poor Egypt. Other clauses specified that Leo release all Muslim merchants and prisoners and that he put no obstacles in the way of slavers bringing their youthful merchandise to the sultan.

Similar considerations prompted Qalawun to issue a proclamation in 1288 giving safe conduct to the Genoese sea traders who shipped slaves from the Crimea and who shared with the Venetians the lucrative trade in spices purchased on the Egyptian market. Brought in by traders from countries such as Ceylon and India, spice was exported to Europe in vast quantities, along with commodities such as silk, linen, and aromatic woods; in turn, the Egyptians imported copper for resale at a handsome profit to the Indians. The huge prices and heavy duties that the sultan imposed on spices contributed greatly to his financial resources, and the wealthy corporation of Muslim merchants who handled the trade provided a convenient source of money when he was short of funds.

Most of the sultan's income was earmarked for the military establishment. The stables alone cost a fortune to maintain. One fourteenth-century sultan kept 7,800 horses, most of which were detailed for the use of his Mamluks, as well as 30,000 sheep, which helped provision the army, and large herds of camels, which were used to carry military baggage. This outlay was not at the expense of home comforts, however: Camels sped ice from the Lebanese mountains to cool the sultan's drinks, and large sums were lavished on diversions such as polo, hunting, and hawking.

The Mamluks also heavily patronized the arts, and their era witnessed a dramatic flourishing of Islamic culture. Metalwork and glasswork both reached new heights, and on a larger scale the Mamluks established numerous mosques, colleges, and retreats for Sufis—Islamic mystics, who commanded a large measure of popular respect. Beginning in Qalawun's reign, such buildings were usually built in local limestone, which withstood decay better than the brickwork of their predecessors and lent itself to brilliantly carved decoration. Much of this construction was carried out by immigrants from Iraq and Asia Minor, who had fled from the Mongols and who by the end of the thirteenth century had helped increase Cairo's population to approximately 500,000. That figure made it the largest city outside China and five times as populous as any in Europe.

Like Baybars before him, Qalawun continued to cherish the idea of driving the Crusaders out of the Holy Land. In 1289, he went some way toward achieving that dream by exploiting differences between Venice and Genoa to capture the busy port city of Tripoli. The immense amount of booty he gained thereby merely served to spur his ambition, and in the final years of his reign he set his eyes on Acre, the last of the Franks' capitals and their greatest port. To protect his flanks during the attack on Tripoli, Qalawun had made a treaty with Acre designed to last ten years, ten months, and ten days—but a pretext for breaking it came to hand in August of 1290. In that month a rabble of newly arrived Italian Crusaders ran riot through the city, murdering everyone they took to be a Muslim. When the sultan's envoys arrived and called for the guilty men to be sent to Cairo, some counselors advised that all the Christians held in Acre's jails be handed over to the emissaries. Public opinion would not allow it, however, and the ambassadors were forced to return to Qalawun empty-handed.

Qalawun was delighted, and he immediately mobilized his army to avenge the outrage. As luck would have it, he was denied the satisfaction; on November 5, 1290, while camped outside Cairo, the seventy-year-old sultan was taken ill with a fever. He died five days later.

It seemed to the inhabitants of Acre that they were saved. Given the factionalism of the Mamluks, it was probable that all their energies would be diverted to the succession struggle—especially since Qalawun's eldest son and nominated heir had died shortly before his father, leaving as the likely claimant a younger brother, Khalil, whom the sultan had openly disliked. It was rumored that Khalil had poisoned his elder brother, and Qalawun had repeatedly refused to sign the decree appointing the young man his heir, insisting, "I will not set Khalil over the Muslims."

Within two days of Qalawun's death, however, Khalil had seized the throne, dashing the Crusaders' hopes and confounding Qalawun's wishes. He had planned well in advance and amassed considerable support through his martial prowess. Even by Mamluk standards he was noted for his horsemanship, archery, and skill in the conduct of war. Khalil spent the winter of 1290 securing his position in Egypt by eliminating his most serious rivals and distributing their wealth to other potential opponents. In the meantime, preparations for the assault on Acre continued under his officers. In all, nearly 100 siege engines had been constructed by the time the sultan led his army out of Cairo in March.

On April 6, 1291, the siege was laid. Although contemporary reports probably overestimated the Mamluks' numbers, citing 60,000 cavalry and 160,000 infantry, the Islamic army dwarfed the defense, which amounted to no more than 1,000 mounted knights and sergeants, about 14,000 foot soldiers, and some 30,000 to 40,000 civilians. Even so, a Mamluk victory was not a foregone conclusion, since Acre occupied a peninsula, with its back to the sea and its one landward side protected by a triple line of walls and strong towers. Moreover, the defenders, who represented nearly all the Crusading powers except Genoa, knew they were fighting for their lives and buried old differences. The Muslims, on the other hand, were weakened by mistrust between Khalil and his Syrian vice-regent, who attempted to desert the siege.

Day after day the great mangonels showered the walls with jars of so-called Greek fire, a highly combustible concoction whose exact components are unknown. As many as 1,000 sappers tried to undermine the fortifications while the defenders poured down retaliatory fire and struck back with their own catapults at the Mamluks'

Heedless of a plowman toiling in the background, picnicking literati depicted in a manuscript illustration find pleasure debating points of grammar. The richness of the Arabic language encouraged cultured citizens to indulge in pastimes such as word games, riddles, and versifying. At a more popular level, professional storytellers installed themselves in markets and other public places, where they attracted audiences eager to hear tales of magic, romance, and bawdy comedy.

CAIRO'S PALACE OF HEALING

Built under the patronage of Sultan Qalawun, the Mansuri Maristan in Cairo was the most sophisticated medical center of its time. While suffering from a serious fever in the Nuri hospital at Damascus, Qalawun had vowed to build an even better institution at Cairo. On his recovery, he did not forget his promise. Work was started in 1284, and with the aid of labor pressed into service off the streets, Qalawun's dream was realized in only eleven months.

Extravagantly funded, the hospital complex included a college mosque and a school for orphans besides incomparable medical facilities. In addition to the convalescent ward shown here, there were separate wards for the treatment of fevers, eye diseases, surgical cases, dysentery, and insanity. The hospital was also provided with laboratories, dispensaries, baths, kitchens, storerooms, and a lecture theater where the chief of medical staff gave instruction.

Fragrant herbs were strewn on the floor in accordance with the physicians' belief that good air was essential to the well-being of their patients, and a natural spring was channeled through the building to cool the atmosphere. All medical treatment was available without charge, and the patients' suffering was further ameliorated by professional musicians who provided entertainment and by fifty men who read the Koran day and night.

siege weapons. A young Syrian prince, Ismail Abu al-Fida, wrote an account of the action: "They brought up a ship carrying a mangonel that fired on us and our tents from the direction of the sea. This caused us distress until one night there was a violent storm of wind, so that the vessel was tossed on the waves, and the mangonel it was carrying broke." For as long as possible the Franks kept the gates open and fought outside them, and when they were forced to close them, they made sallies by night. In the words of Ismail, "The Franks . . . surprised the troops and put the sentries to flight. They got through to the tents and became entangled in the ropes. One of their knights fell into an emir's latrine and was killed there. The troops rallied against them and the Franks fell back routed to the town."

One by one the towers of the outer wall were undermined and abandoned. On May 16, the Mamluks forced their way through, driving the defenders back behind the inner wall. On May 18, 1291, the sultan ordered a general assault on the city. "When the Muslims stormed it," reported Ismail, "some of its inhabitants took flight in ships. Inside the town were a number of towers holding out like citadels. A great mass of Franks entered them and fortified themselves. The Muslims slew and took an uncountable amount of booty from Acre. Then the sultan demanded the surrender of all who were holding out in the towers, and not one held back. The sultan gave the command and they were beheaded around Acre to the last man. Then at his command the city of Acre was demolished and razed to the ground."

Worried that the fall of Acre would provoke another Crusade, as its capture by Saladin had done more than a century earlier, Khalil ordered the destruction of all remaining Frankish possessions that could provide a springboard for reprisal. Tyre, Sidon, Beirut, and Haifa, with the Templar castles of Tortosa and Athlit, were taken and the land around them laid waste. Thus ended nearly 200 years of Crusader rule in the Holy Land.

The fall of Acre and the destruction of the Crusader threat was the signal for a new round of Mamluk infighting. The next twenty years saw a succession of six sultans. The political philosophy they shared was perhaps best summed up by the sultan Salar, whose stated aim was "Have him for dinner before he has you for breakfast." Salar's end was also symptomatic of the period; he was starved to death, ending up eating his own excrement.

Not until 1310 was there some respite. In that year, al-Nasur Muhammad—like Khalil, a son of Qalawun—came to the throne. His reign, lasting a remarkable thirty years, was an interlude of relative stability, but after he died in 1340, the violence resumed with open warfare between the Circassian and the Turkish elements. As the factionalism of the Mamluks increased their quality as soldiers declined. Traditional fighting skills were neglected, and little attempt was made to introduce the new developments of firearms and gunpowder.

Meanwhile, the population of the Mamluk lands was reduced by a series of plagues that also devastated the economy. With villages deserted and agricultural land reverting to waste, the iqta revenue shrank in the late fifteenth century to one-quarter of the level it had been at the beginning of the Mamluk regime. Government interference in commerce, native tribal revolts, and from 1500 on, fierce Portuguese competition for the Indian spice trade helped further impoverish the empire.

Yet for all the evidence of decline, the Mamluks grimly hung onto power until the second decade of the sixteenth century. They were finally overcome not by internal divisions but by a rival Muslim power: the Ottomans of Asia Minor.

THE MAKING OF A MANUSCRIPT

Thirteenth-century Europe developed an insatiable thirst for knowledge. Universities were founded across the Continent, from the towns of Oxford and Cambridge in England to Paris and the Spanish city of Salamanca. Hordes of students—some as young as fourteen—flocked to the academic centers, pursuing scholastic careers that could span many years and several countries. The widening audience for learning in turn created an increased demand for information in the form of the written word.

Manuscripts—literally, "written by hand"—of religious and classical texts had been produced by monks in Europe since before the fifth century for their own study and worship, but now there was a need for a much wider range of texts. Workshops were established in such cities as Paris, Oxford, and Bologna to publish newly written treatises on logic, astronomy, law, mathematics, and music; wealthy individuals could commission psalters and the increasingly popular volumes of personal devotions known as books of hours.

Improved production methods helped meet the demand. Employing fine-quality parchment and the new, angular Gothic lettering that replaced the larger, rounded Romanesque script, bookmakers produced single-volume editions of the Bible—such as the one shown below, measuring about three by five inches—that were small enough to be carried by mendicant Dominican and Franciscan friars on their travels. The flourishing booksellers of Paris made the recently discovered texts of Aristotle and the works of the prolific Dominican theologian, Thomas Aquinas, quickly available to the public.

Although speed and quantity were important factors in this developing industry, the medieval manuscript was not simply a utilitarian object. The skills of professional parchmentmakers, scribes, artists, and bookbinders took years to acquire and were employed with justified pride. The manuscript was one of the main outlets for the creative talents of the time and could be just as precious in its own right as the knowledge it transmitted.

CONSTRUCTING A BOOK

An array of skills were involved in the production of a manuscript. First, the parchment (also called vellum) was made by soaking animal skins—preferably those of cows or sheep—in running water for several days, followed by prolonged immersion in lime and water. Hair was scraped off, the soaking repeated, and the skins stretched on frames to dry. The parchment-maker completed his task by cleaning the skins with pumice and water.

The parchment was folded into leaves and trimmed to size. A number of leaves were then assembled into "gatherings"—standard units, usually of eight, twelve, or sixteen pages—that were stitched together by binders. The series of illustrations here, from a mid-thirteenth-century German Bible, show the stages involved in preparing a manuscript for binding.

A scribe would laboriously transcribe the text from a model manuscript, known as an exemplar, hired from public stationers. Poorer students were able to rent unbound exemplars, a single gathering at a time, and make their own copies; the rich could commission entire manuscripts already illuminated and bound. The accuracy of stationers' exemplars was regularly checked by university authorities to prevent the proliferation of mistakes, which could easily be made during copying.

A parchmentmaker offers a sample of his wares to a monk, who examines it for holes and stains. During its preparation, the parchment was stretched across a wooden frame of the type shown here. The curved knife at the foot of the frame was used to remove hair from the skin.

Having folded the parchment into leaves of the required size and assembled them into sheaves, or gatherings, a scribe trims the edges with a ruler and knife. By the end of the thirteenth century, scribes could buy their parchment already trimmed and packaged in boxes.

With his quill and knife poised above the parchment and an inkhorn at his side, a scribe prepares to write between the guidelines he has ruled. The knife was used to sharpen the quill, to scratch out mistakes, and to hold the page flat while the scribe was writing. Gaps were left for the colored chapter and page headings and the initials, which would be filled in later according to instructions written by the scribe in pale ink beside the text.

Guiding his right hand with his left, an artist paints the head of a man with colors selected from the palette beside his seat. The pigments were ground and then mixed with a binding medium of gelatin, gum, or egg, which gave them a permanent luster.

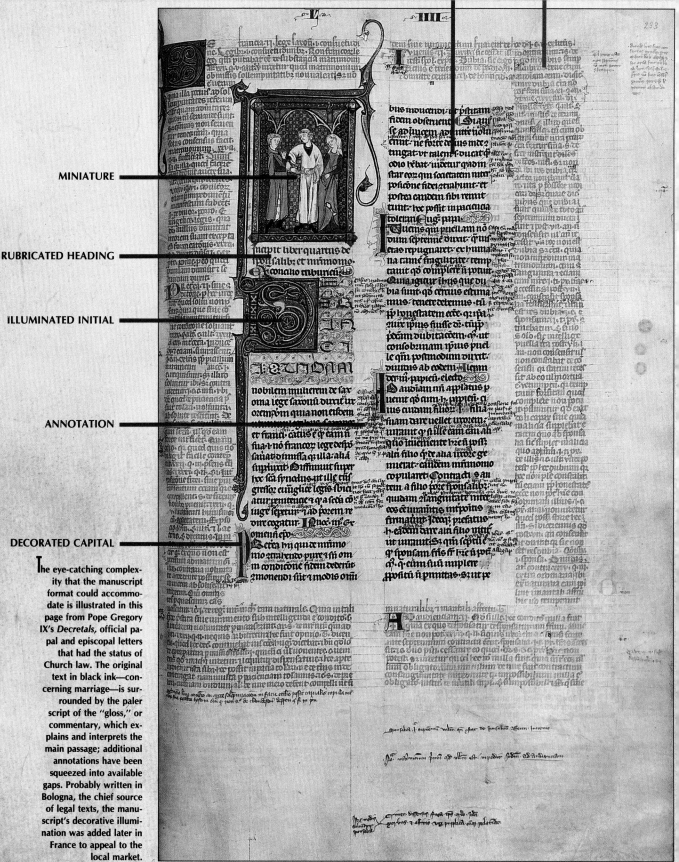

The eye-catching complexity that the manuscript format could accommodate is illustrated in this page from Pope Gregory IX's *Decretals*, official papal and episcopal letters that had the status of Church law. The original text in black ink—concerning marriage—is surrounded by the paler script of the "gloss," or commentary, which explains and interprets the main passage; additional annotations have been squeezed into available gaps. Probably written in Bologna, the chief source of legal texts, the manuscript's decorative illumination was added later in France to appeal to the local market.

DESIGNING A PAGE

The arrangement of the text and decorative effects on a manuscript page were carefully calculated both to enhance its visual appeal and to aid the reader's understanding. The columns and lettering of the text were aligned within a precisely measured grid of guidelines. Intricately worked initials marked the beginning of books or chapters, and headings, known as rubrics, were written in or accentuated by red ink.

Many of the colors used by the rubricators and illustrators were expensive and difficult to obtain. Ultramarine—literally, "from across the sea"—was ground from semiprecious lapis lazuli imported from Persia and Afghanistan; kermes, a red pigment, was made from the dried bodies of certain female insects. Economy and careful integration with the overall design of the page were important. Some artists were warned by the Church against indulging their imaginations too freely lest the reader become distracted from the text.

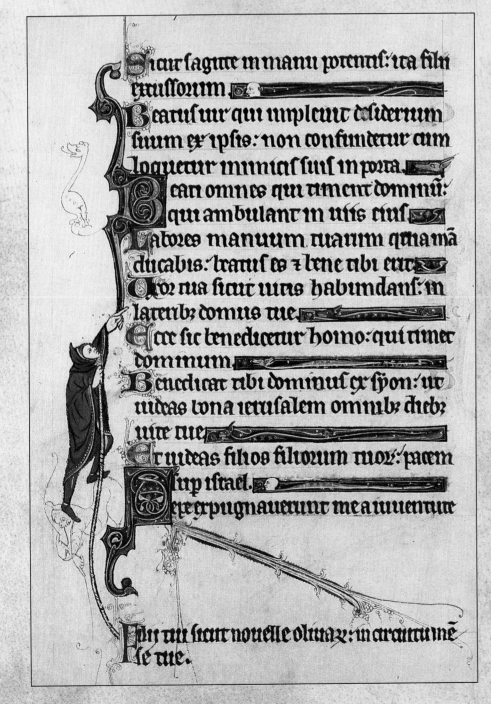

The bottom line of this manuscript page from a thirteenth-century English psalter and book of hours was accidentally left out of the body of the text during copying. The error gave the illuminator an excuse for a playful diversion: The figure wearing a blue cloak and red cap—complementing the colors of the initials and the fancifully elongated men and foxes that end the shorter lines—hauls the omitted line after him on a rope and points out where it should be inserted.

Shimmering with gold, this full-page miniature from the thirteenth-century Oscott Psalter combines majesty with vivid human detail. The two roundels depict the Adoration and the Dream of the Magi; the disproportionately large heads of the figures and the angular folds of their clothing show the influence of French style on the anonymous English artist.

Such miniatures, blazing forth from the text of medieval manuscripts, were primarily intended as an expression of faith. The term *illuminated,* used to describe a gold-decorated manuscript, suggested a text both glorified and clarified by the light reflected from the gold and echoed Saint John's description of the Word of God as "a light that shineth in darkness."

But the miniatures also expressed the skills of the professionals who created them. Following the stages shown by a present-day illuminator on the opposite page, an artist might take four days to complete a miniature similar to the one shown here.

1 A detailed drawing is made in thinned ink or pencil; then size—a primer consisting of a mixture of sugar, plaster, lead, and glue—is applied with a quill to those areas to be covered with gold leaf. When it has dried, the size is carefully scraped with a sharp knife to produce a smooth surface.

2 The illuminator moistens the size with his breath, then presses onto it small sections of gold leaf. Burnishing with a piece of polished agate or a shaped animal tooth set into a handle produces a brilliant shine.

3 The basic colors are blocked in, obscuring the detail of the original drawing. The colors used here include orange lead oxide, ultramarine, malachite, kermes, umber, and raw sienna.

4 Darker shades of the colors already applied are used to pattern the borders and to give shape and substance to the main forms of the illustration.

5 Strong black lines define the areas of color and essential features of the illustration, adding vitality to the almost completed picture.

6 The illuminator applies the finishing touches: fine lines and shading that give character to the faces and hair; thin white bands as well as dots and circles to enliven the border patterns and drapery. The gold leaf is punched with a pointed tool to catch the light.

THE WEST'S EMBATTLED EMPIRE

In the 1230s, strange stories were circulating about Europe's most powerful ruler, the Holy Roman Emperor. It was said that he was curious about the nature of the soul: He had had a condemned man sealed into a wine barrel and slowly drowned while he and his learned courtiers watched carefully for any sign of an escaping emanation; finding none, they concluded that the soul was nonexistent. The emperor had also decided to settle all argument as to the original language of mankind: He had entrusted a group of infant orphans to the care of deaf-mute nurses on an uninhabited island and had visited them a few years later to discover the outcome. (Alas, a lethal outbreak of plague had ruined the imperial experiment.) Some people maintained that the emperor was not even a believer; he had been heard to say that mankind had been deceived by three impostors: Moses, Christ, and Muhammad. Almost as disturbing for a century that regarded personal hygiene as an indulgence, it was rumored that the emperor took a weekly bath.

The man who so shocked and fascinated his contemporaries was Frederick II, grandson of the great emperor Frederick Barbarossa and the third successive member of the south German Hohenstaufen family to have held the imperial throne. Ruling a realm that stretched over much of central Europe, he boasted a title whose origins stretched back to the year 800, when the Frankish king Charlemagne had been crowned in Rome. It had been then and was still an attempt to re-create something of the glory of the original Roman empire, whose ruins were everywhere and whose Latin tongue was still the preferred language of the educated. By Frederick's time, the emperor stood at the pinnacle of the pyramid of feudal obligations within his realm; without him the rest of the structure would have made little sense. But the empire's holiness was important, too, for it was seen as a Christian institution, directly endowed by God: Legally, the emperor was God's vicegerent, or deputy, and not easily subject to any lesser authority.

Yet the emperor had a rival for the leadership of Christendom and one whose mandate was even more directly divine. The pope was Christ's vicar on earth and subject to no lesser authority whatsoever. The church that he directed stood at the heart and center of Western Christendom and was the institution that gave meaning to all the others. By tradition, each new emperor was crowned by the pope; zealous ecclesiastics claimed that it was thereby the pope who gave legitimacy to the secular monarch. This view was controversial, but almost everyone agreed that, at the very least, cooperation between pope and emperor was essential to the well-being of Christendom as a whole.

In practice, though, it was not always easy to attain. Indeed, since the eleventh century, pope and emperor had spent more time in conflict than they had in cooperation. The thirteenth century was to see the disagreements escalate to new levels

Braced for battle in helmet, chain mail, and sleeveless tunic, this thirteenth-century German knight saw action only at banquets, as a bronze aquamanile, or ewer. His live counterparts, armed with lances and lozenge-shaped shields, formed the backbone of an imperial task force with which Frederick II controlled the Holy Roman Empire and challenged the authority of the pope.

89

of bitterness, culminating in internecine warfare. The struggle would cast a shadow over Frederick II's reign and would end, after his death, in an apparently absolute victory for the papacy and in the extermination of the ancient Hohenstaufen family line. Yet the triumph would in turn cost the Church dearly; it, too, was a long-term loser in both power and prestige.

Such a confrontation could hardly have been foreseen in the latter decades of the twelfth century, when papal fears of the emperor's political domination seemed to be on the wane. Although the territories of the emperor were vast, incorporating Germany and its principalities, Bohemia, Burgundy and Provence, and northern Italy, they were too disparate and loosely governed to give him as much power as a map would indicate. The pope, by contrast, ruled directly only the modest Patrimony of Peter—more or less the region of Latium around the city of Rome—and even there his authority was frequently challenged by an unruly citizenry.

To the south of Latium, however, the independent Norman kingdom of Sicily provided an effective counterbalance to imperial power. Previously a Muslim emirate, the island of Sicily had been conquered in the eleventh century by a brave and unscrupulous adventurer, Roger de Hauteville of Normandy. His son, Roger II, took the title of king—his father had ruled as count—and added territories in southern Italy to his domain; from Palermo, where he kept the most splendid court in Europe, he ruled the *regno*, or kingdom, of Sicily, which in fact extended as far north as Naples

When Frederick II became Holy Roman Emperor in 1220, he held sway over the largest feudal conglomeration in Europe: lands that spread from the Baltic in the north to the Mediterranean in the south, encompassing all of Germany and most of the Italian peninsula. Only the Papal States, based at Rome, denied his authority. Eschewing the imperial homelands in Germany, Frederick chose as his base the kingdom of Sicily, where he had been born and raised, turning it into the richest and most cosmopolitan state of his age.

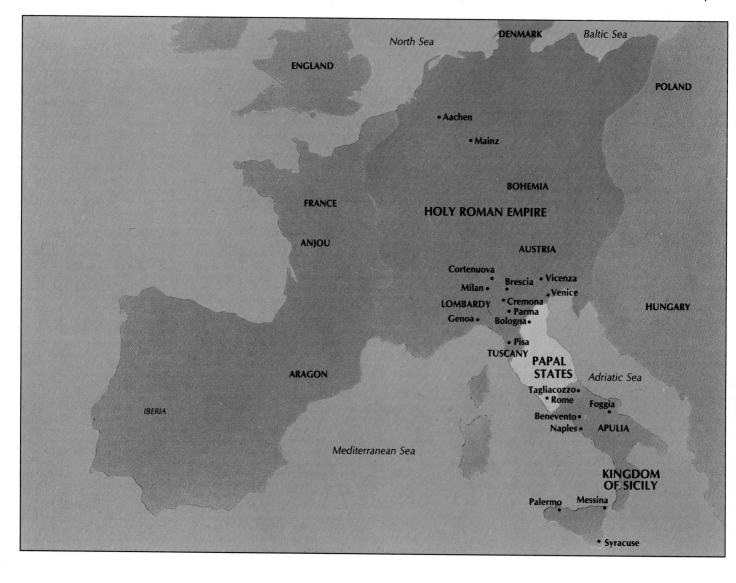

and Abruzzi. And although it was under Norman-style feudal rule, this new realm embraced an open, cosmopolitan society, with an invigorating mixture of Muslim and Christian, Arab and Lombard and Greek.

From Rome's point of view, the Normans were an improvement on their Muslim predecessors. Moreover, they owed no allegiance to the emperor. And after a few violent misunderstandings, the Hauteville family came to enjoy excellent relations with the pope, who became their nominal suzerain and guaranteed their possessions.

A fluke of dynastic succession, though, brought a drastic change to the comfortable status quo. In 1186, Frederick Barbarossa's son Henry married Constance, a daughter of Roger II; four years later her nephew, the king of Sicily, died without an heir, leaving her as the principal claimant to the Sicilian throne. An illegitimate grandson of Roger disputed her title, however, and seized power. In the meantime, Barbarossa had died on Crusade, and the twenty-six-year-old Henry had been elected Holy Roman Emperor as Henry VI. At first he was too involved in German affairs to take the opportunity presented by his wife's Sicilian claim, but in 1194 he swept into Sicily with his German knights, enforcing her title with a ruthlessness that earned him the name Henry the Cruel. All possible rivals were put to death (one, who had died of natural causes shortly before, was hauled from his tomb to suffer public beheading) and at Christmas of that year, Henry, in his capacity as Constance's husband, was crowned king in Palermo. With the exception of the small Papal States, the emperor's power now embraced the entire Italian peninsula. The pope's political position was suddenly precarious.

Constance served her husband well. Not only had she presented him with a kingdom, but in the year of his Sicilian coronation she also gave him an heir. It was an occurrence so unexpected—Constance was forty and had had no children in the first eight years of her marriage—that dark rumors spread of a demonic conception, but Henry was pleased with his baby boy and named him Frederick, after his grandfather. The child was born in Italy (at Jesi, in the district of Ancona); nonetheless, his father was determined to make a good German out of him. In 1196, he had Frederick proclaimed king of Germany at Frankfurt. The following year, he made arrangements to take the boy north for his formal coronation.

But the emperor was not immune to the accidents of mortality that had granted him a new kingdom. On a hunting expedition on the slopes of Sicily's Mount Etna in 1197, he caught a fever and died soon after. Plans for young Frederick's coronation were hastily abandoned: The bear pit of imperial politics in Germany was no place for an infant king. The succession was disputed, and the situation rapidly degenerated into a civil war that set Henry's brother, Philip of Swabia, against a claimant from a rival line, Otto of Brunswick, of the Welf family. The conflict between the Hohenstaufen and Welf houses was an old one. In Germany their respective battle cries had long been used to denote the opposing sides: "Welf!" identified Otto's supporters, and "Waiblingen!"—the title of a family castle in Swabia—became the rallying cry of the Hohenstaufen loyalists. In the coming century, these war cries would move south; Italianized as "Guelph" and "Ghibelline," they would serve as party labels for years of struggle between pope and emperor.

At the time, however, it seemed to the papacy that the hand of God had saved it from imperial domination. Constance, too, was less than grief-stricken at the loss of her husband's northern possessions to civil war: She immediately ordered the expulsion of most of the German aristocrats and administrators brought by Henry to

Italy, amid mass rejoicing that reached almost the level of a popular revolt. Frederick's future was now in his mother's hands. He would grow up as a prince of Norman Sicily, not of Germany.

He had lost one chance at coronation. Constance made up for it with another, when she had him crowned king of Sicily in 1198. But the kingdom he inherited came with a heavy political debt: Ailing and insecure, Constance had entered into an alliance with the papacy shortly after Henry's death. In return for protection and support, she pledged allegiance to Rome and conceded sweeping powers to the Church. When she died, only six months after Frederick's coronation, she left her son under the guardianship of none other than the pope himself—the newly elected Innocent III. Meanwhile, the regno was to be run during Frederick's minority by men nominated by Innocent.

Henry would have been horrified, the more so since Innocent was a fervent exponent of the doctrine of papal supremacy. Moreover, he was well equipped with the industry, intelligence, political shrewdness, and sheer force of personality needed to turn his ambitions into reality. In the course of his pontificate, he was to bring the Church to an unsurpassed level of temporal and spiritual power. He extended the Patrimony of Peter into a substantial territory that embraced most of central Italy. He intervened in the German civil war, affirming the papal right to confirm or depose an emperor. A great jurist, he became the recognized court of appeal for all Christendom. He even forced King John of England to surrender his kingdom and receive it back by papal grace as a fief of the Church.

For the regno and its child-king, Pope Innocent was a disaster. The prolonged regency inflicted years of intrigue and near anarchy on the land and its people. It was Frederick's lot to experience an unhappy upbringing at the hands of various magnates, mostly in the region of Apulia, the heel of the Italian peninsula. His childhood left him with a lifelong love for Apulia and its gentle landscapes and a touchy sense of injured dignity. Innocent himself admitted of his ward that "the need to expound his grievances granted him eloquence at an age when most children are only babbling." Nevertheless, the boy remained under the pope's control. He came of age officially at fourteen in 1208; the following year Innocent arranged his marriage to a Spanish princess.

Almost at once, Frederick began to show dangerous signs of independence: Despite Innocent's objections, he dismissed the last papal regent and began to rule the impoverished regno in his own right. But before the pope could do more than remonstrate, events in the Holy Roman Empire forced him to give his restive pawn a dramatic promotion.

The war in Germany had at last come to an end in 1208 with the assassination of Philip of Swabia, Frederick's uncle, and the next year Innocent had crowned Philip's rival, Otto, in Rome as the new emperor. As an opponent of the Hohenstaufens, Otto was ostensibly the pope's man, but first and foremost he was emperor and was determined to behave like one. Mindful of Henry VI's southern triumph, Otto turned his eyes toward Sicily. Only a few months after his coronation, he led an invading army into the regno.

Innocent was outraged and excommunicated the emperor at once. It was a powerful sanction in an age of faith, not only placing Otto's immortal soul in peril but also encouraging his followers to abandon the allegiance they had sworn to him. Even so, it was not enough to change Otto's plans. Innocent needed a political as well as a spiritual counterattack. The pope's best weapon would be a rival emperor in whom he could invest authority. But there were few candidates who commanded enough respect to challenge Otto seriously.

In fact, there was only one—Frederick. Powerless to resist Otto's invasion, he had had a ship prepared for flight to North Africa when he was invited by German princes, with papal consent, to go north to claim his inheritance. His wife and his counselors advised against acceptance: The risk was too great, and the papal demand that Frederick renounce the throne of the regno in favor of his newborn son, Henry, was unacceptable. But Frederick had his own ideas. In 1212, accompanied by a handful of companions, he traveled northward to claim his inheritance, armed with little more than the pope's blessing and his aristocratic name.

The combination was just enough. The journey itself was difficult and dangerous; several times Frederick came close to capture by Otto or his allies. But once he reached Germany, he received substantial support. He was, for the second time, elected German king at Frankfurt in 1212 and was crowned by the archbishop of Mainz a few days later. Yet the position of the Boy from Apulia—as he was nick-named by friend and enemy alike—was still not secure. It took an alliance with France, engineered by Innocent's astute diplomacy, and two more years of fighting before Otto could be reckoned defeated. In 1215, he was officially deposed, retiring to Saxony, where he could still count on local support. Frederick was crowned once more, this time in Aachen, as tradition demanded; the ceremony was universally accepted as a preliminary to receiving the imperial throne.

Frederick owed much to Innocent, but he had to pay a high price for the pope's support: Rights and privileges that his predecessors, notably Frederick Barbarossa, had enjoyed passed into the hands of the Church. At the moment of his coronation in 1215, though, the new emperor seemed too exalted by the high honor he had received to care. In a mood of religious enthusiasm, he vowed to take the cross and lead a Crusade to liberate the holy places in Palestine. Politics could wait.

For Innocent, Frederick's coronation was a political triumph. He set the seal upon it in 1215, when he called the fourth Lateran Council, named for the Roman palace in which its sessions were held. The greatest assembly of prelates in Church history, the council reaffirmed the pope's supreme authority in ecclesiastical affairs. It also confirmed Frederick's election and Otto's deposition. The conflict between papacy and empire appeared to be over, and there was no doubt about who had won.

Innocent died a few months later, in July 1216, but the proud legacy he left the Church seemed secure enough. For the next few years, relations between Frederick and Innocent's successor, Honorius III, were excellent, although the first signs of imperial backsliding on key promises were already apparent. Despite his oath to Innocent, for example, Frederick remained king of Sicily; far from replacing his father on the throne in Palermo, young Henry was brought north to be proclaimed duke of Swabia—an ancient Hohenstaufen title—and then, at the age of eight, crowned German king in his father's place. Power was vested for the duration of his minority in successive regents. Honorius, a deeply religious man and no politician, let the matter pass. He was more concerned with another unfulfilled promise: Frederick's vow to lead a Crusade.

Instead of realizing his pledge, Frederick chose to remain in Germany until 1220, much occupied with imposing some sort of imperial rule on a country grown dangerously undisciplined during the years of warfare. For the most part, he bought peace, paying with concessions of authority to the ecclesiastical nobility—the great archbishops—and the rising towns. He had little choice, since his military strength was limited. He could consolidate his authority only by diluting it, at least as a temporary measure.

When Frederick returned to Italy in the autumn of 1220, however, it was as a loyal son of the Church. He apologized for his delay in setting off on Crusade: "You will not repent, O Blessed Father," he wrote to Honorius, "of having brought up and loved a son such as I. We are ready to set ourselves at Your Holiness's feet; and soon you will have the fruit you desire from the tree you have planted." The pope allowed himself to be soothed with promises and in April 1220 finally consented to crown Frederick Holy Roman Emperor.

Negotiations were simplified by disorders in Rome itself. The politics of the city were complex and volatile; Honorius had been forced out of Rome six months before by fear of violence following a dispute among the leading Roman families. It was only the escort of Frederick's army that allowed him to return in safety to St. Peter's Basilica for the ceremony.

Apart from renewing his Crusading vows, Frederick swore to act with an iron hand against heretics of all sorts. Germany and Italy were then troubled by the Waldenses, advocates of an austere Christianity who were deeply hostile to the showier aspects of Church life, as well as by the Cathars, believers in the intrinsic evil of the material world. In addition, Frederick reassured the pope by declaring his German and Sicilian dominions to be constitutionally separate. For its part, the Church recognized Frederick's right to both the imperial and the Sicilian crowns. It was a subtlety that would make trouble later, but when Frederick left a subdued Rome to return to his long-abandoned regno, he and Honorius parted on amicable terms.

The kingdom of Sicily had had no real ruler since Henry VI died in 1197, and Frederick found awaiting him a land riddled with banditry, where even minor lords exercised arbitrary and near-absolute power over their petty dominions. He spent two years ruthlessly suppressing his own feudal vassals on the mainland. In 1222, it was the turn of the island of Sicily, where the Muslim population was in full rebellion. It took another two years of desperate warfare before the rebels were crushed and Frederick became king in fact as well as name.

He treated the vanquished Muslims with a leniency that had lasting consequences. Instead of massacre and slavery, their fate was a relatively humane deportation, in entire communities, to northern Apulia. There they were permitted to till the soil and carry on their traditional industries of carpet weaving and arms manufacture. More extraordinarily, they were allowed to practice their Islamic faith unmolested. Frederick's policy turned the former rebels into passionate Hohenstaufen loyalists: From then until the end of the dynasty, the Muslims of Apulia provided the core of every imperial army, as well as the emperor's personal bodyguard. Quite apart from their military prowess, the troops gave their master a valuable advantage in the conflicts that were to come. As Muslims, they were utterly unmoved by threats of excommunication from a Christian pope.

Even while he was pacifying the regno, Frederick was creating a rigid framework of law and administration that would make it the most thoroughly governed state in Europe. There was nothing liberal about his developing constitution: Virtually all powers—except those conceded, with increasing reluctance, to the Church—were

The impassive features in this mosaic portrait of Pope Gregory IX belie the uncompromising determination that he brought to bear in his struggle against the Holy Roman Emperor. Believing that the spiritual authority of the Church would be undermined by the material wealth and political power of the empire, Gregory twice excommunicated Frederick II and even struck an alliance with the northern Italian cities, whose notions of religious freedom he would normally have opposed.

invested in the king himself. But if the king's powers were to be absolute, they were absolute by law and not by whim.

Such a state could function only with the aid of a trained civil service, very much a novelty for the time. Frederick set out to create one to suit his purposes. In 1224, he ordered the foundation of a new university in the ancient city of Naples. It was the first in Europe to be completely free of clerical or monastic control, and although the emperor's sheer love of learning was no doubt one reason for the university's creation, the imperial edict that established it made Frederick's practical needs plain. "It is indeed our purpose that our realm should gain advantage from the University. . . . We will call meritorious and well-praised scholars to our service, entrusting the administration of justice to those who have become learned in the law." These were not just empty words: The year after the edict, the emperor took into his service Pietro della Vigna, a poor scholar who had presented himself at the Palermo court, according to a chronicler, "with neither bread to eat nor clothes to wear." Within a few years, Pietro had become his most trusted counselor.

The university even offered loans to poor students, and Frederick's government guaranteed them decent accommodations. The emperor's new education policy was not entirely free-spirited: The same edict also promised dire penalties for those subjects who dared to study abroad (for fear that they would be contaminated by the papal ideas that dominated other universities) and warned parents that their scholar-children had best return home in short order. But whatever its defects, the university was a cultural landmark, and in time it furnished Frederick with the officials that he needed.

With order restored, southern Italy flourished. It had always been potentially one of the richest areas in the Mediterranean: Sicily was a prosperous exporter of grain, cotton, silk, and much else, while the regno as a whole was a great entrepôt of East-West trade. Frederick's policies ensured that an increasing share of its wealth ended in the hands of the state, which plowed back some of its revenues into mercantile and military fleets that would challenge the merchants of Genoa, Pisa, and Venice for maritime domination.

Not all of Frederick's income was spent on purely practical projects: The court he kept—usually at Foggia, in his beloved Apulia, rather than in the elegant but isolated city of Palermo—reveled in an Oriental splendor that shocked and fascinated the rest of Europe. Frederick lived much like an Eastern potentate, complete with eunuch-guarded harem (his first wife had died in 1222), but the court was as noted for the scholars and philosophers, the poets and musicians who flocked there as it was for the emperor's self-indulgence. Frederick, it was said, could speak nine languages; he is certainly known to have used Latin, Greek, and Arabic as well as German and Italian. He wrote some of the first poetry in that last vernacular—his court was arguably the birthplace of Italian as a literary language—although he used Latin to compose his best-known work, a lengthy textbook on the art of falconry. (His interest in natural history led him to include in his retinue whatever exotic animals he could find: His collection of elephants, camels, giraffes, and leopards traveled with him, making the royal progress somewhat akin to a traveling circus and just as fascinating to onlookers.) By the standards of his time, he had a skeptical and inquiring mind, devoting much energy to the study of astrology and physiognomy and corresponding at length with the supposed masters of these arts. All the facts testified to a monarch of unusual capacity.

Devout Christians, however, were scandalized that the emperor would use his linguistic skills to talk civilly to Arabs, Muslim Arabs at that, and the open-minded atmosphere of his court made him few friends outside the regno; hence the stories about him that circulated around Europe. But in reality, Frederick was less of a freethinker than his enemies suggested. He was emperor under God and in his own eyes the upholder of divine authority on earth. Throughout his reign, he persecuted heretics with zeal, especially in Germany, and his treatment of the regno's Jews was no better—though certainly no worse—than that of other Italian rulers.

In politics, Frederick showed not so much an open mind as a stubborn determination to exercise what he saw as his imperial rights. By 1225, with the regno firmly under control, he was ready to look to the rest of what God had decreed to be his domains. Germany remained a problem, with too much power in the hands of its princes. It could be dealt with when the emperor was strong, but it was not itself a source of much strength. The economy was primitive in comparison with that of Italy, and in the absence of important towns (other than Cologne), not even the kind of efficient tax system Frederick had created in the south could yield much revenue there. For the time being, such imperial authority as remained could be left in the able hands of his young son's regent.

Northern Italy was a different matter. Geographically, the northern Italian plain—Lombardy and the Po valley—was the link between Germany and the rest of the Italian peninsula. It had been at least nominally in the empire's possession for centuries. And it was studded with wealthy mercantile cities that had enriched themselves by the exciting new methods of capitalism, with a handsome cash economy fueled by a banking system that was already providing lucrative loans to many of the crowned heads of Europe. Most of these cities were administered by some kind of self-governing commune, and all of them had taken advantage of a period of imperial weakness to become much too independent.

For Frederick, the obvious next step was to bring them firmly back into the empire's control. He called for a great gathering to be held in the northern city of Cremona at Easter 1226. The princes of the empire, both German and Italian, as well as representatives of all the "free" communes of Lombardy and Tuscany, were commanded to appear. The agenda: imperial rights in Italy. As a sop to the papacy, other subjects for discussion included the repression of heresy and Frederick's much-postponed Crusade. But no one doubted the emperor's order of priorities.

The Diet of Cremona was not a success, to put it mildly. Frederick marched from Apulia with a retinue large enough to enable him to collect so-called taxes from the outraged barons of the Papal States through which he passed. But no delegates from the north appeared, not even Frederick's son Henry from Germany. The imperial proclamation had panicked the northern cities into resurrecting an alliance formed in the preceding century—the Lombard League, with Milan as its head. A league

A HAWKING HANDBOOK

For Frederick II, falconry was not just a pleasant distraction from the affairs of state but a noble and complex art that engaged his talents as a naturalist. From youth he kept a sizable hawking establishment that included peregrines from his native Italy *(above)*, gyrfalcons from the Arctic, and saker falcons from the Middle East. Late in his reign, he set down the knowledge accumulated over thirty years in a treatise, *De Arte Venandi cum Avibus*, or *The Art of Hunting with Birds*. Shortly after he died, a copy of the manuscript was made, complete with some 900 marginal illustrations and, as a frontispiece, the portrait of Frederick with a hooded falcon shown here.

Frederick divided his treatise into six books. In the first, he dealt with the anatomy and habits of birds, supplementing information gleaned from Aristotle's works on natural history with his own observations of flight and migrations. In the remaining five books, he gave practical and comprehensive instructions on the rearing of falcons, their training and management, and the methods of flying them at different quarry. An avid student of Islamic culture, he claimed to have introduced into Europe the Arabic practice of hooding hawks to keep them tranquil during training.

army had blocked the alpine passes and refused to allow the Germans into Italy.

With rare diplomacy, Frederick contrived to turn the situation to his advantage. The behavior of the Lombards, he explained to the pope, was preventing his setting out on the promised Crusade, for which he needed their financial contribution. In fact, the members of the league were reluctant to pay for a great Crusading army, which they feared Frederick would use against their own cities rather than Jerusalem, but the argument carried weight with Honorius. The pope was nearing the end of his life (he was said to be 100 years old) and his Crusade had become an obsession. He swallowed the insult of Frederick's taxgathering and, with threats and interdicts, drove the cities to a compromise. At all costs, the Crusade must go ahead.

Politically, it was not the wisest moment for Frederick to leave Italy, but he could hardly beg for a further postponement. In any case, he had reasons of his own for the journey: In 1225, he had married Isabella, heiress to the Crusader kingdom of Jerusalem, only vestiges of which had survived the fall of the city of Jerusalem to

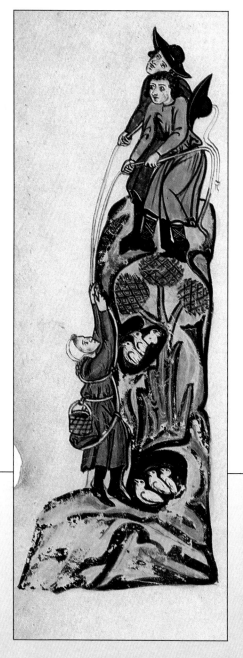

Assistants lower a man over a cliff to steal nestlings from their aeries. If taken too young, Frederick warned, falcons suffered from stunted growth and developed a habit of screaming when hungry.

Carrying one of his hunting birds, a falconer leaves the mews, or hawk house. Frederick stipulated that mews be provided with good ventilation, several perches, and a birdbath.

Saladin some forty years earlier. In September 1227, more than twelve years after his vow on the throne of Charlemagne at Aachen, he sailed from Brindisi.

Old Honorius did not live to see the Crusade's departure; if he had, the outcome would surely have killed him. Within three days, Frederick had returned. He was sick; an epidemic had struck his army. He immediately dispatched an apologetic explanation to the new pope.

Gregory IX, however, was less accommodating than Honorius. An ascetic, something of a mystic, and above all a profound believer in absolute papal supremacy, he was not disposed to listen to Frederick's excuses. In a towering rage, he ordered the immediate excommunication of the "so-called emperor."

Frederick set off again anyway the following spring, an excommunicate with a Muslim bodyguard heading a Christian army on a mission of holy war. It was a paradoxical beginning to what turned out to be a very strange Crusade. Pausing at Crusader-ruled Cyprus to strengthen the island's imperial allegiance, Frederick landed in Palestine in September 1228. His army was small—probably no more than 1,000 knights—and his chances of a military victory were slender.

He did not even attempt one. Instead, he entered into negotiations with Malik al-Kamil, sultan of Egypt, who controlled the Christian holy places. Al-Kamil was a cultured man, interested in poetry and philosophy; so was the emperor Frederick II. Distracted by his own political problems, al-Kamil had no taste for war with so congenial an adversary, and an accord was soon reached. The sultan conceded Jerusalem to Frederick, along with Bethlehem and a corridor from the Mediterranean coast; in return, Frederick undertook not to interfere with the mosques in his new domain. In due course, he crowned himself king of Jerusalem in the Church of the Holy Sepulcher. (He had no choice but to crown himself: Mindful of his excommunication, Jerusalem's Catholic patriarch refused any part in the ceremony and excluded the emperor from the triumphal mass that celebrated his diplomatic victory.)

Falconers demonstrate the correct method of securing hawks to a perch. The leash, tied in a slipknot, is attached to jesses—straps worn on the falcon's legs and fitted with a swivel for freedom of movement.

Predictably, the outcome infuriated Frederick's enemies. There was something unnatural about a Crusade that ended with neither bloodshed nor loot, not to mention a supposedly Christian emperor sipping sherbet and bandying Arabic politenesses with the heathen desolater of the holy places. Indeed, al-Kamil faced a similar reaction from his own Islamic fundamentalists. The agreement was doomed: The sultan's successors were less amenable to a Christian presence, and when Jerusalem fell to them in 1244, it was lost to Christendom forever.

By the time Frederick returned to Italy in 1229, he had no greater enemy than Gregory IX. During his absence, the pope had launched a campaign of calumny against him ("reptile," "basilisk," and "patricide" were among the choicer epithets used), made formal alliance with the Lombard League, and sought to elect a Welf "antiking" in Germany. Finally, Gregory spread a false story that Frederick had died in Palestine, and he ordered troops into the regno, where they met with little resistance from a bewildered population.

But the papal soldiers had no stomach for serious fighting. Frederick, very much alive, scraped up what loyal forces he could find and quickly cleared the regno of the invaders. He called a halt at the border of the Papal States in the hope of reaching a compromise with Gregory, but it took the diplomatic efforts of the grand master of the Teutonic Knights, a powerful Crusading order, and most of the German princes as well as military defeat to force Gregory to agree to a reconciliation. At Ceprano in 1230, the bull of excommunication was at last rescinded, and the "reptile" was transformed, at least in public declaration, into Gregory's "dearest son." Few believed the transformation would endure.

For the time being, Frederick set aside his ambitions for the Lombard cities and turned again to the regno and his own theories about the role of the emperor, the

A sequence of pictures shows the correct stance for handling a falcon. The falconer kneels low to avoid frightening his bird when picking it up and avoids looming over it when offering it a bath.

empire, and its laws. The outcome was the Constitutions of Melfi. Named after the Apulian town where they were first promulgated, they amounted to the first comprehensive legal code that Europe had seen since the time of the Byzantine emperor Justinian, 700 years before. Much of the drafting was the work of Pietro della Vigna, but the constitutions carried the full stamp of Frederick's thought.

At a time when elsewhere justice was regularly dispensed by local aristocrats, all judicial power in the regno was vested by the constitutions in the state; counts and barons had no more right than any other subject to take the law into their own hands. Trades and professions were strictly regulated: Doctors and pharmacists, for example, required state licenses, which were to be issued only to those with genuine qualifications. All citizens had to observe a rigorous code of moral behavior, which forbade, among other things, swearing, gambling, and the making of love potions. The fountainhead of the law was, of course, the sovereign. The source of his authority, however, was no longer the vague "divine right" that served most monarchs but the "principle of necessity": Ever since the fall of Adam and Eve, the constitutions' preamble proclaimed, humankind had had a grave need for a ruler who would regulate them and limit their crimes.

The constitutions were not made of whole cloth. They owed a great deal to the Norman legislation of the previous century, and other ideas were the product of the law school at Bologna, where Pietro had been a student. But in the principle of necessity, they introduced a fresh influence: the political ideas of Aristotle. The long-lost works of the great Greek philosopher were returning to Europe via the scholars of the Arab world: It was only fitting that they should yield their first fruits in Frederick's multicultural court.

Hand in hand with legal developments went the further improvement of the regno's

The behavior of two falcons reveals their unease at being mishandled on horseback. The bird on the left ruffles its feathers while its companion spreads its wings to bate, or attempt flight.

fiscal machinery. In the *collecta*—a regular tax demanded of all his subjects, including the clergy—Frederick created a revenue-gathering system of unsurpassed efficiency, and his state was buttressed by a complex bureaucracy of a type unknown since Roman times. But there was a dark side to his government, too. In the constitutions, heretics of every sort were singled out for especially vicious punishment.

The fact was that the emperor regularly applied a double standard to his own behavior and that of his subjects; however liberal his court, there was a stifling lack of individual freedom in the lands he ruled. Gregory wrote reprovingly, and with some justice, "In your kingdom, no one dares move hand or foot without your order." Cities such as Syracuse and Messina, chafing at the loss of their ancient liberties, rose in revolt and were crushed brutally. Many of the revolt's leaders were burned alive— as heretics. The whole system depended on an army of spies and secret police and rapidly became riddled with corruption.

The constitutions greatly alarmed the northern Italian cities. By now they were virtually independent republics and were loath to be part of Frederick's unified state. Nor did Frederick's attitude toward heresy appeal to them: They were used to a certain amount of religious as well as economic freedom, and they had noted the fate of the Sicilian rebels.

Religious freedom notwithstanding, the cities of northern Italy were supported in their opposition by the pope, who feared a unified empire even more than they did. It was the central irony of the whole brewing conflict: On one side stood the cities of the Lombard League, independent minded, less than religiously orthodox, allied to the passionately orthodox pope, while on the other was the emperor, as independent as and no more orthodox than the cities themselves. But both sides accepted the contradictions and prepared for a showdown.

Events in Germany, however, gave Italy a few more years of peace. Imperial power there was by now in the hands of Frederick's son Henry, who had come of age in 1228 and had struggled since then to hold his own against the overpowerful German princes. Essentially, he was trying to imitate his father's unitary policies in the south, although his method was exactly the opposite: He allied himself with the rising German cities as a counterpoise to the German magnates. But Henry had neither his father's skill nor his resolve. A show of force by the princes was enough to make him back down, and the outcome was an imperial defeat with yet more power delegated to the princes. Embroiled as he was in Italian affairs, Frederick had no desire to start a war in Germany; at Cividale in 1232, he ratified his son's concessions.

With the compromises already made by Frederick in 1220, the Cividale statute set back the cause of German unification for centuries. Henry began to see his father as the author of Germany's misfortunes. In 1234, he came out in open revolt and made an alliance with the Lombard communes. Frederick, backed by few troops but well supplied with good Sicilian gold, marched north with dispatch. He deposed his son— the "boy" languished in various Apulian castles until his death in 1242—replaced him with his younger brother Conrad, and rapidly brought the rebellion to an end.

For two years Frederick remained in Germany, consolidating his imperial position. At the Diet of Mainz in 1235, he managed to extract a recognition of imperial supremacy and a promise of military support from the German princes. In Italy, however, the cities refused to dissolve the Lombard League or to recognize Frederick's rights, and in 1237, the wrath of the thwarted emperor was unleashed on the northern Italian plain.

Nothing could stand against the imperial army: The mercenaries and citizen-soldiers of the league were no match for Frederick's German knights and Saracen archers. He won a string of minor victories against the retreating Lombards. Then, in November 1237, he caught the league army at Cortenuova near the northern Italian lakes and destroyed it utterly. In the wake of the defeat, hostile cities opened their gates to the victorious emperor; entire provinces offered homage. Even the bishops hastened to pledge their allegiance, and Milan itself, the kingpin of the league, sent emissaries of peace. The war should have been over.

But Frederick was not interested in a negotiated settlement: In a catastrophic failure of political judgment, he demanded an unconditional surrender. It was too much for most of the league to take; and once they had recovered their nerve, the outcome was beyond Frederick's power to enforce. For although his army was vastly superior to the league's in the open field, it lacked both the strength and the equipment to capture an array of walled cities. Behind stout fortifications, even untrained citizens could give a good account of themselves.

The emperor called for support from all his dominions—not only Germany and Sicily but Hungary and even Provence. Given his weakness in siege craft, the help made no difference. And while Frederick battered uselessly at the walls of Brescia and Milan, Gregory was concluding a secret treaty with Venice and Genoa, which promised a nine-year war against the emperor in exchange for privileges to be granted, the pope assured them meaningfully, by "the future king of Sicily."

For his part, Frederick called upon the cardinals to save the Church from scandal by rebelling against their master's "dangerous plans," a protest that earned him a second edict of excommunication. Frederick responded by expelling whole religious orders from the regno, while he and Gregory railed against each other with increasing intemperance. Frederick saw himself as the defender of all royal power: "Kings and princes may the more easily be humiliated," he declared, "when the first blow is struck against the imperial authority, which is the shield that protects the others." Retorted Gregory, "A monster has come out of the sea with the claws of a bear and the jaws of a lion. . . . Its mouth only opens to curse God and the saints."

In northern Italy, the Lombard League was now too strong for the emperor to vanquish, although the war continued its destructive course. Instead, he turned his attentions southward, bringing Tuscany under his control and marching through the Papal States as a liberator. Keen to be freed from papal control and sympathetic to Frederick's vision of a unified empire, many cities opened their gates and received him with acclamation. He would never return the conquered territories to the pope, he declared, not even if he lived a thousand years and had to fight the pope for every one of them. Both the Papal States and The Eternal City, he said, would be incorporated in the regno.

But in February 1240, as Frederick and his troops lay outside the walls of Rome, Gregory—then in his ninety-sixth year—contrived the greatest coup of his pontificate. While he was leading a solemn procession to St. Peter's Basilica, he was mobbed by a jeering crowd of people wearing the imperial eagle to show support for Frederick. Holding up a reliquary said to contain the heads of the apostles Peter and Paul, the old pope cried out: "O Saints! You must defend Rome, for the Romans will defend her no more." The crowd was shamed and tore the eagles from their clothes; the defenses were manned, and Frederick, as usual ill equipped for a siege, gave up.

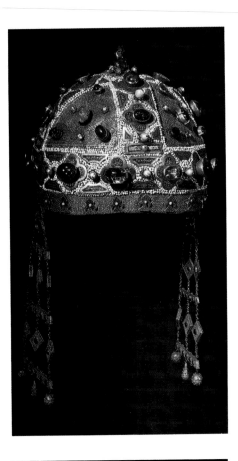

This Byzantine-style crown was sealed in the tomb of Frederick II's first wife, Constance of Aragon, when she died in 1222. The crown illuminates an intimate facet of the emperor's character, for while burial crowns were customarily cheap and tawdry affairs, mere tokens of status, the richness of this specimen indicates the high esteem in which Frederick held his wife. Ten years Frederick's senior when she wed the fourteen-year-old king in 1209, Constance—the widow of the king of Hungary—brought a maturity and cultivation to the marriage that helped Frederick develop the sophistication for which he became renowned.

The war went on. Gregory called a great council of the Church for Easter 1241; Frederick, rightly suspecting that the pope would use it to seek his formal deposition, arranged what amounted to a blockade in order to make the gathering impossible. By now the struggle between pope and emperor was scandalizing all of Europe—and putting it in desperate peril. For in 1240, the Mongol heirs of Genghis Khan had launched a devastating invasion, swallowing Hungary and Poland and annihilating the flower of German chivalry in Silesia. Yet Christendom's two greatest leaders were intent only upon their mutual destruction. As it turned out, the Mongols retired undefeated because of a political crisis in their Asian homeland; neither Frederick nor Gregory had lifted a finger to stop their onslaught.

Both Louis IX of France and Conrad, grand master of the Teutonic Knights, tried to bring about peace, but Gregory paid no heed until the fortunes of war began to tilt

Castel del Monte, Frederick's favorite castle and hunting lodge, dominates the plateau of Apulia in southeast Italy. Believed to have been designed by the emperor himself, its unique octagonal shape with flanking towers reflects the eight-sided form of the imperial crown. Frederick's upbringing in Apulia left him with a special affection for the area, but he was fated to make little use of the castle he raised there: He died in 1250, only a few years after the completion of Castel del Monte.

increasingly toward the emperor. Only after imperialist Padua had defeated the Milanese and Frederick's Pisan allies had destroyed a Genoese fleet carrying delegates to Rome (two cardinals were sent as prisoners to Apulia) did the pope consent to negotiations. But before anything could be settled, Gregory died. Because of the imperial blockade, it was not until 1243 that a successor was elected—Innocent IV.

Frederick was delighted: As a cardinal, Innocent had been prominent among those urging a peace settlement. As a pope, however, he inherited Gregory's implacable hatred toward the emperor. Nevertheless, for a year peace talks went on amid an atmosphere of growing mistrust. Frederick would return the Papal States; the pope would revoke the bull of excommunication. But in which order? A meeting between the two was arranged. Innocent, perhaps rightly, suspected Frederick of planning to imprison him. In June 1244, he fled via Genoa to Lyons in Burgundy, nominally a part of Frederick's empire but far beyond his practical reach. There, in 1245, he summoned the council Gregory had planned, with the results that Frederick had feared. The emperor—the "Antichrist"—was formally deposed, his subjects released from all vows of obedience. The final phase of the struggle had begun.

Throughout the empire, papal envoys fanned the flames of revolt, offering Frederick's titles to anyone with the courage to seize them. In Italy the war degenerated into a series of betrayals and counterbetrayals. Frederick responded violently: Conspirators were mutilated and blinded, hanged, burned alive, and trussed in sacks and flung into the sea. Traitors were everywhere, real or imagined. Even Pietro della Vigna, suspected of treason, was arrested and tortured. The counselor cheated the executioner by suicide; his master said, dismissively, "From nothing he came, to nothing he has returned."

Yet the war remained inconclusive. Frederick suffered grievous defeats: His army was badly beaten during an attempted siege of Parma, and the pro-Innocent Bolognese captured his favorite (though illegitimate) son, Enzo. But the news was not all bad: North of the Alps, King Conrad defeated Innocent's champion, William of Holland, and in renewed fighting in Lombardy, city after city fell to imperial troops. The stakes were higher than ever. An imperial victory would bring unity to Italy, though at the cost of individual freedom, allowing the emperor to turn his energies to Germany; the papacy would be destroyed as a political force, perhaps forever.

But as Innocent saw it, the hand of God was once more at work. Just as the emperor's father had died of a fever in his moment of triumph, so Frederick, with his ambitions still within reach, was taken ill on a journey from his court in Foggia to nearby Lucera. He stopped to rest for a few days at his castle of Fiorentino, in Apulia. On December 13, 1250, he died.

His last testament was an expression of deep religious faith and even of his devotion to the Holy See. But Innocent was in no mood to accept deathbed repentances, or any other kind. In brutal terms, he spelled out his future policy toward the Hohenstaufens: "to destroy to the last descendant that race of vipers, that they may never again assume a crown." And so his terrible vengeance came to pass, although Innocent, who died in 1254, did not live to see it.

The Hohenstaufen line had become a frail plant. Of Frederick's three legitimate sons, the eldest—the disgraced former king of Germany—was already dead, and the youngest died of natural causes in 1253. The following year the one survivor, King Conrad, marched from Germany to recapture Naples and Apulia, which had fallen into papal hands on his father's death. He died en route. Frederick's bastard son

Manfred managed to reclaim most of the old regno and held it until 1266. By then, the papacy had enlisted the aid of the fiercely ambitious French warrior-prince, Charles of Anjou; Manfred was killed in battle against him at Benevento, near Naples. Two years later, Conrad's fifteen-year-old son, Conradin, went south in search of his dangerous inheritance. He was captured by French troops at Tagliacozzo in central Italy; a few months later, Charles of Anjou had the young "viper" publicly beheaded in the Naples marketplace.

Conradin was not quite the last of the Hohenstaufens. There was still Enzo, a prisoner in Bologna. He turned to poetry in his confinement. "Go, my song," he wrote, "go to the plains of Apulia. . . . Where my heart is, night and day." But he never saw Apulia again. He died in captivity in 1272, and with him went the last faint hope for a Hohenstaufen revival.

The destruction of the Hohenstaufens, however, served the papacy little. The sheer bitterness of the long quarrel had stripped it of much of the moral capital with which it had begun the century and, as Innocent IV's successors were to discover, such capital was more easily spent than reearned. The French alliance, which had brought Charles of Anjou and military victory to the south, proved no easier to manage than the emperor had been. Quarrels soon broke out; the Church became something of a pawn in international conflicts, and the way was prepared for the Great Schism of the fourteenth century, with rival popes blasting each other with invective and anathema while Mother Church wandered blindly toward the Reformation.

Nor did Charles and his French entourage gain much from their Italian adventure. By 1282, they had made themselves so unpopular in Sicily that the population rose against them in the massacres known as the Sicilian Vespers. By the end of the century, the island and most of Frederick's regno were in the hands of the Aragonese, who were building their own Spanish empire in the Mediterranean.

As for the Holy Roman Empire, it was never truly reconstituted. For twenty-three years after Frederick's death, there was an interregnum in Germany; when the imperial crown finally passed to an obscure family called Hapsburg, it retained only a shadow of its earlier authority and prestige; real power had passed to the dukes, counts, archbishops, and bishops, who had won virtual independence for their territorial states. It would be more than 600 years before a real national unity could be created from the chaos.

Italy, too, passed through a period of prolonged civil war, a struggle between Guelphs and Ghibellines in which the names of the two great parties became so tangled with local politics that scarcely anyone could remember what they had once stood for. But although national unity was to remain a hopeless dream, in the wake of Frederick's great failure, the rivalries and bickering of Italy's patchwork city-states had a vital, creative side from which, more than a century after Frederick's death, would spring the Italian Renaissance.

What Frederick had sought was a return to the Roman empire of the past. His career had demonstrated that such an ambition was impossible to fulfill. Yet even as Frederick lay on his deathbed, the rising monarchies of England and France were demonstrating how centralized state power could in smaller and more homogeneous societies be reconciled with a vigorous commercial life. Frederick, in the not entirely approving words of the English chronicler, Matthew Paris, had "astonished the world." There were other ways to change it, as the French and English would show.

This marble bust of an elegantly coiffured, bejeweled female courtier reflects the wealth and sophistication of Frederick's Sicilian court; the classical style recalls the majesty of ancient Rome, which Frederick wished to emulate. Although the emperor jealously kept his own wife hidden from sight, women were encouraged to display their skills in music and dancing and enjoyed a prominent position at court. Courtiers of both sexes spent extravagant sums to keep up with the latest fashions in dress, and women of rank wore jewel-encrusted crowns in imitation of their queen.

THE BALTIC CRUSADES

In 1197, the Cistercian abbot Berthold of Loccum, near Bremen, was invested as bishop of Livonia (present-day Latvia), in the eastern Baltic. Far from the comforts of civilization, with a coast that was frequently wrapped in fog or cut off by ice, Livonia was the last place in which the venerable Berthold wished to wrestle for souls. His predecessor, the first bishop, had spent the seventeen years before his death striving unsuccessfully to convert its pagan inhabitants, the Livs, and Berthold took up his new appointment with reluctance. At first, he tried to win over the population with gifts and banquets. The Livs were not impressed: On one occasion they tried to drown him, and when this effort failed, they set fire to a church in which he was preaching.

Having escaped the flames, he went back to Germany and there recruited a Crusader army with which to subdue the Livs. In a battle on July 24, 1198, the luckless Berthold was wounded by a Livonian lance, then torn to pieces by his recalcitrant flock. The Crusaders, enraged by the death of their leader, mounted a campaign of terror against the Livs, forcibly baptizing 150 of them in two days. Once the Crusaders had embarked on the return voyage to Germany, however, the Livs renounced their new faith, plunging into the waters of the Dvina River to wash off their baptism and driving the remaining priests out of the country. Livonia, it seemed, was to remain impervious to the true religion.

Less than a century later, not only Livonia but virtually the whole of the eastern Baltic, from Finland in the north to Prussia in the south, would fall under Christian rule. Fought in inhospitable terrain, with little of the glamor that surrounded the struggle for the Holy Land, the northern Crusades were conducted with a brutal efficiency that would ensure the survival of a Crusader state in the eastern Baltic long after the fall of that in Palestine.

When the thirteenth century began, the eastern boundary of Latin Christendom on the Baltic could be taken as a line running north from the Polish city of Danzig through the island of Gotland to the Swedish coast. Of the territories that lay beyond that line the Western world knew little, and what it did know it did not particularly care for. A twelfth-century traveler who journeyed through the woodlands east of the Oder River wrote that "it was very hard going, on account of the various snakes and huge wild beasts, and troublesome cranes that were nesting in the branches of the trees and troubled and tormented us with their croaking and flapping, and patches of bog that hindered our wagons and carts."

To the north and east, between the Vistula and Dvina rivers, the going was even harder. Here an intractable barrier of lakes, bogs, and primeval forest stretched most of the way from the Baltic shore to the frontier with Russia. Comprising some 1,850 square miles, it was an area in which organized overland travel for large groups was impossible; the only sure routes were the rivers, which provided a passage for boats

Surrounded by his queen and other members of the royal family, King Waldemar II of Denmark holds aloft a cross in this stone relief from Ribe Cathedral in southern Jutland. The Danish monarch was one of many Western Crusaders who traveled east in the thirteenth century to war against the pagan inhabitants of the southern Baltic coastlands. In the 1220s, Danish forces helped a Livonian religious order, the Sword Brothers, subjugate the north of Estonia, which remained in Danish hands throughout the thirteenth century.

in summer and sledges in winter. At other times the rivers were often in flood as a result of autumn rain or spring thaws.

In this wilderness lived a group of peoples who were later to be known collectively as Balts, including Prussians, Lithuanians, and Letts. Settled in tribes, each with its own defined territory, they lived scattered along the coast and in the valleys of the Vistula, Neman, and Dvina rivers, farming, raising cattle, and reaping a regular harvest of furs, honey, and wax from the surrounding forest.

Farther north, between the Dvina and the Gulf of Finland, the country was more open and mountainous, with forests of oak, elm, and ash gradually giving way to pine. This region was the home of three peoples—the Livs, concentrated along the Baltic coast as far as the Au River; the Estonians, occupying the southern coast of the gulf and its offshore islands; and a second group of Letts, wedged between the Livs to the west and the Russians to the east.

Whatever the territorial divisions among these various peoples, Western Christendom saw them as one in their devotion to paganism. They were animists, who worshiped such forces of nature as the sun, the moon, and the stars and whose festivals often involved human sacrifice. Building with stones and mortar was unknown to them, and their dwellings of earth and timber were decorated with animal skulls to ward off the evil eye. One German chronicler of the 1230s was much exercised by such "evil heathens," warning that any Christians who fell into their hands would soon "be robbed of life and property."

But if the eastern Baltic was dangerous, it was also enticing, with a vast supply of natural treasures—fur, fish, timber, honey, beeswax, amber—of which Western traders were anxious to obtain a share. Although the native tribes were willing to do business, exchanging their wares for imported luxuries, such as wool, silver, and iron

Over the course of the thirteenth century, Christian forces brought virtually all the eastern and southern coastlands of the Baltic under their domination. In Finland, opposing armies from Sweden and the Russian principality of Novgorod struggled to be first to convert the pagan population. From their base at Riga, the Sword Brothers conquered Livonia and Estonia; and to the west, the Teutonic Knights struggled with the natives of Prussia. By 1300, the lands of the Sword Brothers had been subsumed in the territory of the Teutonic Knights, creating a formidable military state stretching from Pomerania in the west to the borders of Novgorod in the east. Only in Samogitia did tribes still resist Christian rule, with the aid of neighboring Lithuania, which remained pagan until the late fourteenth century.

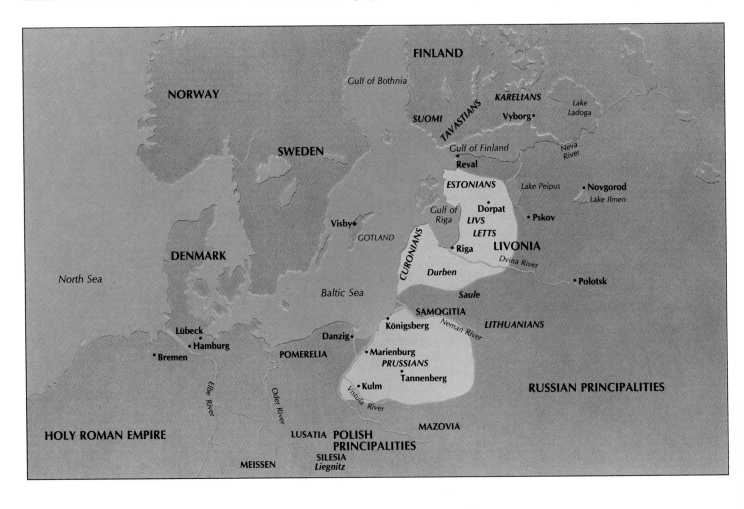

weapons, relations between the two sides were far from harmonious. On the one hand, the local peoples demanded a fairer exchange of goods and less interference in their affairs; on the other hand, the traders clamored for a larger share of the local resources and better protection against marauding tribes.

Another source of concern to Western traders was competition from the Russians—primarily from the principality of Novgorod—who by the twelfth century had already brought several of the Baltic tribes under their control. The Catholic church was also alarmed by the Russians, who, though Christian, owed their loyalty to the Eastern Orthodox church, centered in Constantinople. In the eyes of Rome, such loyalty made them as much in need of salvation as the pagans themselves. Moreover, Russian missionaries were busy carrying out mass baptisms among the Baltic peoples, to the detriment of the Catholic cause.

It was amid the lakes and forests of southern Finland that the confrontation between Orthodox and Latin Christendom was to erupt into all-out warfare. To the southwest, the Catholic Swedes had colonized the region inhabited by the agricultural Suomi, while to the east, the Russians had established virtual sovereignty over the fishing and fur-gathering Karelians. Only the Tavastians, hunters who lived along the central southern coast, remained largely untouched—a situation that both Swedes and Russians were determined to change.

The Russians moved first. In 1227, having taken the precaution of forcibly baptizing the Karelians, Prince Yaroslav of Novgorod led an expedition against the Tavastians. After causing much devastation, the raiders returned home with their plunder. The next year, the Tavastians counterattacked, crossing to the southern shore of Lake Ladoga by boat. They were routed and chased into the surrounding forest, however, by the Russians' Karelian allies. The Karelians were traditional enemies of the Tavastians, and the latter were given little chance of escaping back to the north shore. According to the *Novgorod Chronicle*, a fourteenth-century account of the principality's early years, "It is thought that 2,000 of them had come; God knows, and few of them escaped to their own country; all the rest perished."

Angered by Yaroslav's successes, the pope placed Finland under apostolic protection and, flexing his muscles as spiritual leader of Western Christendom, invoked a trade embargo against Novgorod. The embargo, beginning in 1229, coincided with an autumn frost that destroyed the city's crops, with the result that thousands of the principality's inhabitants died of starvation. As the chronicler described it, "Some of the common people killed the living and ate them; others cutting up dead flesh and corpses ate them; others ate horseflesh, dogs, and cats. . . . Some fed on moss, snails, pine-bark, lime-bark, lime and elm tree leaves, and whatever each could think of."

Fortunately for the Novgorodians, the wealthy trading communities of the western Baltic, such as Bremen, Lubeck, and Visby, had no intention of sacrificing their lucrative eastern trade just to please the pope, and without their support the embargo soon collapsed. The next threat to Novgorod was even more serious. It came in July 1240, when an army of Swedish Crusaders, with Suomi and Tavastian auxiliaries, sailed up the Neva River, intending, as the chronicler recounted, "to take possession of . . . Novgorod, and of the whole Novgorod province. But again the most kind and merciful God, lover of men, preserved and protected us from the foreigners since they labored in vain without the command of God."

The Crusaders also labored without the command of a general able to match the ability of the twenty-one-year-old Novgorodian leader, Alexander, successor to Yaroslav. Rallying his outnumbered forces on the banks of the Neva, he inflicted a crushing defeat on the enemy, winning the title Alexander Nevsky, or Alexander "of the Neva." Nine years later, the Swedes launched a second, more successful Crusade, occupying Tavastia and directly threatening the Russian position in Karelia. Yet it was not until 1292, after more than forty years of fierce but sporadic border fighting, that the Swedes, led by a nobleman, Tyrgils Knuttson, tried to conquer Karelia itself.

Tyrgils failed in his main objective, but he did succeed in establishing a fortress at Vyborg, on the southern tip of Karelia, from which Swedish forces were able to harry the countryside around the lower Neva and Lake Ladoga. The war continued for thirty

A detail from the bronze doors of Poland's Gniezno Cathedral depicts the martyrdom of an early Christian missionary, Saint Adelbert, whose remains were subsequently purchased by the Poles from the pagan Prussians. Before the arrival of the Teutonic Knights, several attempts had been made to convert the Prussians by peaceful means, notably by a Cistercian monk consecrated Bishop Christian of Prussia by the pope in 1215. Ultimately, however, his mission was a failure, and it was Christian himself who called for the first Crusade against the Prussians in 1223.

more years with neither Swedes nor Russians able to gain a decisive victory. They finally agreed to make peace in 1323, and each power received a part of the disputed territory. In fact, the treaty marked not the end of hostilities but merely their suspension, and in less than a generation, the two sides would again be locked in conflict.

For the present, however, the Swedes were content to fold away their banners and await a more propitious time to strike against the heretics. In spite of copious blessings from the pope and the Swedish monarch, the struggle just concluded had not been universally popular. Not so much a Crusade as a series of haphazard skirmishes, it had offered much discomfort, little profit, and no glory. Few knights had been willing to serve on the dismal battlefields of Finland, and those who stayed to settle their new lands became known to the natives as "food Swedes," impressing less with their feats of arms than with their prodigious appetites.

Such was not the case in Livonia, where Crusading warriors established a rather different kind of reputation. Following the debacle of 1198, a young German cleric, Albert of Buxtehude, had been invested as the new bishop of Livonia. Unlike his predecessor, the martyred Berthold, Albert was rich, ambitious, and well connected.

He was, indeed, the personal appointee of his uncle, the powerful archbishop Hartwig of Hamburg-Bremen, and had a ruthless arrogance that boded ill for opponents, whether pagan or Christian. In addition, he possessed remarkable energy and organizing ability, two qualities that he was to display to the full over the next thirty years.

In October 1199, within a few months of being appointed, he had secured a papal assurance that Crusaders—or pilgrims, as they were called—who undertook to fight in Livonia would merit the same automatic remission of sins as those who fought in the Holy Land. Armed with this guarantee, Bishop Albert conducted a recruiting drive throughout northern Germany, and in the early spring of 1200, accompanied by priests, merchants, artisans, and a force of Crusaders 500 strong, he sailed up the Dvina River to begin the conquest of his unruly diocese.

Fighting was no new experience to the Livs. Warfare was endemic to the area and went on not only between the Livs and their traditionally hostile neighbors—the Letts, the Estonians, and the Lithuanians—but among the Livs themselves. So great was the danger of attack by rival tribes that each settlement had its own fortress. Normally this fort served as the residence of the local chief. But at the first sign of danger, it became a refuge for the surrounding population. Located on easily defensible sites, such as hilltops or specially constructed ramparts, and consisting of thick timber walls buttressed with towers and roofed with logs, bark, and clay, these forts were usually strong enough to withstand the spears and arrows of tribal enemies.

They were no proof, however, against the well-organized onslaughts of the Crusaders. Into the wilderness the Western soldiers brought the benefits of a war machine well in advance of the Livs' rudimentary weaponry. Body armor, crossbows, catapults, siege towers, and caltrops—spiked metal balls for laming horses—gave the Crusaders an advantage that far outweighed the superior numbers of the native warriors. Even so, campaigning in Livonia was exhausting and dangerous, involving long marches through a wooded wilderness ideal for silent ambush and swift retreat. Simply getting there, across the pirate-infested Baltic, was a hazardous enterprise.

To compensate, the campaigning season was short, lasting only from June to September. With the approach of the paralyzing winter, the Crusaders would withdraw to Riga, Bishop Albert's new capital at the mouth of the Dvina, to await the coming of spring and the arrival of a fresh batch of recruits.

The men that the bishop brought across the Baltic were a ragbag of professional soldiers and amateur adventurers, but all were perfectly prepared to endure a year's service in Livonia in return for a reasonable amount of plunder and a papal guarantee of complete absolution. No doubt many recruits were also swayed by Bishop Albert's decision to dedicate his primitive diocese to the Virgin Mary—a figure who excited almost as much veneration as the Savior himself. Indeed, in 1215, Pope Innocent III was to declare that he felt the same solicitude for Livonia, "the Land of the Mother," as for Palestine, "the Land of the Son."

A Crusader's yearly expenses in Livonia, including the return passage, averaged ten marks, only half the cost of Crusading in the Holy Land. Still, many of the recruits were poor and had to be subsidized by the merchants of Riga. Few merchants objected to this arrangement, since the Crusaders not only provided them with protection but also sold them the booty captured in raids against the pagans.

Formidable though these summer warriors were, they lacked one vital element: permanence. Because they served for such a short time, their task was to conquer, not to occupy; yet without occupation it was impossible for Bishop Albert to maintain a

PORT OF THE MERCHANT MAGNATES

Many of the towns dominated by the Teutonic Order were members of the Hansa—a league of wealthy trading cities. Centered in Germany but extending to neighboring lands, the league rose to prominence during the course of the thirteenth century. Situated on the Baltic island of Gotland, the port of Visby *(right)*, with its towering limestone warehouses, was one of the league's major entrepôts.

Employing convoys of *cogs*—sturdy vessels that were equipped with hanging stern rudders and that had deep drafts—Hanseatic merchants conducted a lucrative trade in commodities from all over the known world. A major portion of their profits came from the sale of Baltic herring, which was salted in large quantities for the meatless fast days of European Christians.

By the fourteenth century, the power of the Hanseatic League had increased to the point that it minted its own coinage, dealt directly with the rulers of foreign countries (accepting royal regalia as pledges for loans), promulgated its own laws, and was even capable of defeating nations in battle.

hold over the native population. He needed a force that could both spearhead the summer campaigns and garrison the newly won territories in winter. In 1202, therefore, he secured papal approval for the establishment of a military order to be based in Livonia. Officially called the Brothers of Christ's Militia, its knights soon became better known as the Sword Brothers.

Bound by the monastic vows of poverty, chastity, and obedience and clad in distinctive white mantles with red insignia—a cross and a sword—the members of the new order had only one purpose: to defend "Mary's Land" against the heathens. Like the earlier Crusading orders, the Hospitalers, the Templars, and the Teutonic Knights, which had all originated in Palestine during the last century, the Sword Brothers were divided into three classes. The knight-brothers formed the officer corps, from whose ranks were elected the grand master and other senior dignitaries; the priest-brothers served as spiritual advisers to other members of the order and alone had the right to hear confession and grant absolution; the server-brothers, including both foot soldiers and mounted men-at-arms, or sergeants, were often equipped as knights.

The older Crusading orders would accept only Crusaders of noble birth, but the Sword Brothers, faced with competition from such well-established and prestigious rivals, were forced to be less selective. In the eyes of a hostile chronicler, their recruits "were rich merchants banned from Saxony for their crimes, who expected to live on their own without law or king." Certainly the Sword Brothers appear to have had few scruples, and their conduct over the next few years was to scandalize Christian opinion from Riga to Rome. On one occasion, when Bishop Albert persuaded some knights to stage an instructive nativity play for his pagan flock, they inserted such terrifying fighting scenes that most of the audience fled. And as early as 1208, the first grand master, Wenno of Rhorbach, was axed to death by one of his own brethren.

Nevertheless, despite their dubious morals, the Sword Brothers proved to be outstanding warriors for the Christian cause. There were probably never more than 150 knights, yet it was largely due to their efforts that the resistance of the Livs and Letts was broken. Crucial to the Sword Brothers' success was the series of stone and brick fortresses they set up along the Dvina to control the surrounding countryside. Garrisoned throughout the year, these strongholds were impervious to every weapon in the enemy's arsenal, including fire. In addition, the order skillfully exploited old tribal rivalries. By offering to help the Livs and Letts against their traditional enemies, the Lithuanians and the Estonians, Bishop Albert and his men assured themselves of much-needed local support.

By 1206, the Letts were committed to the Christian cause, if only through the prospect of military advantage. Many Livs, however, still resented the foreign intruders. In that year, this resentment flared into bloody rebellion, and scores of Christians, both German and native, were brutally killed. Among the victims were two Liv converts—later proclaimed martyrs by the Church—who tried to negotiate with the rebels and had their arms and legs cut off and their livers torn out.

Helped by fresh troops from Germany and by loyal Livonian tribes, Albert's forces eventually regained control, killing the majority of the rebels and repulsing a Russian army that had taken advantage of the confusion to march on Livonia. With their land safe, the Sword Brothers began looking northward, toward Estonia. They had conquered Livonia on the understanding that they could keep one-third of it for themselves—the other two-thirds were retained by Bishop Albert—and they saw expansion to the Gulf of Finland as an opportunity of securing even greater holdings. To that

A boldly delineated icon of Christ typifies the religious art of Novgorod, one of the principal players on the Baltic stage in the thirteenth century. Proudly styled by its citizens Lord Novgorod the Great, the city dominated the northern end of the river network linking the Baltic to the Black Sea and controlled a fur-trading empire stretching east to the Urals and north as far as the Arctic Circle. Although it paid homage to the Mongol rulers of southern Russia, it retained its independence and, under its able ruler, Alexander Nevsky, expanded its territories into southern Finland and checked the eastward expansion of the Teutonic Knights.

end, in 1208 the Sword Brothers, together with German Crusaders and levies of baptized Livs and Letts, embarked on a series of savage campaigns that steadily reduced the southern half of Estonia to a starving and disease-ridden wasteland.

Their first objective was the frontier province of Saccalia, through which they cut a bloody swath. In 1211, they laid siege to Fellin, the stronghold of the province, where they paraded the prisoners taken en route before the fortifications, offering to spare their lives if the garrison surrendered and accepted the true God. The Estonians refused, jeering at and mocking their attackers and showing off their captured German armor. The prisoners were duly killed and thrown into the moat. The siege continued for six days, with heavy casualties on both sides. Finally, with every surviving defender wounded and supplies of water almost exhausted, the Estonians agreed to surrender, begging, according to one of Bishop Albert's mission priests, Henry of Livonia, "that you spare us and mercifully impose the yoke of Christianity upon us as you have upon the Livonians and the Letts." The survivors were then sprinkled with holy water and catechized as a prelude to baptism.

Such campaigns continued in regular relays, so that over the course of a single summer, nine separate armies rampaged through southern Estonia, burning, torturing, killing, looting, and so devastating the land that "neither men nor food were found there." As Henry explained, the aim of these forays "was to fight long enough so that either those who were left would come to seek peace and baptism or they would be completely wiped from the earth."

By 1219, Bishop Albert had gained tenuous control over the southern half of Estonia, defeating not only the unruly Estonians but Russian armies from Pskov and Novgorod, who were equally keen to gain control of the land. And in 1220, with the help of an army of Danes under the leadership of King Waldemar II, the Crusaders succeeded in subjugating the northern half of the country. "It was now the Bishop's twenty-second year," wrote his faithful chronicler-priest of Albert's campaigning, "and the land of the Livonians rested a bit."

The rest was cut short in 1223, when the Estonians rose against both Danes and Germans. At Fellin, Odenpah, and Dorpat they attacked the Sword Brothers, reducing their ranks by a third; at Jerwa they disemboweled every soldier of the Danish garrison and ate the governor's heart. By now the Estonians had become skilled in the use of war machines, and they used captured German weapons to break through the enemy's fortifications. They were supported by a Russian army, which marched in from Novgorod and Pskov to besiege the main Danish stronghold of Reval.

It was to take another year of warfare for the Crusading armies to regain control. In 1224, the Crusaders took the fortress of Dorpat by storm, killing all but one of its defenders, a Russian who was given a good horse and sent back to Novgorod to report on the triumph of the Latins. The victory was an unmistakable demonstration of the Crusaders' prowess, and both the Russians and Estonians hastened to make peace. In the aftermath, the victors divided the country according to an agreement decided two years earlier, whereby the Danes received northern Estonia and the Sword Brothers retained their southern conquests. Arguments between the two allies soon broke out, however, with the land-hungry order seizing Danish territory. In 1225, in an attempt to end the dispute, the pope placed both parts of the country under the control of a papal legate.

This arrangement, too, soon led to conflict. In 1229, a new legate, Baldwin of Alna, arrived in Riga. Bishop Albert had died earlier that year, and Baldwin's brief was to look into the controversy that had arisen over the election of a successor. Unfortunately, Baldwin was ambitious, intemperate, and meddlesome, and his relations with the Sword Brothers rapidly deteriorated. Matters came to a head in 1233, when the order refused to relinquish the castle of Reval, which they had seized from the Danes. Baldwin tried to take the castle by force, and in the ensuing battle, the papal troops were defeated and Baldwin himself was captured.

Though soon released, the outraged prelate was in no mood to forgive his enemies. Instead, he brought an ecclesiastical lawsuit, charging them with disobedience, rebellion, and heresy. Specific offenses included killing converts, assaulting monks, and preventing would-be Christians from receiving baptism. The verdict went against the Sword Brothers, and they were censured by Pope Gregory IX, who directed them to return to King Waldemar the Danish provinces of Estonia seized in 1224 and pay compensation to the victims of their misdeeds. In the event, the order did not survive long enough to carry out either of these directives.

In the summer of 1236, Grand Master Folkwin was persuaded by his Crusading reinforcements to launch an invasion into Lithuania. Proceeding as far south as the Saule River, the Christian forces, in the words of a contemporary chronicler, "robbed and burned wonderfully in many bands, and ravaged up and down the land freely." But when the Lithuanian warriors appeared, Folkwin's Crusader allies lost their nerve and were "cut down like women," so the chronicler reported. More than 2,000 Crusaders died, including the grand master and some 50 of his comrades. It was a disaster from which the Sword Brothers never recovered. Condemned by the pope, opposed by the Danes, and now defeated by the Lithuanians, the surviving brethren began negotiations to become absorbed into another order, the Teutonic Knights.

The Teutonic Knights, also known as the Cross Bearers from the black cross

The Holy Beggars

A new element in thirteenth-century Christendom was the mendicant friars— wandering monks dedicated to preaching, poverty, and scholarship and who relied on begging as their only means of sustenance. The first order to be founded was the Dominican, established by a Castilian cleric in 1216 to evangelize the Cathars of southern France. At about the same time, the young Saint Francis of Assisi, son of a rich Italian cloth merchant, converted to the cause of voluntary poverty and gathered a band of followers that formed the basis of the Franciscan order. In a time of growing ecclesiastical wealth, the asceticism of the mendicants was said to have won acclaim from clergy and laity alike.

Though new to Christendom, the mendicants' way of life was paralleled in other religions. The Islamic countries harbored mystics belonging to the Sufi order, who wandered the roads seeking ecstatic union with God. In India, the disciples of Jainism vowed to renounce all worldly goods, to injure no creature, and to remain chaste in order to reach a state of freedom from all mental and bodily encumbrances. And throughout Asia, roving Buddhist monks sought enlightenment through a life of contemplation and self-denial.

Part of a series depicting Saint Dominic—founder of the Dominican order—at prayer, this miniature shows two images of the saint continuing his devotions even while traveling.

emblazoned on their white mantles, had been founded in 1198 by German Crusaders to the Holy Land. With headquarters at Acre, the order had enjoyed a rapid growth in wealth, power, and prestige, due in no small measure to the veteran Crusader Herman of Salza, who was elected grand master in 1210. Born around 1170 in Thuringia, Fra Herman was described by an admiring contemporary as "eloquent, affable, wise, careful and far seeing, and glorious in all his actions." Certainly, he knew how to impress the influential, winning the favor both of the pope and of the Holy Roman Emperor. From the former, the Teutonic Order received papal privileges, and from the latter, land—in Italy, Greece, Germany, and Palestine.

The order's involvement in eastern Europe began in 1211, when King Andrew II of Hungary invited it to defend part of his frontier against the warlike Cumans of central Asia. In fact, the Cumans proved to be less of a menace than the Teutonic Knights, who having defeated the nomads proceeded to set up an independent state of their own, even bringing in German farmers to colonize the land. By 1224, King Andrew was determined to rid himself of the danger. Describing them as "fire under the shirt,

Spoils of the Spanish Crusade

In Spain as in the Baltic, Christian knights fought a continuous Crusade throughout the thirteenth century. There, though, the enemy were the Islamic forces who had held much of the country since the eighth century. The victory at Las Navas de Tolosa, about sixty miles north of Granada, in 1212—when the caliph's banner, shown here, was taken as a battle spoil—was a turning point in the long struggle between the two religions. For the first time since the Muslim invasions, Christian forces controlled most of the Iberian Peninsula.

The remaining Muslim strongholds offered stern resistance, however. It took the armies of Ferdinand II of Leon and Castile and James I of Aragon another thirty-five years to recapture the island of Majorca and the towns of Córdoba, Valencia, Murcia, and Seville. Firm control of the Strait of Gibraltar was not achieved until 1344, and Granada was in Muslim hands until 1492.

mouse in the bag, viper in the bosom," he told the knights to leave, and when they refused, he descended on them with his army and expelled them by force.

They received another invitation almost immediately, this time from the Polish duke Conrad of Mazovia, who wanted them to tame his heathen and hostile neighbors, the Prussians. All previous attempts had had only limited success. Various missions seeking to win converts through persuasion rather than force had made modest inroads; nevertheless, the vast majority of Prussians remained implacably hostile. In 1220, therefore, inspired by the example of the Sword Brothers, the Poles had founded the Knights of Dobrzyn to provide some protection against pagan attacks. But the new military order, consisting of little more than a dozen knights, was scarcely able to defend its own castle. Although it had launched a Crusade in 1223, the Prussian reprisal raids had been so savage that the borders of Mazovia and the other adjoining Polish duchies were in greater jeopardy than ever before.

Now, in return for their help, Conrad offered the Teutonic Knights the province of Kulmerland, including the fort of Kulm, together with any other territory they might conquer. Grand Master Salza wanted no repetition of the Hungarian debacle, however, and it was not until Emperor Frederick II himself had guaranteed the order's right to retain all conquered territory—a guarantee later confirmed by Pope Gregory IX— that the Teutonic Knights were given the signal to march north.

The main contingent, consisting of 20 knights and 200 sergeants under the command of one of the order's greatest heroes, Herman Balke, arrived at Kulm in 1230. Like the Sword Brothers in Livonia, they used the rivers as invasion routes, marking their advance with a string of forts from which to strike into the surrounding forest. As each new district was conquered, it was settled with a community of German knights and burghers, who not only helped to colonize the land but provided the order with a ready source of income and military service.

One advantage that the Teutonic Knights had over the Sword Brothers was independence. The Sword Brothers had been created as the instrument of Bishop Albert, with the duty, not always undertaken with great zeal, of obeying and protecting him. The Teutonic Knights, on the other hand, were an autonomous order, free from episcopal restraints. In addition, the Teutonic Knights had a plentiful supply of Crusading allies. Whereas the Sword Brothers had had to rely on the reinforcements that Bishop Albert had been able to scrape together on his annual preaching tours of North Germany, the Teutonic Knights had a vast network of convents, castles, and commanderies to serve as recruiting centers. Moreover, many German Crusaders who had quailed at the idea of sailing through the dangerous waters of Livonia were prepared to make the overland journey to Prussia. The Teutonic Knights also had close ties with many powerful nobles, Polish now as well as German, and they sent a steady stream of men and supplies.

Despite these advantages, campaigning against the Prussians was far from easy. Although their wicker shields and wooden forts were no match for the crossbows and siege engines of the Crusaders, the native tribes fought back with the ferocity of desperation. Accompanying the Crusader armies were Dominican priests who offered peace in return for conversion, but rarely was their offer accepted. The Prussians asked for no quarter and they gave none. The chronicles of the Teutonic Order, for instance, describe the fate of two knights who had the misfortune to be captured by the Prussians. One was placed in a cleft tree trunk held apart by ropes. The ropes were then released so that the knight was crushed, and the tree was set ablaze. The other captive was tied to his horse and hoisted with his luckless mount to the top of an oak, beneath which a great fire was lighted. The Crusaders dealt out justice in the same summary manner, usually hanging or beheading their prisoners.

The dominant motive of the Teutonic Knights was redemption through battle. "Who fights us," proclaimed the order, "fights Jesus Christ." The enemy was not just the unrepentant pagan, however—it was the Satan within themselves.

In an effort to vanquish this unseen but deadly foe, the knight-brother submitted himself to a Draconian regime of prayer, discipline, and self-denial, which applied on the campaign as well as in the convent. He owned no property but was issued a sword and armor, as well as a pair of breeches, two shirts, two pairs of boots, one surcoat, one sleeping bag, one blanket, one breviary, and one knife. He could have two or four mounts, as he required, but these mounts, like his clothing and equipment, belonged to the order. He was forbidden to consort with laymen, and he had to remain silent at meals, in the dormitory, on the march, and in the latrines. He was not permitted to joust. He could hunt solely those animals that attacked the crops and livestock of the settlers—the wolf, the lynx, and the bear, for example—and only if he forfeited the assistance of hounds. His one lawful amusement was woodcarving.

All forms of vanity, such as the displaying of personal coats of arms, were strictly forbidden. Hair had to be short, although beards were permitted. The knight-brother had to sleep in his shirt, breeches, and boots, with his sword at hand, and he was required to rise four times a night to recite the offices. On Fridays, he took the discipline, flagellating his own body until blood was drawn. Derelictions, spiritual or military, were dealt with by a senior officer, the marshal, using his rod in camp and his club on the battlefield.

Besides the usual Lent abstinence, the knight-brother was not allowed to eat meat during most of November and December, or on any of twenty specified fast days, or on Monday, Wednesday, Friday, or Saturday at any time of the year. For the most part his diet consisted of eggs, milk, porridge, and water. In addition, he was expected to resist all temptations of the flesh: One postulant trained himself to curb his carnal desires by choosing the prettiest girl he could find and sleeping beside her for a year without touching her. Others suppressed their longings through pain, wearing their chain mail under their shirts until the raw skin rusted the metal.

Despite such privations, the knights made an awesomely effective fighting force. In 1235, their order swallowed up the remnants of the Knights of Dobrzyn. By 1236, after six years of warfare, they had penetrated as far as the Vistula delta and were ready to start advancing eastward along the Baltic shore toward the Neman River. But the union with the Sword Brothers in May 1237, following their defeat at Saule, brought the Teutonic Knights a Baltic dominion that stretched far beyond the borders of Prussia. A few weeks later, the master of Prussia, Herman Balke, arrived in Riga to take charge of the Crusade in Livonia.

His first priority was to pacify the Danish ruler, King Waldemar, who was still demanding the return of his Estonian territories. In 1238, both sides agreed to the original partition scheme of sixteen years earlier, with the Danes receiving the northern provinces and the order retaining the Sword Brothers' conquests in the south. Estonia still remained under the protection of the Holy See, however, and the price for papal approval was a promise by the Danes and the Teutonic Knights to join in a grand Crusade against the Russians of Novgorod. Accordingly, in 1240 a combined German and Danish force marched out of Livonia and, having captured the cities of

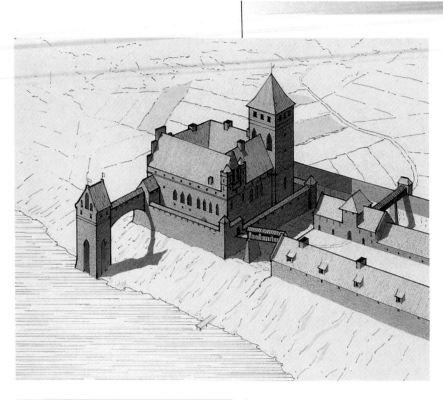

The castle of Lochstedt, near the port of Königsberg, was just one of many that the Teutonic Order placed strategically along the Baltic coast and in river valleys as bases for subjugating Prussia. Built of brick, the fortress featured a chapel, a dining hall, an armory, a chapter house for meetings, a kitchen, and a dormitory for the knights, as well as a latrine tower; the tower drained directly into the sea, was separated from the main body of the castle, and was reached by a covered passageway. An adjoining complex contained estate offices for the steward, who administered the surrounding farmland, barns, workshops, stables, a hostelry for visitors, and quarters for the other ranks. The castle would have held a total garrison of about sixty men, including priests, sergeants, and some ten to twenty knights.

Izborsk and Pskov, prepared to overrun Novgorod. It was a time of mortal peril for the principality, which faced an invasion not only from the Crusaders but from the Mongols under Batu Khan, who had spent the previous three years devastating southern and central Russia.

But Batu, instead of advancing on Novgorod, decided to head west into Poland and Hungary, and the Crusade against the Russians was temporarily superseded by the Crusade against the Mongols. On April 9, 1241, an army of Poles and Germans, including a strong detachment of the Teutonic Knights under the Prussian master Poppo of Osterna, clashed with the Mongols at Liegnitz in Silesia. Disdaining to wait for reinforcements, the mailed knights made a valiant charge at the dense ranks of the enemy, only to be cut down by a hail of arrows. Poppo escaped, but others were not so lucky. The severed head of the Christian commander, Duke Henry of Silesia, was born aloft on a lance, and the ears of his dead comrades were cut off, gathered into nine sacks, and presented to Batu.

Fortunately for Catholic Europe, in late 1241 the Great Khan Ogedei died—an event that sent Batu hurrying back to Mongolia for the ensuing succession dispute. The Novgorodians, relieved of immediate danger from the Mongols, took the opportunity to settle accounts with the Crusaders. Early in 1242, two years after his resounding victory over the Swedes on the Neva, the prince of Novgorod, Alexander Nevsky, recaptured the Russian territory occupied by the Danes and the Germans.

In a doleful account of the fall of Pskov to the Russians, a German chronicler claimed that only two knight-brothers had been left to defend the town. "If Pskov had been held, it would have benefited Christianity to the end of the world. It was a mistake to have taken the land and not have occupied it properly. He cries most about the pain who could have avoided it easily."

Worse was to follow. On April 5, 1242—almost a year after the disaster at Liegnitz—the two Christian armies clashed beside Lake Peipus. At first the Crusaders' heavily armored cavalry had the best of it, breaking through the Russian ranks. But they were overwhelmed by Nevsky's superior numbers and, according to one chronicle, were driven onto the frozen lake, where the majority were killed or captured.

The Crusaders had barely recovered from this latest defeat when they were confronted with an even more serious crisis—a rebellion by the Prussians. The insurgent tribesmen destroyed all but three of the order's forts and settlements, and it took the brethren a full seven years to suppress the uprising.

Anxious to avoid future trouble, the papacy persuaded the Teutonic Knights to deal generously with the vanquished tribes. Under the Treaty of Christburg, in 1249, Prussians who renounced paganism and accepted the faith were guaranteed the same rights as Germans and Poles. They could buy, sell, litigate, and worship on an equal basis with the immigrant burghers, and they could become priests and knights.

It was around this time that the Lithuanian chieftain, Mindaugas, whose powerful and well-organized state was under attack from Poles, Russians, Mongols, and Crusaders, decided to neutralize at least one of his enemies by accepting the embrace of Rome. So delighted was Pope Innocent IV that he gave the new convert a royal crown. Mindaugas, for his part, invited German merchants and settlers to enter Lithuania and even arranged for the Teutonic Order to take over his lands should he die without an heir—a likely event, given the murderous inclinations of the Lithuanian nobles. More important, he offered to cede the brethren the coastal territory of Samogitia, which would complete the land link between Prussia and Livonia.

The Samogitians refused to accept Christian rule, however, and in July 1260, they routed a Crusader army at Durben, in western Curonia. It was the worst defeat the Teutonic Knights had suffered since coming to the Baltic—150 knight-brothers were killed, including the master of Livonia and the marshal of Prussia—and it sparked another general uprising by the Prussians. The revolt spread to other tribes, and even Mindaugas, seeing a chance for further self-aggrandizement, decided to resume his war against the Christians. Although he was murdered by his brother-in-law in 1263, his death had little effect on the military situation, since many Lithuanians continued to support the rebels. Indeed, so desperate was the plight of the Teutonic Knights that Pope Urban IV, who had been planning a Crusade against the Mongols, urged all those who had taken the cross to go to the assistance of the order, promising full remission of sins for any length of service, no matter how short.

By now, the pagan warriors had learned the techniques of modern war from the Christians; they were well armed, well led, well organized, and able both to attack the enemy's fortresses and to engage them in open battle. The Crusaders thus met with some heavy defeats; nevertheless, they usually inflicted more casualties than they received. In 1290, after thirty years of war, they finally brought their subjects to heel, although the Samogitians and Lithuanians remained defiantly belligerent.

With the Teutonic Knights firmly in control, the trickle of settlers into their territory became a flood. Livonia, because of its forbidding location, was largely ignored by the newcomers, but Prussia was a different story. Lured by the prospect of large landholdings for low rents, peasant colonists from north Germany arrived in such numbers that within half a century they had founded some 1,500 towns and villages, with an estimated population of 150,000. (The indigenous population, decimated by years of war, was scarcely larger.)

To ensure efficient cultivation of the Prussian wilderness, the Teutonic Knights employed locators, or colonizing agents, whose job was to recruit the peasants, allocate the plots, and organize the villages. For this service, a locator received his own village plot—usually one-tenth of the whole—the position of village judge and headman, and often the ownership of the local mill or inn. A village was made up of about twenty families, each holding between 100 and 150 acres. In Germany, the peasant was bound by his duty to the lord of the manor, whereas in Prussia he was largely free to come and go at will. His only obligations were to pay his annual rent on time and to perform military service.

The local merchants, based mainly in Riga, were also left to pursue their affairs. As a result, they built a prosperous trade network that stretched from the wealthy ports of northern Germany to the landlocked cities of Hungary, Lithuania, and Russia. (Trade continued with the

Presented to the cathedral of Plock by Conrad, ruler of the Polish province of Mazovia, this gold paten, used to hold the bread for the service of mass, bears on its upper right quadrant the image of its donor offering a chalice. Disturbed by Prussian border raids, Conrad invited the Teutonic Order to subdue his pagan neighbors in 1225. The order's knights arrived in 1230 and in the ensuing fifty years made Prussia an independent state under their direct control. Their success eventually jeopardized Poland's own position, and bitter enmity grew up between the two powers. Not until the fifteenth century was the situation resolved, after a combined Polish and Lithuanian army defeated the Teutonic Knights at the battle of Tannenberg.

BATTLE ON THE ICE

The campaigns of the Baltic Crusades were fought in difficult terrain and often in intemperate weather conditions that could hardly have been more different from the blazing heat of the Holy Land. A typical encounter took place on April 5, 1242, when a group of Teutonic Knights and native allies clashed with the Russians at Lake Peipus, in eastern Estonia. Returning from a raid into the principality of Novgorod, some thirty mounted knights, with the same number of mounted sergeants and about 250 Estonian foot soldiers, met a force of 300 Russians under the leadership of Alexander Nevsky.

Clad in distinctive white mantles emblazoned with a black cross, the knights were equipped with helmets, mail coats, swords, and spears. Confident of their superior armor and weaponry, they charged in a wedge formation into the Russian ranks, only to be encircled and driven back. According to one chronicle, they were forced onto the frozen lake, where most of the knights were captured or slaughtered.

Lithuanians and Russians despite wars and religious differences.) Though required to pay customs duties, the merchants could transport their goods without charge in Prussia and Livonia, using the roads or the rivers, which were patrolled by brethren.

The Teutonic Order itself carried on a large and lucrative trade, maintaining a merchant fleet to take its goods across the Baltic. Its main exports were grain and Prussian amber—the latter, a monopoly of the order, being much prized for rosaries. The order also minted its own coinage, set up an internal postal service, and enforced a uniform system of weights and measures. Matters of policy were decided by the master of Prussia and his senior officials, but the day-to-day running of the country, such as the collection of taxes, the administration of justice, the organization of defense, was left to local commanders, each supported by a convent of at least twelve brothers. Many of these brothers were skilled bookkeepers, who made sure that the financial affairs of the convent were in order. They submitted weekly accounts to the commander, and he in turn submitted monthly accounts to a senior administrator. The commander also compiled a personal dossier on each brother, sending the information to the main archives at Marienburg castle.

Whatever the demands of their role as scribes and clerks, the Teutonic Knights never lost sight of their main priority: the defense of the realm against heathens and unbelievers. The benefits of Christian rule were meant only for Christian subjects; accordingly, no Jew or necromancer was allowed to settle in the order's domains. In addition, the native Prussians continued to be regarded with fierce suspicion. The small minority who had remained loyal during the great rebellion were treated no differently from the German settlers themselves, receiving lands and liberties appropriate to their rank. But Prussians who had reverted to paganism or were suspected of being less than wholeheartedly Catholic—and they constituted the vast majority— were recruited as menial laborers on German estates and denied the right even to open a shop or an inn. Indeed, so deep-rooted was the distrust of the natives that whenever Prussians and Germans were drinking together, the Prussians were required to drink first to reduce the risk of poisoning.

As the thirteenth century entered its final decade, the Teutonic Order had never appeared more secure, with greater wealth, power, and prestige than most secular monarchs. But appearances were deceptive. In 1291, the Muslims stormed Acre, overrunning the order's headquarters and forcing it to establish a new base in Venice. This melancholy event was followed by more trouble in the Baltic—and it came not from the resentful pagans of Prussia but from the Christian burghers of Riga.

The Rigans and the Teutonic Knights had been set on a collision course for some time, with the former demanding more independence and the latter refusing to give up their sovereignty over the city. The issue came to a head in 1297, when the knight-brothers demolished a bridge the Rigans had built over the Dvina River. In the ensuing violence, blood flowed on both sides, and houses were burned, merchants arrested, and goods impounded. Angry citizens stormed the local convent of the order, destroying it and throwing six captured brethren into prison. In response, the knight-brothers devastated the surrounding farmlands, burned manors and barns, cut down fruit trees, drove off livestock, and killed the burghers who tried to intervene. On Christmas Eve, they routed a force from the city and then mocked the terrified inhabitants by shouting, "Where is your pope?" In desperation, the Rigans turned to the knight-brothers' most implacable foes, the Lithuanians, who immediately invaded Livonia, killing the Livonian master and sixty of his knights. Although the Lithuanians soon returned home, the conflict between the Rigans and the brothers continued.

Appalled at the turn of events in the Baltic, Pope Boniface VIII demanded an explanation, and in July 1299, representatives of both sides pleaded their case before him. According to the Rigans, the Teutonic Knights were mere ruffians, more interested in making money than in fighting the heathens. Archbishop John III of Riga, whose estates had been seized by the brethren and who had been imprisoned by them for thirty days, was especially vehement in his denunciation. The order was given Livonia, he claimed, to assist in the work of converting the natives and to defend the country from attack; instead, it had hindered the task of conversion and refused to fight the pagans. It was the Teutonic Knights, he insisted, who had driven King Mindaugas into the wilderness, and who, by their "savagery, cruelty, and tyranny," had deterred the population from accepting the Christian faith.

The order indignantly denied the accusations, arguing that the knight-brothers had paid with their blood to achieve the conversion of Livonia. Such was their success, they claimed, that if one of the natives were asked, "Do you believe in God?" he would reply, "I believe in God and the Holy Roman Church, and in the catechism, like other true and good Christians." Pope Boniface tried to arrange a compromise between the two sides, persuading the archbishop and the Rigans not to pursue their charges in return for a promise by the order to give back what it had taken.

In 1306, however, the quarrel was revived by Archbishop John's successor, who added witchcraft, sodomy, and genocide to the original list of charges against the order. Previously, the Teutonic Knights had been able to rely on their standing with the curia to help them through their difficulties with awkward prelates. But Pope Clement V, elected in 1305, was a close ally of Philip IV of France—and Philip's declared aim was to abolish the existing military orders and set up a new one with himself at its head. In October 1307, he arrested all the members of the Templar order then resident in his realm and had them tried for heresy. A year later, he prevailed on the pope to authorize the arrest and trial of Templars throughout Europe. Although the charges were groundless, confessions were often obtained by torture, and many knights who had fought gallantly against the infidel were burned at the stake.

The lesson was not lost on the Teutonic Order, which in 1309 hastily transferred its headquarters from Venice to Marienburg castle in Prussia, beyond the reach of either pontiff or monarch. The move came just in time. The following year, Clement appointed a commission to investigate all outstanding charges against the Teutonic Knights, who "shaming all the faithful, and damaging the faith, have become . . . familiars of the enemy, not fighting in the name of Christ against the enemies of the faith, but rather, astounding to hear, waging war on behalf of such people against Christ, with various cunning ruses."

In actuality, there was little the pope could do against the knights. Without signed confessions, there were insufficient grounds for proscribing the order, and its enemies had to be satisfied with a papal directive banning the knight-brothers from Riga—a directive that was rescinded only a few months later.

The brethren's problems with the papacy did not keep them from pursuing expansionism in the Baltic. In 1308, they had occupied the province of Pomerelia, including the city of Danzig, starting a prolonged if intermittent conflict with Poland. They also pressed the war against the Lithuanians, united now under the powerful Liutaras dynasty. With the loss of Acre, it was not possible to take the cross to Palestine, so adventurous nobles from all over Europe flocked to the Baltic Crusade.

The Teutonic Knights, though themselves abstemious, were lavish in their hospitality to such guests, for whom they provided sumptuous banquets and entertainments, with music, juggling, and jousting. The main event of the program—the *reysen,* or raids, against the Lithuanians—depended on the season. The *winter-reysa,* involving from 200 to 2,000 Crusaders, was a rapid foray, aimed at clearing and plundering an area as quickly as possible. There were usually two winter-reysen a year—one in December, the other in January or February, with a break for Christmas.

The *sommer-reysa,* held in August or September, was a larger and more elaborate undertaking, its object being to conquer new territory, either by destroying an existing stronghold or by building a new one. One of the French knights who took part in a reysa saw it as "a grand affair, and very honorable and beautiful," what with the "great assemblage of knights and squires and noblemen, both from the kingdom of France and elsewhere."

Despite their theatricality, reysen were not for the fainthearted or the physically unfit. No matter what the season, the Crusaders had to spend several weeks hauling their armor and supplies through dense forest to reach their objective. Although they were usually accompanied by Prussian guides, Crusader armies sometimes lost their way and were never seen again. And always there was the risk of the unexpected: a sudden flood in summer or a thawing of the ice in winter, an attack by wild beasts, an ambush by the Lithuanians. But such rigors seem to have had little effect on the ardor of the Crusaders, who fought with their usual remorseless savagery.

Although captured Lithuanians were often ransomed by the Crusaders, as were captured Crusaders by the Lithuanians—the Teutonic Order promised to pay for the release of any Christian knight who fell into enemy hands—this courtesy was extended only to the rich and the highborn. The common soldier and the hapless peasant could expect less tender treatment. Indeed, such was the reputation of the Crusaders that on one occasion the inhabitants of a Lithuanian village decapitated one another rather than be captured by the besieging Christians. One old woman killed over 100 warriors in this way, and when the Crusaders finally broke in, she used the ax to split her own head.

Throughout the early and mid-fourteenth century, the Teutonic Knights enjoyed a high summer of unprecedented power and prestige. But by 1386 their downfall was in sight. In that year, the Lithuanian leader, Grand Duke Jogaila, became a Catholic, married the Polish queen Jadwiga, and was crowned King Vladislav IV of Poland. Not only was it now difficult for the Teutonic Knights to justify the continuation of a Crusade against a Christian ruler, but the dynastic union of Poland and Lithuania posed a serious military threat to the order.

A day of reckoning was inevitable, and it came on July 15, 1410, at Tannenberg (present-day Grunwald), near the Prussian border with Poland. In a bloody, ten-hour encounter, a Polish and Lithuanian army annihilated the forces of the Teutonic Order. Among the fallen were the grand master, the chief officials, and some 400 brethren. The triumphant allies failed to take Marienburg, however, and after a fifty-seven-day siege, the Poles and Lithuanians withdrew, leaving the order with most of its territories intact. It would, indeed, be another century and a half before the order, overwhelmed by enemies from both within and without, was forced to cede the last of its lands to Poland. But Tannenberg was the turning point, marking the start of the order's decline and effectively ending the Baltic Crusade.

THE GOTHIC ZENITH

As men sought to provide an ideal setting for the worship of God, thirteenth-century Europe witnessed a proliferation of art and architecture of a dramatic new style. The pioneers of this style—known today as Gothic, the name bestowed on it by hostile Renaissance writers who identified it with medieval barbarism—aimed to create an earthly prefiguration of paradise.

Churches became crowded with images of saints, prophets, and martyrs. Artists adopted an arresting realism, abandoning the stylized Romanesque figures of the eleventh and twelfth centuries. Painters and sculptors showed an interest in the humanity of Christ, whose actions—for example, crowning his mother, Mary *(right)*—were invested with a new tenderness.

At the same time, architects sought to create buildings whose soaring spaces would emphasize the mystery and immensity of God. They were inspired above all by the symbolism of light, the element they believed most resembled God's power, illuminating the darkness of creation.

Conceived at the abbey of Saint Denis outside Paris in the years after 1137, the mode attained an aesthetic peak in a series of great cathedrals built in northern France under the patronage of the French kings. With pronounced local variations, the style spread at the same time to England, Germany, and other neighboring lands.

Previously churches had been places of gloom and shadow. To support the immense weight of masonry and roof, Roman-esque builders had had to rely upon the rounded arch, sustained with the aid of massive walls and thick internal pillars. The Gothic style introduced such technical innovations as the flying buttress—an external stone brace supporting the walls—and the pointed arch, which reduced lateral thrust and could sustain a skeleton of stone ribs to bear the weight of the roof.

Relieved of some of their load-bearing function, the outer walls of churches could then be transformed into delicate shells that encompassed wide expanses of stained glass. Soaring to unprecedented heights, the windows created an architecture of light, drenching church interiors in a multicolored radiance.

A gallery of saints and apostles frames the main portal of Bourges Cathedral. In the tympanum—above the twin doors—Christ presides in majesty over the Last Judgment.

Visible to the faithful for miles around, the towers and spires of the Gothic cathedral stood as beacons of the faith. Beneath them, statue-thronged portals served symbolically as thresholds separating the realm of God from the world of man. Rising out of each gable and pediment, a multitude of crockets and finials—finely carved stone spears and buds—led the eye upward to the heavens.

Height was achieved by spreading the weight of walls and roof across a wide foundation by means of flying buttresses. Connected to the walls of the church by arches of masonry, the buttresses, which served to brace the outward thrust of the structure, developed into a delicately chiseled form of scaffolding in stone. It was these supports that enabled the architects of Rheims to raise their roof to a height of 125 feet and those of Amiens to a height of almost 140 feet. Only at Beauvais Cathedral did the quest for verticality reach its limit when in 1284 the great vaults of the choir—almost 160 feet high—collapsed because of inadequate foundations.

Slender flying buttresses support the eastern end of Bourges Cathedral, bracing the walls and making it possible for them to be pierced by many windows.

rows to heaven, a side aisle parallel to the nave of Rheims Cathedral draws the eye inexorably to the glow of stained glass at its eastern end.

Bathed in a richly hued glow, the interior of the Gothic cathedral was intended as a theater for the performance of the Christian liturgy. Typically, builders achieved the effect by the insertion of at least two rows of windows—one near ground level to illuminate the nave and aisles, the other immediately below the roof—separated by a pillared gallery. The columns that bore the weight of the roof were carved into clusters of delicate shafts, surmounted by stone ribs that sprang out to meet in pointed arches at the center of the vault. The angle of the arch could be widened or narrowed to support roof areas of differing widths at the same height—a feat impossible with the earlier system of rounded arches and barrel vaults.

Buttercups adorn a capital in Southwell Minster.

Carried on slender pillars the nave of Bourges Cathedral soars to a height of 130 feet in three tiers— an arcade at ground level a pillared gallery known

Pennanted cross, an allegorical statue from Strasbourg Cathedral symbolizes the Church's role in dispensing the sacraments.

A realistic statue adorns Naumburg Cathedral.

Placed inside the cathedral or arranged in rows on its outer walls, statues functioned as sermons in stone, reminding the faithful of a biblical character or a benefactor or illustrating theological messages. For example, juxtaposing Old Testament prophets with the Gospel writers emphasized the continuous transmission of the Word of God. In this way, stone carving served not only to provide a visual reference for congregations who were largely illiterate but also to convey ideas by means of sculpted parables and allegories.

A pair of statues from the west facade of Strasbourg Cathedral show a foolish virgin preparing to accept an apple from a handsome tempter.

Juxtaposed with the figure that represents the Church *(opposite)*, this symbolic statue of the Synagogue, shown with eyes blindfolded, was intended to emphasize the superiority of the New Testament faith over that of the Old.

The crowning glory of Gothic architecture was the stained glass that turned church windows into lustrous visions of a better world. Enclosed within a tracery of lead, the windows were held in place by supporting spokes of iron driven into the surrounding masonry. Various pigments were added to the glass to create its rich colors, the most popular being a brilliant sapphire made from cobalt oxide sand imported from Bohemia. A brown resin was used to sketch in details such as faces and drapery. The characteristic ruby red was produced from copper oxide so deep in hue that sheets of clear glass had to be laminated onto layers of the red to make it transparent. The end product was a gemlike radiance that in the words of a contemporary English scholar, Robert Grosseteste, transformed light into "the mediator between bodiless and bodily substance, at the same time spiritual body and embodied spirit."

Circled by apostles, angels saints, and martyrs, Chris is portrayed in glory at the center of the south rose window of Notre Dame the cathedral church of Paris, which was completed in the year 1230

A roundel, or small circular window, from the north choir of England's Canterbury Cathedral depicts an incident during the siege of the city by the Danes in 1011.

The greatest monument to the Gothic passion for stained glass, the Sainte-Chapelle in Paris, was built by King Louis IX to house one of Christendom's holiest relics, Christ's crown of thorns. The king bought the crown in 1239 for 135,000 livres—more than three times the chapel's cost.

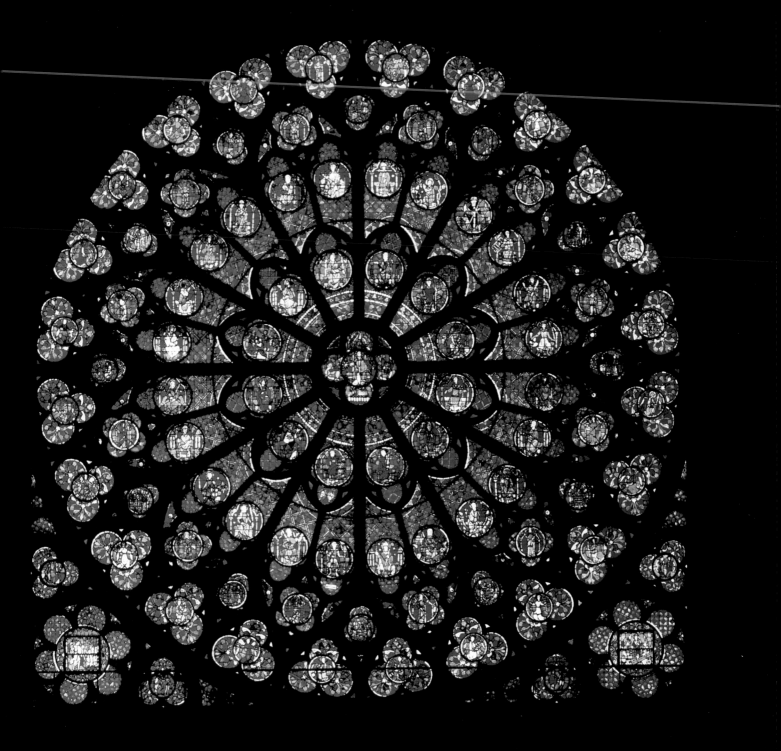

EUROPE'S NEW MONARCHIES

At first glance, Louis IX of France and Henry III of England would seem to have been remarkably similar. They were closely related by blood, both being descendants of Henry II of England and Eleanor of Aquitaine. Both commanded territories in France for the better part of the thirteenth century, and thus their fates were inextricably entwined. Each acceded to his throne when he was a boy, and each had redoubtable regents during his minority: Chief among Henry's was William Marshall, earl of Pembroke, the most famous knight in Christendom; Louis's regent was his mother, the masterful Blanche of Castile. The kings—and their brothers—married sisters, daughters of Raymond of Provence. Both were pious men who sponsored the construction of soaring churches that were the flower of the Gothic style—Westminster Abbey in London, the Sainte-Chapelle in Paris. Both men had to deal with an unruly feudal nobility and with a powerful clergy. Both presided over the beginnings of true nationhood for their countries.

But the differences between the monarchs' fates—and those of their kingdoms—were profound. Henry Plantagenet died bereft of authority, reviled by the chroniclers. Louis Capet died in the fullness of his power, so revered that he was canonized shortly thereafter. Henry left territories that were a great deal smaller than they had been in his grandfather's day and a monarchy that was held in check by England's baronage: The parliamentary system had been born. The French royal domain, by contrast, grew from a relatively small area surrounded by often hostile feudal dependencies into an enormous state, united under monarchs whose absolute authority only increased as the century came to a close.

Some of the reasons for the differences may be found in the natures of the two countries: France was large and diffuse, a condition that worked to a strong king's advantage. England was compact and much more homogeneous. Thanks to their diversity, the French never established a tradition of communal resistance to the king; thanks to their similarity, the English did. As important as these factors, however, were the characters of the kings who reigned during the age of change. The successes and failures of Henry and Louis depended in large part on their own personalities—and on those of their fathers and grandfathers.

Few in France could have foreseen the developments of the thirteenth century as the twelfth drew to its close. When Philip II, Louis's grandfather, came to the throne as a fourteen-year-old in the year 1180, the French monarchy was weak. Europe was a continent still in the process of settling down after centuries of disorganization and terror. When the migrations and invasions that had shattered the structures of the ancient world at last slowed to a stop, in about AD 1000, they left behind a fragmented continent in which a contractual, or feudal, relationship of mutual support

In this detail from an illuminated Bible commissioned by King Louis VIII of France, a king is depicted holding the orb and scepter that symbolized his office. Reigning for only three years before his death in 1226, Louis was one of five monarchs to ascend the French throne in the course of the thirteenth century—a period that saw a consolidation of royal authority not only in France but in the realm of its old rival, England.

between local warlords and their dependent vassals was the best guarantee of security. The relationship of the king to his lords had the same character: support and protection in return for allegiance and service.

But the degree of allegiance could vary widely. When Philip became king, he acquired two quite separate levels of authority over different parts of his realm. In territories forming the royal domain—those lands that answered directly to him as their lord—royal power was indeed a reality, but the territory concerned was small. Centered on the Île-de-France and the city of Paris, the royal domain covered less than 10,000 square miles—about the size of the modern-day state of Vermont.

Beyond the borders of the royal domain, the king reigned in little more than name. In theory, he was the feudal overlord of all the various counties, duchies, and other territories that made up the land of France. In practice, however, the great lords who controlled these regions ruled as virtually independent monarchs and resisted the encroachment of royal power. They acknowledged a formal allegiance to the king as their overlord but did all they could to maintain their independence.

One such vassal lord was particularly well placed to challenge the French king, and that was the king of England, who had substantial landholdings on the French mainland. Since the Norman conquest of 1066, the English throne had had close links with the duchy of Normandy. The French connection had become much stronger after 1154, when the throne passed to Henry II, the son of the count of Anjou, one

At the dawn of the thirteenth century, France was a tangled web of duchies and counties ruled by local magnates recognizing a largely theoretical bond to their feudal overlord, the king. Only in the royal domain—the landlocked Île-de-France around Paris—did the ruler exert unchallenged authority. With Normandy, Anjou, and Aquitaine under his control, the greatest of his vassals was none other than the king of England, whose territory on both sides of the Channel formed the powerful Angevin empire. By the end of the century, however, the situation was very different. Under a series of strong kings, France had wrested from the Angevins virtually all of their continental possessions except Gascony, leaving an English realm that was considerably shorn of power, although it now included Wales.

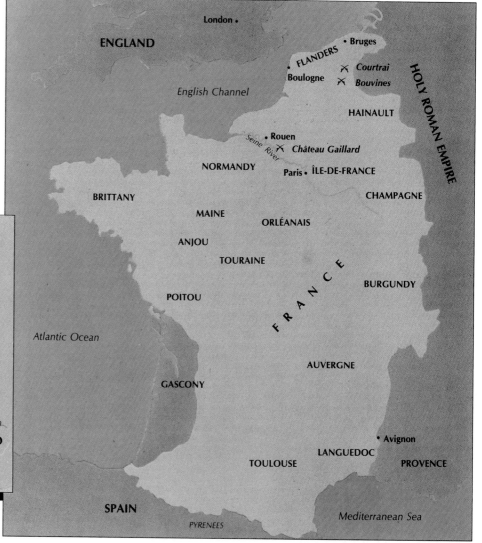

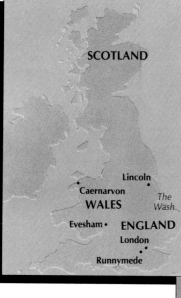

of France's magnates. With him had come a disparate empire that besides Anjou incorporated Maine, which included Mayenne, Sarthe, part of Orne and Eure-et-Loir; the Touraine; Aquitaine, including Gascony and Poitou; and from the 1160s, Brittany. In effect, it constituted the entire western seaboard of France, with its hinterland stretching as far as the Massif Central. Together with England, Normandy, and parts of Ireland, these lands made up the so-called Angevin empire.

The Angevin territories in France, held for the most part in vassalage to the French king, were actually far more extensive than Philip's own domain. Henry's heir, Richard the Lion-Hearted, had underlined the fact by building a showpiece fortress, Château Gaillard, on the Seine at Les Andelys, a mere day's march from Paris. Employing the most advanced military architecture of its day, the castle was a direct challenge to Philip's authority; "I could hold Château Gaillard," boasted Richard, "if it was made of butter."

Philip could scarcely break the Angevin stranglehold while the warrior Richard held the throne. His chance came in 1199, when Richard died and was succeeded by his brother John. The new king's ill-understood character, more complex than that of the ruthlessly effective Richard, led him into diplomatic blunders from which Philip adroitly profited. John soon alienated the lord of Poitou by snatching the lord's betrothed bride for his own wife. The offended noble appealed to Philip, his suzerain, for satisfaction, and in 1202, Philip arraigned John as his vassal to answer the charges against him. John refused, giving Philip the excuse he needed to appropriate his lands and initiate the process of uniting France under a French king.

Philip began by invading Normandy. Château Gaillard fell after a seven-month siege in 1204, and with his strongest defensive position gone, John could no longer control his fiefs. Philip's triumph, aided by well-placed concessions to the English king's former vassals, was soon complete. By 1205, all of John's territories north of the Loire River had fallen, and the richest and most advanced parts of the Angevin empire were in Philip's hands.

John's overriding purpose was now to regain his lost lands in France, and it was this determination that led him into a disastrous campaign. Joining with other of Philip's enemies, he set out to conquer the French king.

The decisive battle took place on Sunday, July 27, 1214, near the tiny Flemish village of Bouvines, where the boundaries of France, Germany, and Flanders converged. The harvest had already begun on the broad, sloping fields of the monastery of Cysoing, a small foundation dating from the ninth century, but no one was at work among the sheaves. Glinting across the empty grainfields, two armies confronted each other, committed to battle after days of maneuvering.

With the sun burning their backs stood the feudal host of France—some 1,300 knights, with the same number of mounted sergeants and several thousand foot soldiers, all under the command of the experienced King Philip. The oriflamme, or sacred banner of France, had been hurriedly brought from its usual home in the abbey of Saint Denis near Paris to the king's side in the center of the front rank.

Opposite the French ranks were arrayed France's enemies. At their center stood the Holy Roman Emperor, Otto, with the glittering standard of his authority: an eagle perched on a dragon, raised on top of a lofty pole. On the right wing, the earl of Salisbury—illegitimate brother and right-hand man of King John—commanded a select body of English troops as well as a horde of Flemish mercenaries paid for with English silver. At Salisbury's side was the energetic count of Boulogne, Renaud de

A KEY FORTRESS FALLS

In February 1204, after a seven-month siege, the army of France's Philip II dealt a crushing blow to the Angevin empire by breaching the walls of Château Gaillard, about fifty miles northwest of Paris.

The castle—built at great expense in the 1190s by King Richard of England—was the main stronghold in a chain of forts guarding the duchy of Normandy, then ruled by England. Modeled on Crusader castles Richard had seen in the Holy Land, it had the most up-to-date military architecture of the time, with two wards, or courtyards, a citadel, and a keep, all boasting walls up to thirteen feet thick. Perched on a rocky spur more than 300 feet above the Seine and flanked by cliffs, it seemed impregnable.

But in 1199, the English throne passed to Richard's inept brother, John, leading Philip to invade Normandy. In August 1203, Philip laid siege to the castle, ordering a boat barricade across the Seine to deny the garrison river-borne relief. While French crossbowmen fired deadly salvos at the garrison, sappers mined beneath the walls, weakening their foundations by setting fires in the tunnels. In February 1204, the outermost tower was brought crashing down, and Philip's troops poured into the outer ward, as shown here. A latrine window gave access to the second ward, and using catapults and mines, the invaders took the citadel. On March 6, the remaining 186 defenders surrendered. Château Gaillard's fall sealed the fate of the duchy: Four months later, it was in Philip's control.

Dammartin. Count Ferrand of Flanders took the left wing with many Flemish knights of battle-proven courage and skill.

John himself was not present but was more than 300 miles away to the southwest, in Poitou. He had planned to trap the French king with a pincer's movement between his own force and that of his allies. Philip's son Louis, however, had pinned him down, and his army had made little headway.

On the sweltering battlefield the commanders stood ready, each surrounded by a bodyguard of specially chosen knights of skill and rank. But even before the trumpets sounded for the onset of battle, fighting began. King Philip's most active and resourceful adviser, the bishop of Senlis, sent a force of mounted sergeants to harry Ferrand's Flemish knights in preparation for a French cavalry charge. The Flemings, indignant at confronting common soldiers instead of their knightly equals, refused to ride out to meet them. Instead they waited for Philip's forces to charge before driving them back contemptuously.

A vast dust cloud, stirred up by the charging horses, soon obscured the fighting that ensued, so that it was impossible for an observer to gain a general impression of the fray. Under the masking dust, individual knights picked out worthy opponents to challenge in combat; foot soldiers dashed in where they could to strike at a knight's horse or pin down a fallen warrior until a knight came to take his submission. From time to time, tired by bouts of fierce combat, the knights retreated to regain their breath before rejoining the ranks. Well protected by their armor and by the battlefield convention that captured opponents of noble stock be taken alive for ransom, they could afford a sporting attitude toward warfare, secure in the knowledge that barring accidents, they would live to fight again. Typically, most of the casualties of Bouvines were foot soldiers; even the mounted sergeants sent to harass the Flemish ranks suffered only two fatalities when their attack was so brusquely repulsed.

The tide of battle swept back and forth. At one point, John's allies came close to victory, when Otto's German knights made a determined push to reach the French king. Philip's bodyguard held them off, but as they fought, German foot soldiers slipped through unnoticed to surround Philip and cut his horse from under him. The royal standard-bearer swung the oriflamme wildly to summon assistance, and Philip's assailants were put to flight.

Taking a fresh mount, the king urged his men to attack the German emperor. Otto was less fortunate than Philip. Wounded in the fighting, his horse bolted; his retainers followed their master, leaving the imperial standard behind them. Leaderless, the German knights continued to fight bravely until sundown, but the emperor's departure was a heavy blow to their cause.

On the allies' left wing, the twenty-eight-year-old count of Flanders was also wounded and was subsequently captured by the French. On the right, the count of Boulogne fought on, gathering his knights within a protective circle of closely packed and heavily armed foot soldiers, tough and battle-hardened mercenaries from the Netherlands; the circle opened to allow sorties against the enemy and to receive knights returning to safety when sorely pressed. But by now the odds were telling against the allies. As evening drew on, their ranks became thinner, until eventually the brave count was left with only half a dozen men to continue the unequal struggle. The end came when a French foot soldier managed to lift the section of mail that protected the count's horse and drive his sword up into its belly. The beast fell, trapping its master under it. After an unseemly squabble among several French knights as to who should take him prisoner, the count was able to yield to the bishop of Senlis himself and was led off to join Count Ferrand in captivity. The earl of Salisbury was also taken, and by nightfall the alliance was vanquished.

Back in the French camp, the prisoners taken in the battle were brought before the king. They included five counts and twenty-five lords of sufficient rank to fight under their own banners. Magnanimous in victory, the king granted them their lives and dispersed them in bonds to strongholds throughout the country to await ransom.

Confronted with the collapse of all his plans, King John had no choice but to conclude a truce with his victorious enemy and return to England. His defeat was the death knell of his hopes. Although no additional land was lost, the English monarch's territories on the French mainland were now decisively restricted to the lands south of the Loire River—territories where an unruly local nobility made overlordship a comparatively profitless business.

Philip, by contrast, won for himself a security on which he could build. In Paris, a storm of rejoicing for the victory broke out; it was not stilled for a week. Reorganization of the administration followed, and Paris was established as the Capetian capital. The name Bouvines became the cornerstone of a royal propaganda edifice. The great day was celebrated again and again in literary works, of which the *Phillipide*, written by William the Breton, Philip's chaplain and an onlooker at the battle, was the earliest. It was William who gave his master the sobriquet Augustus, or "the Majestic," and it was as Philip Augustus that this effective ruler was to be remembered by his people.

The chronicle was completed in Latin by 1224, a year after Philip's death. The monarch was succeeded by his son Louis VIII, whose brief reign almost seamlessly continued his own. Louis had been actively associated for many years with the policies of his father. It was Louis's successful southern campaign that had pinned John's forces down in 1214; he had followed King John's retreat to England by crossing the Channel at the invitation of a faction of rebellious English barons. The invasion of England was short-lived, however, and Louis devoted his three years' rule to problems in France.

In 1224, at the end of the ten-year truce following the Battle of Bouvines, Louis overran Poitou and started the process of binding that traditionally anti-Capetian region to the throne by grants of money and privileges to nobles, churches, and towns. Next he turned to the project of extending Capetian dominance into the south of France—a region more foreign to the northern French than even England in climate, culture, and mental outlook.

The pretext for annexation of the south was a war against heresy. In the Languedoc, the doctrine of Catharism—a dualistic religion—was a serious threat to the Catholic church. Its doctrine, that God ruled only the spiritual realm of heaven while Satan held power in the physical world on earth, was obviously incompatible with orthodox beliefs. The pope, after failing to limit the spread of Catharism by political and diplomatic pressure, had offered to endorse whoever would take up arms against its adherents, and northern French barons had been fighting in Languedoc since 1208. By the time Louis joined them after returning from his abortive invasion of England, much progress had been made in destroying the ruling families of the south and transferring their lands to their northern attackers, but the French monarchy had not yet gained a real foothold. In 1226, Louis mounted a massive expedition to the Languedoc. Battered by nearly twenty years of savagery and war, the south collapsed.

Honnecourt's mechanical drawings ranged from designs for a water-powered saw and a perfectly accurate crossbow *(top)* to a lectern-mounted eagle that would face the deacon whenever he read the Gospels *(bottom, left)*.

Compiled between 1220 and 1235, the sketchbook of the French architect Villard de Honnecourt provides a fascinating insight into the mind of a medieval artist. Combining the roles of designer, sculptor, and engineer, a master mason such as Honnecourt directed and often personally participated in every stage in the erection of a building, from drafting plans, laying foundations, making scaffolding, and building machines for transporting stone to decorating the finished design. Grouped in lodges—exclusive professional bodies with secret archives of formulas and methods—such artisans enjoyed high social status.

Like many of his colleagues, Honnecourt was constantly on the move, executing commissions as far afield as Switzerland and Hungary, searching for new materials, examining new designs, and consulting with fellow architects. In an age when copyright was nonexistent, designs were often imitated in distant lands. Honnecourt's sketchbook—intended as an exemplar for his apprentices or possibly for his lodge—contained a rich fund of knowledge on proportion, measurement, ground plans, elevations, and architectural learning gleaned from Byzantine and Arab as well as European sources, in addition to his own pictorial musings on the nature of mechanics and anatomy.

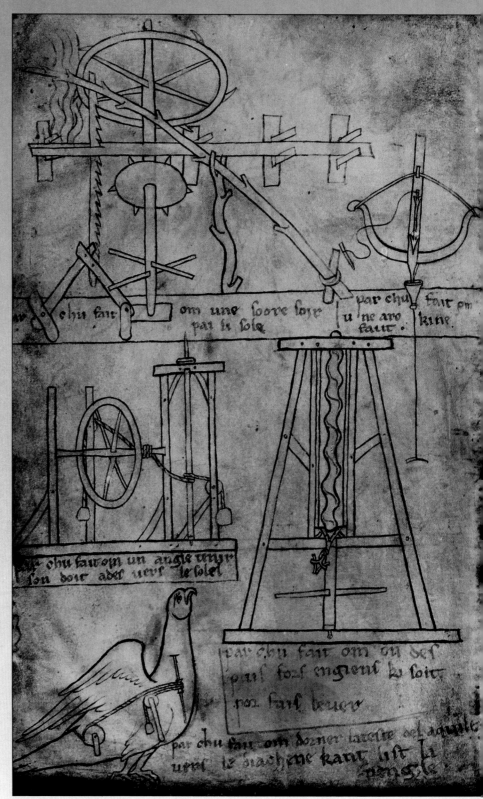

Expressive of complete exhaustion, a figure of Christ lies prostrate. Honnecourt's notebook had many such drawings, intended as models for sculptural decoration.

A sketch of Laon Cathedral's towers accurately depicts two statues of oxen, perhaps a reminder of the beasts used in the cathedral's construction. But the huge hand at right is Honnecourt's whimsy.

Revolving around a central axis, four masons chisel one another's feet in Honnecourt's design for a bell-striking mechanism.

Louis died that year while his army was still in the field, but the independence of the Languedoc—although the province remained restive and unruly—was already a thing of the past.

Louis IX now succeeded to a royal domain that thanks to his father and grandfather extended from the English Channel to the Mediterranean. The glories of his reign could hardly have been predicted at the time, for Louis was a child of twelve when his father died, and the barons and princes who had seen their position compromised by the growing power of the throne recognized an opportunity to regain some of the ground they had lost. So did King John's son, the young Henry III of England, who responded to overtures from the French rebel barons by unsuccessfully attempting to fight his way back into Poitou. But Louis's mother, Blanche of Castile—herself a granddaughter of Henry II of England—emerged as a resolute and able stateswoman; the barons could not agree among themselves long enough to make any lasting gains, and Blanche's prompt and authoritative actions steered the monarchy safely through Louis's minority. So fierce and resolute was Blanche that street songs described her as a she-wolf. And even after Louis came of age and married Margaret of Provence, Blanche remained his most valued adviser until her death in 1252.

Blanche's piety was the formative influence in Louis's upbringing. He impressed his contemporaries with his good humor and wit but above all with his devoutness and his generosity in almsgiving. Although he had strong convictions as to the overriding prerogatives and duties of royalty and lived amid much magnificence, his personal style was austere and simple. It was said that his clothes, once he had finished wearing them, were not worth handing on to anyone else.

An impressively moral, responsible, and religious monarch, Louis made an early start on a series of magnificent endowments and building projects, which enhanced the splendor of the monarchy along with the glory of God. Perhaps the most notable was the Sainte-Chapelle in Paris, designed to house one of Christendom's most sacred relics, the crown of thorns supposedly worn by Jesus.

Louis also embarked on an extensive program to unite France under royal administration. Relations with Henry of England were made more stable, and the disruptive lords who had caused so much trouble in his minority were soon brought under control. In 1247, as an aid to public justice, he sent commissioners, more often than not friars, around his territories to receive and deal with complaints against the bailiffs and provosts who processed provincial administration.

Louis showed a concern for just dealing that few of his contemporaries could demonstrate. His friend and chronicler, Jean de Joinville, described his way of giving audience: "In summer, after hearing mass the king went often to the wood of Vincennes, where he would sit with his back against an oak. . . . Those who had any suit to present could come to speak to him without hindrance from any man." Probity was to emerge as Louis's dominant characteristic.

Unlike many other kings of the period, Louis answered the papal call to liberate the Holy Land. When Blanche heard that her son had taken the cross, she mourned (in the words of Joinville) "as if she had seen him lying dead." He did return alive—although she did not live to see him—but only after suffering disastrous reverses that left an ineradicable mark.

Louis's Crusade, the best-prepared and most-expensive expedition ever mounted to the Middle East, set out in August 1248. His forces landed in Egypt, where they soon captured the delta port of Damietta, but from then on, the expedition found itself

Medieval bestiaries—manuscripts describing animals and their behavior—combined text and pictures to produce so-called pocket zoos that often drew parallels between animal conduct and the correct moral deportment of mankind. Based on an early Greek prototype, the *Physiologus,* such books relied more upon popular mythology than accurate observation, describing real animals alongside such creatures as the unicorn and the phoenix. Hedgehogs *(below)* were presented as models of parenthood, feeding their hungry infants with grapes shaken from vines and then impaled on their prickles. Barnacle geese *(right)* had no apparent moral significance, but according to the tenets of Aristotle, they ripened in an underwater nursery, sprouting like fruit from the arms of the barnacle.

in trouble. Disabled by scurvy and an epidemic of dysentery, much of the army, including the ailing king himself, was captured by the Muslim forces while attempting to retreat from an ill-judged advance inland. Louis's queen, Margaret, left at Damietta in an advanced state of pregnancy, saved the venture from complete disaster by promising large sums of money to the captains of the Italian ships that had brought them, thereby preventing their desertion. A vast ransom secured Louis's freedom, but he had lost many of his men. He spent the next four years fruitlessly engaged in Middle Eastern warfare and diplomacy before finally returning home in 1254, having received news of his mother's death the year before.

Louis had been away for six years all together. He could not forgive himself for his failure to free the holy places and for the loss of Christian lives that the attempt had incurred. For the remainder of his reign, he devoted himself to living out the role of a Christian king, practicing and preaching the ideals of justice and charity and living an increasingly ascetic life.

The king's concern with just government was everywhere apparent. A reforming edict issued in 1254 not only bound the administrators of the royal lands by oath to behave honestly but more practically instituted a machinery of appeal should they fail to do so. At the same time, the hearings of his peripatetic commissioners, or *enquê-teurs,* were put on a regular annual schedule. The 1254 ordinance was proclaimed throughout the realm of France, the first to be so. Louis intended to rule as king of the whole nation. The barons were less than happy, particularly when Louis insisted on

149

making them, too, subject to royal justice. He made persistent efforts to eradicate the practice of judicial duels, by which disputes between nobles were settled by force of arms; in their stead, he encouraged disputants to submit their cases to the Crown.

By now the royal court was the undisputed seat of authority in France. With his officers, Louis devised a variety of means of tapping the riches of the growing towns, whose wealthy professional guilds increasingly stood outside the rigid structures of feudal society. To the traditional royal sources of income—proceeds from the royal domain, now greatly extended, and feudal services in money form—were added subventions cajoled out of the towns, special levies, and the proceeds from judicial processes, including fines and the revenues of confiscated properties. In addition, the Church was subjected to heavy taxation. King Louis's piety was no bar to the exercise of his prerogatives.

Louis's foreign affairs, however, were less successful. Relations with the English king, who had launched two failed expeditions to Poitou in 1230 and 1242, continued to strike a sour note. Not until the Treaty of Paris, made in 1259 between Louis and John's successor, Henry III, was the reality of French domination given formal accord. But even then, the terms pleased neither king's supporters, and the discord between the two sovereign powers continued. Six years later, Louis involved France in the troubled affairs of the Italian peninsula, when he allowed his ambitious brother, Charles of Anjou, to accept a papal offer of the crown of Sicily, contested between supporters of the papacy and the German imperial house of Hohenstaufen.

Louis was by then growing old. In 1270, ill and failing, he set off again on Crusade but got no farther than Tunis before he died. His bones were brought back and buried in the abbey of Saint Denis, to become the object of intense veneration.

Following his death, the French monarchy was left in a state of such spiritual and political dominance that it looked unchallengeable, not only in France but in Europe. Under the two kings whose reigns saw out the century, the movement toward territorial enlargement and centralization of power swept on with a new ruthlessness.

During the fifteen-year tenure of Louis's son Philip III, the royal lands were swelled by important acquisitions, most notably the county of Champagne. Long one of the richest and most independent of the great principalities and geographically central to the consolidation of royal territories, the county was united with the domain by the betrothal of its three-year-old heiress to the king's son and successor. By the time of Philip's death, in 1285, the royal domain far outweighed in size and wealth the remaining duchies of Brittany, Burgundy, Gascony, and the county of Flanders.

The new king, Philip's seventeen-year-old son, Philip IV, continued the trend toward centralization. Under the relentlessly efficient influence of a new breed of university-trained lawyer-politicians who were guided by Roman civil law rather than the clerical tenets of Louis IX's time, a naked determination to extend direct royal control into all corners and all levels of France emerged as the chief preoccupation of the government.

One of the major targets was the power of the papacy in France. King and pope were soon at odds about the right of the monarch to exact levies from the Church without the pope's permission. The argument escalated into a conflict over the fundamental issue of papal authority. Not until 1303 was the issue settled, when Philip took the drastic step of abducting the pope. When a Frenchman was elected pope in 1305, the papacy was transferred to Avignon, just outside French territory.

To combat the papal threat to his sovereignty, Philip and his advisers sought to

In a detail from the statued façade of Rheims Cathedral, a Crusader receives consecrated bread and wine from the hands of a priest. The Crusades, launched in 1095, continued to draw thousands of Christian warriors throughout the thirteenth century. Of the many European notables who took the cross, the most ardent was King Louis IX of France—canonized a mere twenty-seven years after his death—who even built a port at Aigues-Mortes on the Rhone delta from which his Crusading armies could depart. The two Crusades on which he embarked were failures, however: In 1250, Louis was captured in a fruitless assault on Egypt, and in 1270, he died while besieging the North African port of Tunis. By the end of the century, the last Christian territories in Palestine had fallen to the Mamluk rulers of Egypt, and the movement was virtually at an end.

recruit the sympathies of the three estates of the realm: clergy, nobles, and townspeople. Representatives of all three were several times summoned to meetings with the king. The expedient provided an invaluable two-way channel of communication: The king was able to explain his case and to receive in return the endorsement of the people for his policies. The meetings, however, had no legal power to bind the French king; among his own people Philip's sovereignty was untrameled.

Philip's mastery of his remaining feudal vassals was less certain. The two most powerful were the duke of Gascony alias the king of England (by this time Edward I, Henry III's son) and the count of Flanders. In 1297, goaded by Philip's interference in their affairs, the two powers came together in an alliance reminiscent of the Bouvines campaign. Edward and the Flemish count were at first outmaneuvered by Philip. But the Flemings so resented the way the French wielded their resulting control that in 1302 they massacred occupying Frenchmen and collaborators in Bruges. The revolt continued, bringing down on them in vengeance a thundering host of fully caparisoned French knights.

Yet times were changing. When the two forces met at the battle of Courtrai in 1302, the overweening French cavalry, careless in their knightly superiority, foundered on the bristling pikes of ranks of Flemish foot soldiers. Philip was forced to settle with Edward and failed in renewed efforts to subdue Flanders.

The financial costs of Philip's campaigns were crippling. They led him ever further

A Pagan Survival

A popular subject for sculptors working in the new Gothic style during the thirteenth century was the foliate head, or Green Man, whose face, shrouded in leaves, appeared in the stonework and woodwork of churches throughout Europe.

A pagan leftover, probably evolving from Celtic or Roman gods, the Green Man originally presented a demonic countenance to inspire fear in early churchgoers, who associated the natural world with lust and sin. Gothic sculptors transformed the leafy head into a benign image symbolizing renewal and resurrection. The elevation of the Green Man's character enabled sculptors to portray him in central positions within churches and even in association with Christianity's most sacred figures, Christ and the Virgin Mary.

A profusion of carved acanthus leaves forms a foliate head in Bamberg Cathedral in Germany. This Green Man adorns the console of "The Bamberg Horseman," an equestrian statue that dominates the cathedral.

into new exactions, which alienated and alarmed important groups. Mounting provincial resentment greeted the continuing encroachments of his central control. Trouble was brewing that would boil over in the dark century to come.

In the time of Henry III's grandfather, England seemed to have a much more promising future than France—and a much stronger throne. For one thing, England had been conquered in the eleventh century by William, duke of Normandy, who had replaced its Anglo-Saxon landholding nobility with his own Norman vassals. These lords, having received their lands by direct royal grant, were beholden to the monarchy. As a result, the feudal system had a clearer shape than in France.

The situation grew more complicated in the mid-twelfth century, when young Henry Plantagenet, count of Anjou, added the throne of England to his existing French possessions. The task of administering lands that stretched from the Scottish border to the Pyrenees conditioned the nature and development of Angevin rule. Outlying regions, such as Ireland and Brittany or the Welsh and Scottish marches, were left under the control of virtually independent lords. In the Angevin heartlands of England, Normandy, Anjou, Maine, and Touraine, however, the king governed through local officials—in England a justiciar, on the Continent seneschals—who answered directly to him. Written instructions were sent to these local officials, traveling commissioners monitored the workings of the organization, and the king

A Green Man takes a rare aggressive attitude.

Foliage adorns a Poitiers choir stall.

A foliate head in Winchester exudes benign calm.

himself was ceaselessly on the move. With his itinerant court, he migrated from one province to another to review the whole process, try cases, and answer complaints, halting to see the queen through another confinement or even perhaps to gather the scattered family together for a brief Christmas reunion before moving on again.

The administration of England was only one of an Angevin king's preoccupations, albeit an important one. The English vassals now part of this empire resented the expansion of the Angevin administration, the demands for money, the interference in local and personal affairs, but at least the king was not always present to irritate them. Richard, Henry's heir, was in England only about one year in his eleven-year reign, and John, Richard's brother and successor, stayed away for the first four years of his rule, apart from a three-week visit for his coronation in 1199.

These circumstances changed after the loss of the French provinces to Philip II and the defeat at Bouvines in 1214. Deprived of his favorite continental lands, John was now forced to reside more or less permanently in his English realm. Equally, many of the king's vassals who had held lands spread widely through the Angevin territories now found themselves confined to their English possessions.

John never gained the affection of his vassals, although some of his advisers were conspicuously loyal. His enemies pictured him as a villain of cruelty, lechery, avarice, and cowardice, perhaps because his continual conflicts with the Church—he was excommunicated in 1208 and regained favor in 1213 only by making his kingdom a papal fief—alienated the monasteries where the chronicles detailing his crimes were composed. More objective documentary evidence of John's reign shows him to have been at his best an energetic and meticulous administrator. He was an educated man who was always surrounded by books—often historical chronicles—but he had the ungovernable temper typical of the Angevin family. Minor vexations had been known to send his father, Henry II, into tantrums in which he would tear off his clothes and chew the straw covering the floor beneath his feet. John was no more stable, alternating between bouts of energetic decisiveness and an inexplicable, disabling lethargy.

It was not just John's personality, though, that caused problems on his return to England in 1214. Lacking the enormous resources of the Capetians, he had exhausted his exchequer by the export of huge quantities of silver to pay for the French expedition. Many of the lords and barons whom he had summoned to feudal service had failed to campaign and had sent none of the knights they owed. During his absence, the kingdom had been left in the hands of administrators—some of them not English—who were unaccountable to anyone but the monarch.

The result was a sharp increase in friction between the king and the powerful magnates of the land. John resorted to ever-more-savage fiscal measures in order to remain solvent. During his reign, succession dues, payable by a baron on accession to his title, rose from 100 marks to sums that were as high as 10,000 marks. The fines exacted by the king's justices for even the most minor of misdemeanors spiraled upward alarmingly. King John was eminently capable of stooping to outright blackmail to raise funds; a record from his exchequer reveals that one northern baron had to offer the king five first-class palfreys in 1210 "that he would keep quiet about the wife of Henry Pinel," paying in addition a large sum to regain the "goodwill" of the king. John was also prepared to use the nobles' own wives in his questionable dealings; another record reveals that "the wife of Hugh Neville promises the lord king two hundred chickens that she might lie one night with her husband." The monarch's exactions raised a growing discontent that peaked following the defeat at Bouvines.

During the winter that followed John's return from France, he attempted to collect payments in lieu of service from those who had refused to campaign. The barons resisted openly, demanding that the despotic innovations of the Angevin regime be thrown out and that the customs of Anglo-Norman days be restored. John played for time, even going so far as to take Crusading vows, thus putting himself and his property under the protection of the Church. Meanwhile he sent hastily to Aquitaine and Flanders for mercenaries to crush the rebels. Before they could arrive in force, the barons repudiated their oaths of fealty and took up arms. They failed to capture the important town of Northampton, but Bedford opened its gates to them, and they were also able to occupy London, never a stronghold of loyalty to the Angevins. Under pressure from moderate advisers in his court, John asked for a truce.

In June of 1215, the two sides conducted detailed negotiations at the meadow of Runnymede, about twenty miles up the Thames River from London. By the terms of the agreement they finally reached, the barons renewed their loyalty to the king in return for the issue of the document that came to be known as the Magna Carta, the Great Charter. Its sixty-three clauses consisted of specific promises extracted from the king to redress the barons' complaints.

The force of the charter's most important provisions was to assert the supremacy of the rule of law over the arbitrary power of the king. So, in the thirty-ninth clause, the king proclaimed, "No free man shall be taken or imprisoned, or stripped of his rights or possessions, or outlawed or exiled, or in any way ruined, nor will we go or send against him, except by the lawful judgment of his peers or by the law of the land." There was no abstract attempt to define the law; ancient customs such as trial by ordeal or judicial duel were not dead, yet objective inquiries and the taking of evidence were well established, too. What the king's opponents forced him to concede was that he was not entitled to proceed against free men on his own whim.

Another central provision was the stipulation that no extraordinary payments be made to the crown, whether in lieu of military service or for special needs as they arose, except with the consent of "the common counsel of our realm"—an advisory body comprising, in theory, all who held land directly from the king. Many clauses were devoted to making the justice of the royal courts more promptly and effectively available; others limited the numerous devices that the Angevins had developed for transferring money from their subjects' pockets to their own. Certain paragraphs were no more than restatements of time-honored customs that the autocratic Angevins had come to ignore; some simply named hated royal agents and announced that their careers were henceforth at an end. The merchant community of London was rewarded for its support of the barons with guarantees of freedom of movement for goods and an attempt at standardizing currency and weights and measures. Perhaps the most limiting feature of the whole agreement from the royal point of view was that twenty-five of the barons were nominated as a tribunal, to which complaints could be addressed concerning breaches of the charter. As such, it had the power to restrain the king, if necessary by force.

In retrospect, the Magna Carta can be seen as a milestone on the path away from autocracy. In the short term, however, the momentous charter could not prevent England from collapsing into chaos. It was impossible for John's government to cope with the volume of work called for, and some ambitious barons, still hoping to

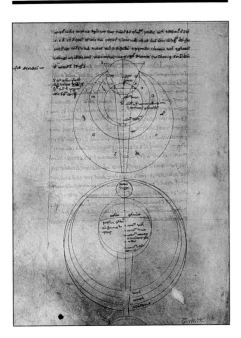

An ardent experimenter, the English scientist Roger Bacon diagramed the refraction of light entering the human eye. Realizing the potential of artificial lenses, Bacon noted that convex lenses could be helpful for reading, a suggestion that heralded Europe's first use of spectacles. He even theorized that huge refractive mirrors might be built so nations could spy on their enemies. A mathematician, alchemist, and practitioner of the occult, Bacon was born around 1214 and lived at a time when the works of Aristotle and other Greek philosophers were being rediscovered in the West.

overthrow John, actively sought to renew the conflict. Despite the assistance of Prince Louis's invading French troops, who temporarily occupied London, the barons failed to make much headway. John had had time to put an effective mercenary force in the field, and the French invasion bogged down.

But John was by now ill with dysentery and weakening fast. Disaster struck on October 12, 1216. Returning with his army from breaking a rebel siege at Lincoln, John became separated from his baggage train in the fenlands of Cambridgeshire, near the coast of the great bay called the Wash. Attempting a shortcut across the tidal estuary of the Wellstream River, the packhorses and their drivers came to grief. In the words of a contemporary chronicler, "Many members of his household were submerged in the waters of the sea and sucked into the quicksand there, because they had set out incautiously and hastily before the tide had receded." In the accident, John lost a great deal of his harshly exacted wealth, as well as many of his household effects. He did not long survive the disaster. Within just one week's time, in the castle of Newark, he was dead.

His nine-year-old son was speedily crowned king as Henry III; a decisive victory over the invaders and their allies in May of 1217, followed by the destruction of a fleet of reinforcements in August, sent Louis back to France with a face-saving truce; and the Magna Carta was reissued (though without the committee of twenty-five barons) to confirm that the gains of the civil war were not to be reversed. The party of the rebels melted away.

During Henry's minority, a degree of order returned to England under the regency of William Marshall. After the regent's death in 1219, the young king began increasingly to assume power. England was still under the theoretical protection of the pope, however, and it was 1223 before the king got papal approval to rule the country "principally by the counsel of his own servants." That Henry derived his authority from the pope rather than his people was greeted with suspicion by the great lords; they also mistrusted their exclusion from the king's confidence by an inner circle of royal advisers—skilled, ambitious men who were often not even English, although they might be rewarded with English lands and titles. In 1225, a further reissue of the Great Charter in return for a general grant of money reassured the barons; nevertheless, the gulf between king and magnates continued to widen.

At twenty, with the approval of the pope, Henry came of age. For almost all his long reign—he died in 1272—he faced his near-contemporary Louis IX across the Channel, and the rivalry he felt for the French king was a lasting theme of Henry's life. He did not profit by the comparison, for Louis easily outdid him in piety and prestige as well as political achievements. Yet he was a generous and perceptive patron of the arts, and although Henry's reign saw a renewed episode of civil war, he left the kingdom at his death more united and prosperous than it had been at his accession.

Nonetheless, as a young king, he was soon alienating the barons by his high-handed actions. He dispensed with his moderate and trustworthy justiciar, Hubert de Burgh, and deprived that office of its former power; new appointees carried out a thorough reform of the administration, both local and central. The chief organ of government became the king's council, a restricted group whose members took a formal oath of office. It included both magnates and ministers, but it was the full-time administrators who held the greatest influence, thanks to their professional expertise and their closeness to the king.

Henry also infuriated his subjects by his apparent love of foreigners. In 1236, he

Figures of an apostle and a saint, adorning the sumptuous ecclesiastical cloak known as the Syon Cope, exemplify the style of embroidery known as *opus Anglicanum*, or "English work." Richly decorated with gold and silver thread and studded with precious stones, such garments were prized by popes and emperors and were considered sufficiently valuable to be accepted as security for loans. Merchants made special arrangements for their export, concealing them within bundles of ordinary cloth before risking them upon the pirate-infested seas of Europe.

married Eleanor of Provence, a sister of the French queen, who brought a number of her relatives with her from Savoy to England. Two years later, the king's own sister, also called Eleanor, took a French husband, Simon de Montfort. Increasingly, the English barons were pushed to one side as Henry appointed his new French relatives to earldoms and bishoprics.

To the barons it appeared as if all the gains of 1215 were being rapidly eroded. The king was becoming more and more autocratic, and the foreign administrators who had been a hated hallmark of John's reign seemed once more to be getting the upper hand. Moreover, Henry appeared to be uncomfortably dominated by the pope. He was reported to have said, "I neither wish nor dare to oppose the lord pope in anything." By 1238, Henry's unpopularity had reached such heights that to safeguard against assassins, he thought it prudent to have bars fitted not only to the windows of all his chambers but to the outflow of the royal lavatory at Westminster.

The nationalistic emotions that Henry aroused among his barons were not assuaged by his attempts to regain the Angevin territories in France. In 1242, Henry became involved in a campaign in Poitou on the instigation of his mother, who had married a French lord with claims to the province. It ended disastrously, leading ultimately to the Treaty of Paris in 1259, with Henry paying homage to his brother-in-law Louis for Gascony and formally renouncing all claim to the remaining Angevin lands.

The barons were strongly opposed to Henry's French adventures and to other extravagant foreign undertakings in which he dabbled—especially his acceptance of Pope Innocent IV's offer of the crown of Sicily for his son Edmund (prior to its acceptance by Charles of Anjou). This ill-judged project involved Henry in an expensive and embarrassing failure that further increased the barons' resentment of the pope's political influence over the king. Henry had similarly disturbed the English bishops by his willingness to allow the pope to bestow offices and raise money from the Church in England without deference to their wishes. When one papal legate arrived in 1245 to impose levies on the clergy, the English magnates told him that he would be torn to pieces if he did not depart.

In 1258, a crisis arose. Resentful at the growing number of foreigners at the court, dissatisfied with the way the country was being governed, and stung by their lack of influence with the monarch, the magnates refused to grant Henry the money he desperately needed to finance his rash enterprises abroad. Specifically, they took exception to a demand for a tax to subsidize Henry's Sicilian ambitions and to the activities of Henry's fortune-seeking half-brothers, who had arrived from Poitou in 1247. Exerting pressure that stopped just short of armed coercion, the barons made the king promise to obey their advice in all matters, placing him under the direction of fifteen baronial councilors. They went on to make detailed and significant proposals for reform. Regular meetings of the council of magnates, now coming to be known as parliaments, were to be held three times a year for baronial representatives to discuss the affairs of the realm. The chief officials of the kingdom were to be responsible to the council. At a local level, knights were to hear complaints and present them to a justiciar appointed by the barons. Knights representing the shire communities—where the lesser gentry had long played a part in local administration—

Vignettes of a Prosperous Era

In England and France, the thirteenth century was a time of burgeoning populations and widening horizons. Forests were felled and marshlands drained to provide new land for cultivation. Relative political stability encouraged the spread of agricultural technology: Windmills, introduced into Europe during the twelfth century, now became widespread, and increased use was made of such fertilizers as the mineral-rich sediment marl.

Towns expanded, fed by agricultural surpluses and enriched by profits from fairs and markets. Many larger cities purchased charters for self-government, thus freeing themselves from exploitation by feudal overlords or the Church.

This prosperous world, embellished with the glories of Gothic architecture and enriched by a growing number of schools and universities, is reflected in the pages of the Luttrell Psalter. Vignettes of English life crowd the margins of this book of psalms produced for an English noble in the early fourteenth century.

were summoned to some parliaments. A regular forum was developing for consultation on the affairs of the realm, and the practice of selecting representatives of large groups was gaining currency.

But Henry's resentment at the controls imposed on him led inevitably to renewed conflict. After skirting civil war for several years, in 1263 the barons and the king agreed to refer their dispute to independent arbitration. Their choice of mediator was Louis IX of France, whose reputation for moral rectitude had become such that even his old rivals accorded him their grudging admiration. Louis's own belief in royal sovereignty brought him down against the barons, and his judgment released Henry from all the restrictions they had laid on him. The barons—now led by Simon de Montfort, a man of stature whose idealism had separated him from the self-interest and incompetence of the king—could not accept the negation of their achievement, and there was no escape from war.

Initially the barons were successful, capturing the king in battle at Lewes in 1264. But the provisional government set up by Montfort in the king's name lacked popular support, and the next year, further hostilities resulted in a final defeat for the king's opponents at Evesham, where Montfort was slain and brutally mutilated.

Among the heroes of the day at Evesham was Henry's son and heir, Edward. Unlike his father, Edward was a courageous and effective military leader who loved war and tournaments and cherished the traditions of chivalry. Tall and curly-haired, the young prince's imposing presence was marred only by a slight lisp and a drooping left eyelid. A true Angevin, Edward had a volatile temper—on one occasion he chased a hunting companion with drawn sword for failing to control a falcon properly—but this flaw was tempered by a deep sense of piety and a keen intelligence, which he honed with games of chess.

After the victory at Evesham, Edward emerged as an influential force in the governing of the land, and he duly ascended the throne as King Edward I on his father's death in 1272. Despite the defeat of the reformers, in the intervening years he had shown an awareness of the need for change, and throughout his reign he continued and extended the practice of summoning parliaments. As the highest court in the land, Parliament became the arena in which Edward enacted a great series of statutes aimed at providing remedies for specific grievances, from measures for preventing subinfeudation—a process by which lands were split up through inheritance into ever-smaller circles of feudal obligation—to provisions for the care of the roads.

Sheltered from the elements and from prying eyes, the ladies of a royal court travel in a carriage large enough to accommodate many servants and lap dogs.

Each parliament was summoned for a range of purposes: to hear petitions and judicial appeals, to grant taxes, and to assent to acts of the king. Magnates and bishops were individually summoned; knights of the shire and burgesses from the boroughs were sometimes called to act as representatives of their communities; and later in the century, members of the lesser clergy were also given a voice.

Edward's reign saw many investigations into the way the country was governed. The first of these, initiated in 1274, sent out royal commissioners to establish who was wielding what powers throughout the realm. Though designed to determine whether the rights of the crown were being usurped, the investigation produced numerous examples of the abuse of power; a prior of Spalding in Lincolnshire, for instance, was discovered to have detained a man unjustifiably and in such bad conditions that his feet had rotted away. The scandals were subsequently dealt with by parliamentary legislation. More important still were the quo warranto inquiries, initiated in 1278, which established the principle that all jurisdictional rights were delegated by the Crown. As in France, regional authority was being transmuted into that of the realm.

The main task for which the borough and shire representatives were required was to grant the king money for wars that could no longer be waged solely with the resources provided by traditional feudal obligations of military service. Succeeding English kings had tried to extend their dominion into the unassimilated corners of the British Isles, but both Wales and Scotland had resisted effective intrusion into their Celtic hinterlands—though at the price of formally acknowledging the overlordship of the English king. The Welsh chieftains in particular had taken advantage of the chaos during the later years of Henry III's reign to renounce their allegiance and had risen in revolt. Their leader was Llywelyn ap Gruffudd, recognized by a treaty with the English in 1267 as prince of Wales, the first time such a title had been used. When Llywelyn refused homage to Edward, the scene was set for a showdown that was to prove disastrous to the Welsh cause.

Edward launched a crushingly effective invasion in 1277 that deprived Llywelyn of all but a portion of his lands. Leniently treated after his first defeat, the prince revolted again in 1282 in resentment at the spread of English influence in the principality. This time Edward determined to show no mercy, revealing a newly aggressive and expansionist side to the power of the English state. By 1284, he had destroyed forever the ability of the Welsh to resist and had built a chain of new towns and castles to integrate the land into the English administration.

Servants prepare a banquet for their masters, whose rich diet was often enhanced by the addition of Oriental spices.

His army reinforced by large bodies of Welsh archers, Edward next looked to Scotland, which, traditionally linked with France, was a potentially dangerous neighbor. For most of the thirteenth century, English interference had been negligible; successive Scottish kings, married to English princesses, were considered allies. But the death of Alexander III in 1286, followed by that of his only heiress, a little girl of six, left the way open for Edward to make a move. Between 1296 and 1306, he sent eight armies of invasion to Scotland; the harshness of the English commanders left in charge led to grim and savage revolts. The final uprising, in 1306, under the able Scottish baron Robert Bruce, was Edward's undoing. Sixty-seven and already terminally ill, the king dragged himself northward to deal with it. He died on the way in July 1307, and his son and successor, Edward II, lacked the character to combat Bruce's resourceful leadership. His faltering efforts were disastrously repulsed at the Battle of Bannockburn in 1314, leaving Bruce to dominate England's northern boundary as king of a still-independent Scotland.

The repeated and sustained campaigns required to subdue Celtic resistance to the king's territorial ambitions, as well as excursions into France to protect Edward's rights in Gascony, damaged the generally harmonious relationship between the king and his subjects. Such wars could no longer be represented to feudal vassals as shared necessities requiring their loyal support, nor could they be concluded within the forty days of service that feudal custom sanctioned. Payment for military service was unavoidable, whether it was given to barons and knights to keep them in the field after their customary service had expired or to foreign mercenaries. The need to raise revenues for such purposes led to a confrontation in the year 1297, when Edward was forced to mollify an angry nation by reissuing the Magna Carta once again, this time with the additional provision that no taxes over and above the traditional feudal levies would be raised without the "common assent of all the realm and for the common profit thereof." The king later reneged on the agreement, winning a papal dispensation to cancel his promise, but a precedent nonetheless had been set for future generations to pursue.

The century during which the monarchies of England and France thus began to move into a postfeudal world was one of continuing economic vigor and expansion. The population was growing, marginal land was being brought into cultivation to support the extra mouths, and bigger agricultural surpluses encouraged the development of urban centers. New towns came into being, and existing ones burgeoned into cities.

A group of English villagers take turns at archery practice.

Money now circulated in ever-increasing quantities, with far-reaching effects on every aspect of daily life.

In the century to come, the growing population of Europe would contribute to food shortages, urban unrest, and declining living standards, but for the moment, it was against a background of relative prosperity that France and England led the way in the development of national spirit.

The implications of the national monarchy were many and various. Each country sought to assert its rights over the Church within its boundaries, occasioning conflicts with the papacy. The scale of government activity increased on both sides of the Channel; there were more officials at work and there were also increased attempts—in France via the enquêteurs, in England through Edward's administrative investigations—to keep a check on their activities. The study of Roman law, which emphasized civic responsibility and the good of the state, was spreading in both lands, and its concepts slowly started to oust older feudal views of personal obligation.

Both nations managed to consolidate the lands they controlled into more practical geographical entities. Indeed, Henry's failure to regain England's French territories ultimately produced a more manageable and coherent realm. The English conquest of Wales and the French annexation of the Languedoc helped to create states approximating more closely the nations that now bear the names of France and England than the oddly shaped feudal conglomerates of the year 1200. Gascony, however, remained in the hands of the English king. Its retention was to prove a running sore in relations between the two lands; in the course of the next century, it would plunge them into the horrors of the Hundred Years' War.

Despite many similarities, there were also significant differences between the two emergent nations, most notably the nature of their rulers. In France, an autocratic monarch ruled through a large body of royal administrators, his actions little hindered by the need to consult with local assemblies. In England, the king was held in check by his own subjects, and a tradition of opposition, growing out of the Magna Carta, resurfaced regularly throughout the century in the demand for a more general consultation. By the year 1300, the seeds of future constitutional development in the two lands had been sown and were already beginning to germinate.

Soldiers brave the waves in a turreted warship that resembles a seaborne fortress.

The thirteenth century was a great age for castle building in Europe, especially in contested lands, where the strongholds—and the soldiers they housed—could be used to impose a ruler's will on recalcitrant subjects for many miles around. This strategy of conquest was never more thoroughly employed than in the subjugation of Wales by King Edward I of England.

Long after Norman invaders had asserted their dominance over southern Wales in the eleventh and twelfth centuries, the northern lords of Gwynedd remained defiantly independent, isolated from their English neighbors by language, culture, and the formidable mountain barrier of Snowdonia. Unable to subdue them by military means, King Henry III of England recognized the most powerful, Llywelyn ap Gruffudd, as prince of Wales in return for an oath of fealty to the English crown. But Llywelyn consistently refused to pay homage, and Henry's successor, Edward, determined to crush his unruly vassal and impose his supremacy over all of Wales.

In 1277, Edward mounted a great campaign of conquest, cutting through Llywelyn's territory to seize the island of Anglesey in the northwest, whose vital grainfields had enabled the rebels to sit out previous sieges in their mountain fastness. A truce was called, but in 1282 rebellion again erupted, resulting in a crushing defeat for Llywelyn, who was slain; with him died the hope of Welsh independence.

The previously independent parts of Wales were reduced to the status of a colony, governed from London. English law was introduced, English taxes were levied, and Welsh troops were recruited into English armies. A rebellion in 1294 failed, and seven years later Edward sealed his conquest by making his own son and heir prince of Wales.

By 1300, Edward had secured the wild hinterland of Snowdonia with a ring of great castles on or near the coast, shown on the map opposite: Hope, Flint, Rhuddlan, Conwy, Criccieth, Harlech, Beaumaris, Caernarvon, and Aberystwyth to the south. Beneath the walls of each, he created new towns in which English immigrants were encouraged to settle by grants of land and other privileges. Edward already had experience in creating fortified towns in Gascony, and the castle-town complexes he erected in Wales were imposing statements of military, economic, and social domination. Linked to the castles by strong walls, the towns provided secure havens from which their inhabitants were able to trade in deliberately favored competition with the indigenous peoples.

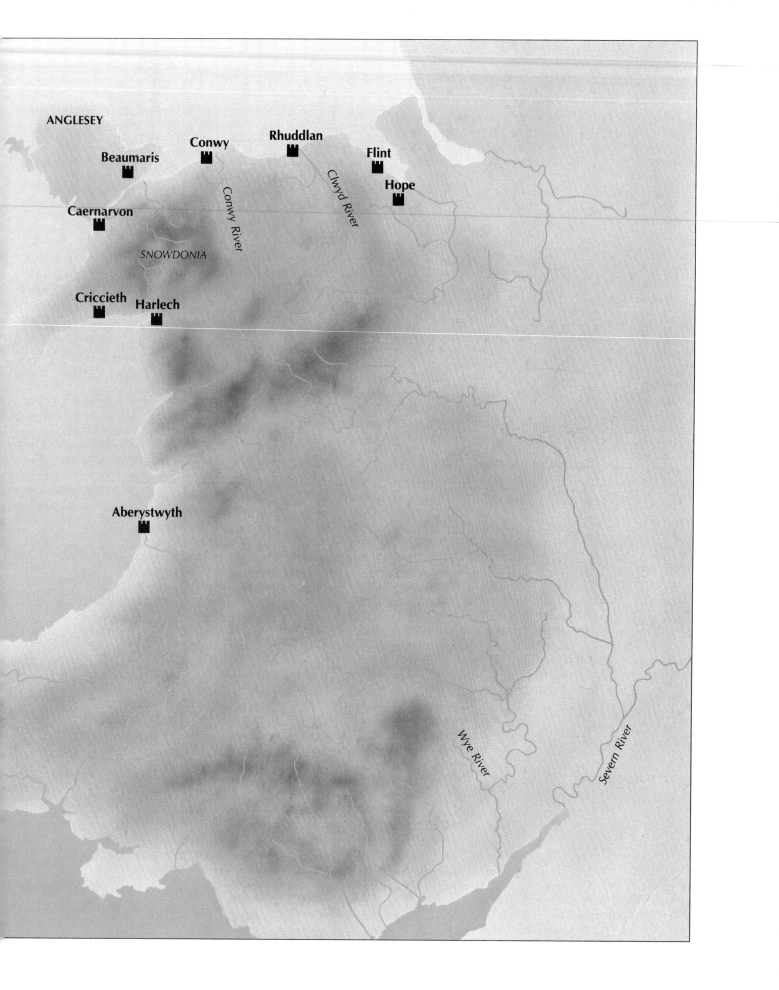

ANGLESEY

Beaumaris

Conwy

Rhuddlan

Flint

Hope

Caernarvon

Conwy River

Clwyd River

SNOWDONIA

Criccieth

Harlech

Aberystwyth

Wye River

Severn River

CAERNARVON: OUTPOST OF THE ENGLISH

Massively fortified and strategically situated on the Menai Strait, Caernarvon was the mightiest link in Edward's chain of castles, designed to resist any attack. Its sandstone-banded walls and multiangular towers were modeled on those of Constantinople, built in the fifth century and still reputed to be the world's strongest fortifications.

At its base, the town was also protected by a sturdy wall, almost half a mile long, behind which lay a grid of cobbled streets dividing the land into regular plots measuring sixty by eighty feet. These so-called burgages were granted to English settlers, who were encouraged to construct houses, to cultivate the surrounding countryside, and to rent stalls in the newly built market and around the harbor. The town had its own civic buildings and law court, under whose partisan jurisdiction the trade of immigrant leatherworkers, tanners, and wool merchants flourished.

STRUCTURES DESIGNED FOR DEFENSE

Using the latest military designs, Edward's Savoyard architect, James of St. George, linked Caernarvon's seven towers and two gates with a system of galleried curtain walls, giving defenders great freedom of movement. Arrow slits commanded every approach, some allowing a single archer to shoot in many directions, others focusing the aim of several bowmen on a single target. All entrances were heavily protected; the King's Gate was equipped with a drawbridge, five sets of massive doors, six portcullises (vertically sliding fortified gratings), arrow slits in the walls, and so-called murder holes in the ceiling through which projectiles could be hurled.

Caernarvon was more than just a defensive structure, however. As the seat of royal government in North Wales and the site of the exchequer and judiciary, it held offices, capacious living quarters, and six chapels.

Queen's Tower

A view of the castle's western bailey as it was in 1300 shows the Queen's Tower and the triple-turreted Eagle Tower, the highest in the castle. A cutaway of the wall—against which the Great Hall would later be built—reveals two tiers of passages from which archers could fire at the enemy.

Eagle Tower

A first-floor cross section of the Eagle Tower reveals both the bastion's main chamber and the complicated construction of its fifteen-foot-thick walls, honeycombed with small chambers and passages. The stairs serving the tower were accommodated within the walls; so was a private chapel.

1200-1210	1210-1220	1220-1230	1230-1240	1240-1250

WESTERN EUROPE

1200-1210	1210-1220	1220-1230	1230-1240	1240-1250
King John of England loses Château Gaillard to the French (1204); within a year, the French take all English territory on mainland France north of the Loire River. Pope Innocent III calls the Albigensian Crusade against the Cathars of Languedoc in southern France (1208).	At Bouvines, Philip II of France decisively defeats a coalition of his enemies brought together by King John of England (1214). English barons force King John to sign a charter of rights, the Magna Carta (1215).	Frederick II is crowned Holy Roman Emperor (1220). Louis IX ascends the throne of France (1226).	Frederick II defeats the Lombard League—a coalition of northern Italian cities—at Cortenuova (1237).	Pope Innocent IV formally [de]poses Frederick II as Holy [Ro]man Emperor (1245).

THE BALTIC

1200-1210	1210-1220	1220-1230	1230-1240	1240-1250
Bishop Albert of Riga establishes the military order of the Sword Brothers (1202). Bishop Albert's forces subdue the Livs and the Letts and march on Estonia (1209).	Christian forces destroy the Estonian stronghold of Fellin (1211).	The Sword Brothers, reinforced by Danish forces, finally conquer Estonia (1224). The pope places Finland under apostolic protection and invokes a trade embargo against Novgorod (1229).	A military religious order, the Teutonic Knights, arrives to subjugate the pagan Prussians (1230). The Sword Brothers are all but annihilated by the Lithuanians at Saule (1236). The Teutonic Order absorbs the territory of the Sword Brothers (1237).	Alexander Nevsky of Novg[orod] defeats the Swedes on the [banks] of the Neva (1240). The Mongols defeat a Chri[stian] army at Liegnitz in Poland[, then] proceed to invade Hungar[y but] withdraw on the death of [the] great khan (1241). Alexander Nevsky defeats [the] Teutonic Order on Lake Pe[ipus] (1242).

CENTRAL ASIA AND THE FAR EAST

1200-1210	1210-1220	1220-1230	1230-1240	1240-1250
The Hojo clan gains control of the military government, effectively ruling Japan from Kamakura (1203). Temujin unites Mongolia and takes the title Genghis Khan (1206). The Mongols invade northern China (1207).	The Mongols take the Jin capital of Zhongdu (1215). Power in Japan passes from the shoguns, or military leaders, to their regents (1219).	In the Jokyu War, the Kamakura military government defeats an uprising of the imperial forces based in Kyoto, who resent Kamakura control (1221). Genghis Khan dies on a campaign against the Tanguts (1227) and is succeeded by his son Ogedei (1229).	The military rulers of Japan draw up the Joei Formulary, a new legal code (1232). The Mongols extinguish the Jin Kingdom in North China (1234).	

AFRICA AND THE MIDDLE EAST

1200-1210	1210-1220	1220-1230	1230-1240	1240-1250
		The Mongols overwhelm the Iranian empire of Khwarizm (1221). Frederick II gains Jerusalem by diplomacy in the Sixth Crusade (1229).		The Mongols defeat the Sel[juks] of Rum (1242). On the Seventh Crusade, L[ouis] IX of France takes Damiett[a in] Egypt but is later captured (1249).

TimeFrame AD 1200-1300

k II dies (1250).

rovisions of Oxford,
l of England agrees to
plishment of a baronial
with the power of veto
actions (1258).

Prince Edward defeats rebellious
English barons at Evesham
(1265).

The Sicilian Vespers rebellion
ousts Charles of Anjou and gives
Peter III of Aragon the crown of
Sicily (1282).

Edward I invades Scotland
(1296).

ty of Paris gives formal
o Louis's domination of
France (1259).

Charles of Anjou takes the
throne of Sicily (1268).

Edward I ascends the throne of
England and initiates a series of
administrative reforms (1272).

Edward I of England completes
the conquest of Wales (1284).

Louis IX of France is canonized
(1297).

The Samogitians defeat the Teutonic Knights at Durben, spark-
ing a native uprising against
their Christian rulers in the
southern Baltic (1260).

The southern Baltic tribes are
finally subjugated by the Teutonic Order (1290).

The Swedes establish the strate-
gic fort of Viborg in the region
of Karelia, disputed with the
Russians (1292).

In China, Kublai Khan declares
himself first emperor of the
Yuan dynasty (1271).

The first Mongol invasion of Japan ends in the withdrawal of
the attacking forces (1274).

ngols campaign against
g of southern China

Genghis's grandson Kublai defeats his brother to become
great khan (1264).

The Mongols complete the conquest of Song China (1279).

A second Mongol invasion of
Japan fails because of a typhoon
that became known as the *kamikaze*, or "divine wind" (1281).

Kublai Khan dies (1294).

mluks seize power in
om the Ayyubids (1250).

Following the death of Mongke
Khan, Mamluk forces defeat the
Mongols at Ayn Jalut (1260).

Louis IX dies at Tunis in the
course of the Eighth (and final)
Crusade (1270).

ngols capture Alamut
eat the Assassins (1257).

The Mamluk sultan Baybars re-
establishes the caliphate in
Cairo (1261).

The Mamluks defeat the
Mongols in Asia Minor and temporarily occupy Caesarea
(1277).

ngols sack Baghdad and
the Abbasid caliphate

The Mamluks take Antioch from
the Crusaders (1268).

The Mamluk sultan Qalawun
comes to power (1279).

Qalawun defeats the Mongols at
Homs (1281).

The Mamluks take Acre, the last
Crusader outpost in Palestine
(1291).

BIBLIOGRAPHY

THE BALTIC

Brundage, James A., transl., *The Chronicle of Henry of Livonia*. Madison, Wisconsin: University of Wisconsin Press, 1961.

Christiansen, Eric, *The Northern Crusades: The Baltic and the Catholic Frontier, 1100-1525*. London: Macmillan, 1980.

Evans, Geoffrey, *Tannenberg, 1410-1914*. London: Hamish Hamilton, 1970.

Michell, Robert, and Nevill Forbes, transls., *The Chronicle of Novgorod, 1016-1471*. London: Camden Society, 1914.

Probst, Christian, *Der Deutsche Orden und Seine Medizinalwesen in Preussen*. Bad Godesberg: Verlag Wissenschaftliches Archiv, 1969.

Riley-Smith, Jonathan, *The Crusades: A Short History*. London: Athlone Press, 1987.

Setton, Kenneth M., ed., *The Fourteenth and Fifteenth Centuries*. Vol. 2 of *A History of the Crusades*. Madison, Wisconsin: University of Wisconsin Press, 1975.

Seward, Desmond, *The Monks of War: The Military Religious Orders*. London: Eyre Methuen, 1972.

Steinbrecht, Konrad, *Schloss Lochstedt und Seine Malereien: Ein Denkmal aus des Deutschen Ritterordens Blütezeit*. Berlin: Königliche Technische Hochschule zu Berlin, 1910.

Urban, William, *The Baltic Crusade*. De Kalb, Illinois: Northern Illinois University Press, 1975.

Vernadsky, George, *Kievan Russia*. New Haven, Connecticut: Yale University Press, 1959.

Zamoyski, Adam, *The Polish Way*. London: John Murray, 1987.

WESTERN EUROPE

Anderson, William:
Castles of Europe. London: Paul Elek Productions, 1970.
The Rise of the Gothic. London: Hutchinson, 1985.

Barlow, Frank, *The Feudal Kingdom of England, 1042-1216*. Harlow, England: Longman, 1972.

Barraclough, G., *The Origins of Modern Germany*. Oxford, England: Blackwell, 1946.

Branner, Robert, *Manuscript Painting in Paris during the Reign of Saint Louis*. Berkeley, California: University of California Press, 1977.

Brunskill, R. W., *Illustrated Handbook of Vernacular Architecture*. London: Faber and Faber, 1971.

De Hamel, Christopher, *A History of Illuminated Manuscripts*. Oxford, England: Phaidon, 1986.

Duby, G., *Le Dimanche de Bouvines*. Paris: Gallimard, 1973.

Götze, Heinz, *Castel del Monte*. Munich: Prestel-Verlag, 1984.

Hallam, Elizabeth, *Capetian France, 987-1328*. Harlow, England: Longman, 1980.

Hampe, K., *Germany under the Salian and Hohenstaufen Emperors*. Oxford, England: Blackwell, 1973.

Harvey, John, *The Master Builders: Architecture in the Middle Ages*. London: Thames & Hudson, 1971.

Jackson, Donald, *The Story of Writing*. London: Barrie & Jenkins, 1981.

Kantorowicz, E., *Frederick the Second*. New York: R. R. Smith, 1931.

Lassus, M. J. B. A., *Facsimile of the Sketch-Book of Wilars de Honecort*. London: John Henry and James Parker, 1859.

Leuschner, J., *Germany in the Later Middle Ages*. Amsterdam: North-Holland, 1980.

Lobel, M. D., ed., *Historic Towns*. Vol. 1. London: Lovell Johns, 1969.

MacDermott, M., *Military Architecture*. Transl. from the French of E. Viollet-Le-Duc. Oxford, England: James Parker, 1879.

Masson, Georgina, *Frederick II of Hohenstaufen: A Life*. London: Secker & Warburg, 1957.

Morris, J., *The Matter of Wales*. Oxford, England: Oxford University Press, 1984.

Norgate, Kate, *England under the Angevin Kings*. London: Macmillan, 1887.

Previt-Orton, C. W., *The Shorter Cambridge Medieval History*. Cambridge, England: Cambridge University Press, 1952.

Robb, David M., *The Art of the Illuminated Manuscript*. London: Thomas Yoseloff, 1973.

Roderick, A., ed., *Wales: A History*. London: Michael Joseph, 1986.

Royal Commission on Ancient and Historic Monuments in Wales and Monmouthshire, *Central Caernarvonshire*. Vol. 2 of *Caernarvonshire*. London: Her Majesty's Stationery Office, 1960.

Simpson, W. D.:
Castles in England and Wales. London: Batsford, 1969.
Exploring Castles. London: Routledge and Kegan Paul, 1957.

Swaan, Wim, *The Gothic Cathedral*. London: Paul Elek Productions, 1969.

Toy, S., *Castles of Great Britain*. London: Heinemann, 1953.

Van Cleve, T. C., *The Emperor Frederick II of Hohenstaufen*. Oxford, England: Clarendon Press, 1972.

Vaughan-Thomas, W., *Wales through the Ages*. Llandybie, Wales: Christopher Davies, 1959.

Warner, Philip, *Sieges of the Middle Ages*. London: G. Bell and Sons, 1968.

Warren, W. L., *King John*. London: Eyre Methuen, 1978.

Wilkinson, B., *The Later Middle Ages in England*. Harlow, England: Longman, 1969.

Wood, Casey, and Marjorie Fyfe, transls., *The Art of Falconry*. Boston: Charles T. Branford, 1955.

CENTRAL ASIA AND THE FAR EAST

Bloom, Alfred, *Shinrans's Gospel of Pure Grace*. Tucson, Arizona: University of Arizona Press, 1965.

Brent, Peter, *The Mongol Empire*. London: Weidenfeld and Nicolson, 1976.

Cameron, Nigel, and Brian Brake, *Peking: A Tale of Three Cities*. New York: Harper and Row, 1965.

Chambers, James, *The Devil's Horsemen*. London: Weidenfeld and Nicolson, 1979.

Dumoulin, Heinrich, S. J., *A History of Zen Buddhism*. New York: Pantheon Books, 1963.

Duus, Peter, *Feudalism in Japan*. New York: Alfred A. Knopf, 1969.

Encyclopedia of Japan. Tokyo: Kodansha, 1983.

Frederic, L., *Daily Life in Japan at the Time of the Samurai*. Transl. by Eileen M. Lane. London: Allen & Unwin, 1972.

Gabriel, Ronay, *The Tartar Khan's Englishman*. London: Cassel, 1978.

Gascoigne, Bamber, and Christina Gascoigne, *The Treasures and Dynasties of China*. London: Jonathan Cape, 1973.

Gibson, Michael, *Genghis Khan and the Mongols*. London: Wayland, 1973.

Hall, J. W., and J. P. Mass, eds., *Medieval Japan: Essays in Institutional History*. New Haven, Connecticut: Yale University Press, 1974.

Humble, Richard, *Marco Polo*. London: Weidenfeld and Nicolson, 1975.

Hurst, G. C., *Insei: Abdicated Sovereigns in the Politics of Late Heian Japan, 1086-1185*. New York: Columbia University Press, 1976.

Ipsiroglu, M. S., *Painting and Culture of the Mongols*. Transl. by E. D. Phillips. London: Thames & Hudson, 1967.

Ishii, Ryosuke, *A History of Political Institutions in Japan*. Tokyo: University of Tokyo Press, 1980.

Jien, *The Future and the Past*. Berkeley, California: University of California Press, 1979.

Kidder, J. Edward, Jr., *The Art of Japan*. Tokyo: Shogakukan, 1981.

Kitagawa, H., and B. Tsuchida, transls., *The Tale of the Heike*. Tokyo: Tokyo University Press, 1975.

Kitagawa, Joseph M., *Religion in Japanese History*. New York: Columbia University Press, 1966.

Kyotaro, Nishikawa, and Emily J. Sano, *The Great Age of Japanese Buddhist Sculpture, AD 600-1300*. Fort Worth, Texas: Kimbell Art Museum / Japan Society, 1982.

Latham, Ronald, transl., *Marco Polo: The Travels*. London: Penguin, 1958.

Lewis, Suzanne, *The Art of Matthew Paris in the Chronica Majora*. Cambridge, England: Scolar Press, 1987.

Lu, David John, *Sources of Japanese History*. Vol. 1. New York: McGraw-Hill, 1974.

Mass, J. P., *Warrior Government in Early Medieval Japan*. New Haven, Connecticut: Yale University Press, 1974.

Mass, J. P., ed., *Court and Bakufu in Japan*. New Haven, Connecticut: Yale University Press, 1982.

Mills, Douglas E., transl., *A Collection of Tales from Uji: A Study and Translation of Uji Shui Monogatari*. Cambridge, England: Cambridge University Press, 1970.

Miner, Earl, *An Introduction to Japanese Court Poetry*. Stanford, California: Stanford University Press, 1968.

Mori, Hisashi, *Sculpture of the Kamakura Period*. Tokyo: Weatherhill / Heibonsha, 1964.

Okudaira, Hideo, *Narrative Picture Scrolls*. New York: Weatherhill, 1973.

Peking (The Great Cities series). Amsterdam: Time-Life Books, 1978.

Phillips, E. D., *The Mongols*. London: Thames & Hudson, 1969.

Rockhill, William Woodville, ed., *The Journey of William of Rubruck to the Eastern Parts of the World, 1253-55*. London: Hakluyt Society, 1900.

Sadaie, Fujiwara no, *The Little Treasury of One Hundred People, One Poem Each*. Transl. by Tom Galt. Princeton, New Jersey: Princeton University Press, 1982.

Sadler, A. L., transl., *The Ten Foot Square Hut and Tales of the Heike*. Sydney: Angus and Robertson, 1928.

Sansom, G.:
A History of Japan to 1334. Stanford, California: Stanford University Press, 1958.
A Short Cultural History. London: Cresset Press, 1946.

Saray-Alben, *Diez'sche Klebebände aus den Berliner Sammlungen*. Wiesbaden: Franz Steiner Verlag, 1964.

Sato, Kanzan, *The Japanese Sword*. Tokyo: Kodansha International and Shibundo, 1983.

Saunders, J. J., *The History of the Mongol Conquests*. London: Routledge and Kegan Paul, 1971.

Shinoda, Minoru, *The Founding of the Kamakura Shogunate*. New York: Columbia University Press, 1960.

Smith, Bradley, and Wan-go Weng, *China: A History in Art*. London: Studio Vista, 1973.

Suann, Peter C., *An Introduction to the Arts of Japan*. Oxford, England: Bruno Cassirer, 1958.

Totman, Conrad, *Japan before Perry: A Short History*. Berkeley, California: University of California Press, 1981.

The Travels of Marco Polo. London: Sidgwick and Jackson, 1984.

Turnbull, Stephen:
The Book of the Samurai. London: Arms & Armour Press, 1982.
The Samurai: A Military History. London: George Philip, 1988.
Samurai Warriors. London: Blandford Press, 1987.

Yule, Sir Henry, *The Book of Ser Marco Polo the Venetian Concerning the Kingdoms and Marvels of the East*. London: John Murray, 1921.

AFRICA AND THE MIDDLE EAST

Ashtor, E. Liyahn, *A Social and Economic History of the Near East in the Middle Ages*. London: Collins, 1976.

Atil, Esin:
Art of the Arab World. Washington, D.C.: Smithsonian Institution Press, 1975.
Renaissance of Islam: Art of the Mamluks. Washington, D.C.: Smithsonian Institution Press, 1981.

Coste, Pascal, *Architecture Arabe ou Monuments du Kaire, 1818-1826*. Paris: Didiot Frères, 1837.

Creswell, K. A. C., *The Muslim Architecture of Egypt*. Vol. 2. Oxford, England: Clarendon Press, 1959.

Ettinghausen, Richard, *Treasures of Asia: Arab Painting*. Lausanne, Switzerland: Éditions d'Art Albert Skira, 1962.

Glubb, John Bagot, *Soldiers of Fortune: The Story of the Mamlukes*. London: Hodder & Stoughton, 1973.

Holt, P. M., *The Age of the Crusades: The Near East from the Eleventh Century to 1517*. New York: Longman, 1986.

Holt, P. M., A. K. S. Lambton, and B. Lewis, *The Cambridge History of Islam*. Vol. 1. Cambridge, England: Cambridge University Press, 1970.

Irwin, Robert, *The Middle East in the Middle Ages: The Early Mamluk Sultanate, 1250-1382*. London: Croom Helm, 1986.

Leaf, William, and Sally Purcell, *Heraldic Symbols*. London: Victoria & Albert Museum, 1986.

Lewis, Bernard, ed., *The World of Islam*. London: Thames & Hudson, 1976.

Mayer, L. A., *Mamluk Costume*. Geneva: Albert Kundig, 1952.

Runciman, S., *A History of the Crusades*. Vol. 3. Harmondsworth, Middlesex, England: Penguin Books, 1987.

Ruthven, M., and the Editors of Time-Life Books, *Cairo* (The Great Cities series). Amsterdam: Time-Life Books, 1980.

Shaw, M. R. B., transl., *Joinville and Villehardouin: Chronicles of the Crusades*. London: Penguin Books, 1963.

ACKNOWLEDGMENTS

The following materials have been reprinted with the kind permission of the publishers: Page 42: "Everyone had waited expectantly . . .," quoted in *The Future and the Past*, by Jien (Brown and Ishida eds.), Berkeley, California: University of California Press, 1979. Page 44: "Sorry not to see . . .," quoted in *The Little Treasury of One Hundred People, One Poem Each*, as compiled by Fujiwara no Sadaie, translated by Tom Galt (ed.), Princeton, New Jersey: Princeton University Press, 1981. Page 50: "At the New Year, ill omens . . ." and page 55: "Saiko, aged eighty-five . . .," both quoted in *Japan: A Short Cultural History*, by G. Sansom, London: Cresset, 1946. Page 61: "They care only about raiding . . .," quoted in *The Middle East in the Middle Ages*, by Robert Irwin, London & Sydney: Croom Helm, 1986. Page 80: "They brought up a ship . . ." and "The Franks . . ." and "When the Muslims stormed it . . .," quoted in *The Age of the Crusades: The Near East from the Eleventh Century to 1517*, by P. M. Holt, New York: Longman, 1986.

The editors also wish to thank the following individuals and institutions for their valuable assistance in the preparation of this volume:
Denmark: Copenhagen—Marianne Poulsen, Danish National Museum. Ribe—Per Kristian Madsen, Antikvariske Samling.
England: Cambridge—Christel M. Kessler; Phillip Lindley, St. Catherine's College. Cheltenham—Kate Fleming. Leeds—Stephen Turnbull. London—Marian Campbell, Department of Metalwork, Victoria & Albert Museum; David Carpenter; James Chambers; Nicola Coldstream; Jeremy Davies; Christopher de Hamel, Illuminated Manuscripts, Sotheby's; Nikolai Dejevsky; Alistair Duncan, World of Islam Festival Trust; Ian Eaves, The Royal Armouries, H.M. Tower of London; Timothy Fraser; John Gillingham, London School of Economics; Lindy Grant, The Courtauld Institute; Victor Harris, Department of Japanese Antiquities, British Museum; Clive Hicks; Gillian Hutchinson, National Maritime Museum; Beth McKillop, Department of Oriental Manuscripts, British Library; David Morgan, Department of History, School of Oriental & African Studies, University of London; Berwick Morley, English Heritage; Suzanne O'Farrell; Readers Digest Association Ltd.; Eugénie Romer; Kenneth Teague, The Horniman Museum; Brian A. Tremain, Photographic Service, British Museum. Loughborough—David Nicolle. Maldon, Essex—Lt. Cdr. Peter Kemp. Oxford—William Leaf; Nick Vincent.
Ireland: Dublin—David James, Chester Beatty Library.
Japan: Tokyo—Yuri Fukusawa.
Poland: Warsaw—Bogdan Turek.
Spain: Madrid—Jane Walker.
Sweden: Visby—Mrs. Gun Westholm, Gotland's Historical Museum.
U.S.A.: Fort Worth—Emily Sano, Kimbell Art Museum. Washington, D.C.—Barbara Shattuck, *National Geographic* Magazine.
Wales: Cardiff—Peter Humphries. Monmouth—Donald Jackson, Calligraphy Centre; Brodie Neuenschwander.

PICTURE CREDITS

INDEX